William Blake

William Blake.

From the Painting by T. Phillips. R.A. engraved by L. Schiavonetti.

WILLIAM BLAKE

A CRITICAL ESSAY

BY

ALGERNON CHARLES SWINBURNE

A NEW EDITION

LONDON
CHATTO & WINDUS
1906

203143

PRINTED BY
SPOTTISWOODE AND CO. LTD., NEW-STREET SQUARE
LONDON

PREFATORY NOTE

THERE are men whose fame is as universal as the appeal of their work to the sympathy and gratitude of all men but such as seek their single chance of notoriety by denying or decrying the claim and the station of the greatest among all the sons of men. There are others whose fame is as limited as the appeal of their work to the sympathies of those alone who can appreciate and assimilate the exceptional influence and the peculiar charm of it. These may not impossibly be liable to overvalue the actual excellence which the average critic will assuredly depreciate or deny. The greatest English poet except Collins who had the fortune or misfortune to be born into a century far greater in progress than in poetry—in the advance of humanity than in the ascent of imagination—is perhaps the most notable example on record of this hardly less happy and only less illustrious class of poets, or of artists, or of men.

The genius of William Blake—and his genius is one with his character: at one with it on all

points and in every way—has so peculiar a charm
that no one not incapable of feeling its fascination
can ever outlive his delight in it.   While we were
able to regard this Londoner born and bred as not
only a fellow-townsman of Milton's but a fellow-
countryman of Shakespeare's, it did seem an
almost insoluble problem to explain or to con-
jecture how so admirable and adorable a genius
could be so deeply flawed and so continually
vitiated by such unutterable and unimaginable
defects.   But if we regard him as a Celt rather
than an Englishman, we shall find it no longer so
difficult to understand from whence he derived his
amazing capacity for such illimitable emptiness
of mock-mystical babble as we find in his bad
imitations of so bad a model as the Apocalypse:
his English capacity for occasionally superb and
serious workmanship we may rationally attribute
to his English birth and breeding.   Some
Hibernian commentator on Blake, if I rightly
remember a fact so insignificant, has somewhere
said something to some such effect as that I, when
writing about some fitfully audacious and fanci-
fully delirious deliverance of the poet he claimed
as a countryman, and trying to read into it some
coherent and imaginative significance, was inno-
cent of any knowledge of Blake's meaning.   It
is possible, if the spiritual fact of his Hibernian
heredity has been or can be established, that I

was : for the excellent reason that, being a Celt, he now and then too probably had none worth the labour of deciphering—or at least worth the serious attention of any student belonging to a race in which reason and imagination are the possibly preferable substitutes for fever and fancy. But in that case it must be gladly and gratefully admitted that the Celtic tenuity of his sensitive and prehensile intelligence throws into curious relief the occasional flashes of inspiration, the casual fits of insight, which raise him to the momentary level of a deep and a free thinker as well as a true and an immortal poet.

The vein of sound reason in Blake's eccentric and fitful intelligence has never been adequately acknowledged or perceived. He assailed Voltaire as a mocker : but he said the best and truest and deepest thing ever said of that great deliverer when he affirmed, after his fashion, that Voltaire had said to him in a vision, ' I blasphemed the Son of Man, and it shall be forgiven me ; but my enemies blasphemed the Holy Ghost in me, and it shall not be forgiven them.' He brought the same charge against Rousseau, with whom he had more in common than with any other con- temporary man of genius ; but to match the antitheistic audacity of his passionate theanthropy we must turn from these milder heretics to Diderot himself. Antitheism, opposition to the

God of man's making and man's worshipping,
could hardly find bolder or better expression than
in this memorable deliverance of 'a memorable
fancy':

'The worship of God is, Honouring his gifts
in other men each according to his genius, and
loving the greatest men best: those who envy
or calumniate great men hate God, for there is
no other God.'

So hard-headed a materialist as Diderot is
no fiercer or more fervent an antagonist of all
religions built on creeds and propped by sacra-
ments than so imaginative an irrationalist as
Blake.   Underneath all his incessant denunciations
of 'the holy reasoning power' which comes to its
consummation in grammars of assent and creeds
of things incredible, there was actually a spiritual
bedrock of natural righteousness and reason which
preserved his intelligence and delivered his
conscience from the farthest aberration and the
worst perversion of all.

DEDICATION

To WILLIAM MICHAEL ROSSETTI

THERE are many reasons which should make me glad
to inscribe your name upon the forefront of this book.
To you, among other debts, I owe this one—that it
is not even more inadequate to the matter under-
taken; and to you I need not say that it is not de-
signed to supplant or to compete with the excellent
biography of Blake already existing.   Rather it was
intended to serve as complement or supplement to
this.   How it grew, idly and gradually, out of a mere
review into its present shape and volume, you know.
To me at least the subject before long seemed too
expansive for an article; and in the leisure of
months, and in the intervals of my natural work, the
first slight study became little by little an elaborate
essay.   I found so much unsaid, so much unseen,
that a question soon rose before me of simple alter-
natives : to do nothing, or to do much.   I chose the
latter ; and you, who have done more than I to serve

and to exalt the memory of Blake, must know better how much remains undone.

Friendship needs no cement of reciprocal praise ; and this book, dedicated to you from the first, and owing to your guidance as much as to my goodwill whatever it may have of worth, wants no extraneous allusion to explain why it should rather be inscribed with your name than with another.   Nevertheless, I will say that now of all times it gives me pleasure to offer you such a token of friendship as I have at hand to give.   I can but bring you brass for the gold you send me ; but between equals and friends there can be no question of barter.   Like Diomed, I take what I am given and offer what I have.   Such as it is, I know you will accept it with more allowance than it deserves ; but one thing you will not overrate—the affectionate admiration, the grateful remembrance, which needs no public expression on the part of your friend

A. C. SWINBURNE.

November, 1866.

CONTENTS

WILLIAM BLAKE

Tous les grands poëtes deviennent naturellement, fatalement, critiques. Je plains les poëtes que guide le seul instinct ; je les crois incomplets. Dans la vie spirituelle des premiers, une crise se fait infailliblement, où ils veulent raisonner leur art, découvrir les lois obscures en vertu desquelles ils ont produit, et tirer de cette étude une série de préceptes dont le but divin est l'infaillibilité dans la production poétique. Il serait prodigieux qu'un critique devînt poëte, et il est impossible qu'un poëte ne contienne pas un critique.—CHARLES BAUDELAIRE.

I

LIFE AND DESIGNS

IN the year 1827, there died, after a long dim life of labour, a man as worthy of remark and regret as any then famous. In his time he had little enough of recognition or regard from the world ; and now that here and there one man and another begin to observe that after all this one was perhaps better worth notice and honour than most, the justice comes as usual somewhat late. Between 1757 and 1827 the world, one might have thought, had time to grow aware whether or not a man were worth something. For so long

B

there lived and laboured in more ways than one
the single Englishman of supreme and simple poetic
genius born before the closing years of the eighteenth
century ; the one man of that date fit on all accounts
to rank with the old great names. A man perfect
in his way, and beautifully unfit for walking in the
way of any other man. We have now the means of
seeing what he was like as to face in the late years
of his life : for his biography has at the head of it
a clearly faithful and valuable likeness. The face is
singular, one that strikes at a first sight and grows
upon the observer ; a brilliant eager old face, keen
and gentle, with a preponderance of brow and head ;
clear bird-like eyes, eloquent excitable mouth, with
a look of nervous and fluent power ; the whole
lighted through as it were from behind with a strange
and pure kind of smile, touched too with something
of an impatient prospective rapture. The words
clear and sweet seem the best made for it ; it has
something of fire in its composition, and something
of music. If there is a want of balance, there is
abundance of melody in the features ; melody rather
than harmony ; for the mould of some is weaker
and the look of them vaguer than that of others.
Thought and time have played with it, and have
nowhere pressed hard ; it has the old devotion and
desire with which men set to their work at starting.
It is not the face of a man who could ever be cured
of illusions ; here all the medicines of reason and
experience must have been spent in pure waste.
We know also what sort of man he was at this time

by the evidence of living friends. No one, artist
or poet, of whatever school, who had any insight
or any love of things noble and lovable, ever passed
by this man without taking away some pleasant
and exalted memory of him. Those with whom he
had nothing in common but a clear kind nature and
sense of what was sympathetic in men and acceptable
in things—those men whose work lay quite apart
from his—speak of him still with as ready affection
and as full remembrance of his sweet or great
qualities as those nearest and likest him. There
was a noble attraction in him which came home to
all people with any fervour or candour of nature in
themselves. One can see, by the roughest draught
or slightest glimpse of his face, the look and manner
it must have put on towards children. He was
about the hardest worker of his time; must have
done in his day some horseloads of work. One
might almost pity the poor age and the poor men
he came among for having such a fiery energy cast
unawares into the midst of their small customs
and competitions. Unluckily for them, their new
prophet had not one point they could lay hold of,
not one organ or channel of expression by which to
make himself comprehensible to such as they were.
Shelley in his time gave enough of perplexity and
offence; but even he, mysterious and rebellious as
he seemed to most men, was less made up of mist
and fire than Blake.

He was born and baptized into the church of
rebels; we can hardly imagine a time or scheme of

B 2

things in which he could have lived and worked
without some interval of revolt. All that was
accepted for art, all that was taken for poetry, he
rejected as barren symbols, and would fain have
broken up as mendacious idols. What was best
to other men, and in effect excellent of its kind, was
to him worst. Reynolds and Rubens were daubers
and devils. The complement or corollary of this
habit of mind was that he would accept and admire
even small and imperfect men whose line of life and
action seemed to run on the same tramway as his
own. Barry, Fuseli, even such as Mortimer—these
were men he would allow and approve of. The
devils had not entered into them ; they worked, each
to himself, on the same ground as Michael Angelo.
To such effect he would at times prophesy, standing
revealed for a brief glimpse on the cloudy and
tottering height of his theories, before the incurious
eyes of a public which had no mind to inhale such
oracular vapour. It is hard to conjecture how his
opinions, as given forth in his " Catalogue " or other
notes on art, would have been received—if indeed
they had ever got hearing at all. This they naturally
never did ; by no means to Blake's discouragement.
He spoke with authority ; not in the least like the
Scribes of his day.

So far one may at least see what he meant ;
although at sight of it many would cover their eyes
and turn away. But the main part of him was, and
is yet, simply inexplicable ; much like some among
his own designs, a maze of cloudy colour and

perverse form, without a clue for the hand or a
feature for the eye to lay hold of. What he meant,
what he wanted, why he did this thing or not that
other, no man then alive could make out. Never-
theless it was worth the trying. In a time of critical
reason and definite division, he was possessed by
a fervour and fury of belief ; among sane men who
had disproved most things and proved the rest, here
was an evident madman who believed a thing, one
may say, only insomuch as it was incapable of
proof. He lived and worked out of all rule, and
yet by law. He had a devil, and its name was
Faith. No materialist has such belief in bread and
meat as Blake had in the substance underlying
appearance which he christened god or spectre,
devil or angel, as the fit took him ; or rather as he
saw it from one or the other side. His faith was
absolute and hard, like a pure fanatic's ; there was
no speculation in him. What could be made of
such a man in a country fed and clothed with the
teapot pieties of Cowper and the tape-yard infidelities
of Paine? Neither set would have to do with him ;
was he not a believer? and was he not a blasphemer?
His licence of thought and talk was always of the
maddest, or seemed so in the ears of his generation.
People remember at this day with horror and pity
the impression of his daring ways of speech, but
excuse him still on the old plea of madness. Now
on his own ground no man was ever more sane or
more reverent. His outcries on various matters of art
or morals were in effect the mere expression, not of

reasonable dissent, but of violent belief. No artist of equal power had ever a keener and deeper regard for the meaning and teaching—what one may call the moral—of art. He sang and painted as men write or preach. Indifference was impossible to him. Thus every shred of his work has some life, some blood, infused or woven into it. In such a vast tumbling chaos of relics as he left behind to get in time disentangled and cast into shape, there are naturally inequalities enough ; rough sides and loose sides, weak points and helpless knots, before which all mere human patience or comprehension recoils and reels back. But in all, at all times, there is the one invaluable quality of actual life.

Without study of a serious kind, it is hopeless for any man to get at the kernel of Blake's life and work. Nothing can make the way clear and smooth to those who are not at once drawn into it by a sincere instinct of sympathy. This cannot be done ; but what can be done has been thoroughly and effectually well done in this present biography.* A trained skill, an exquisite admiration, an almost incomparable capacity of research and care in putting to use the results of such long and refined labour, no reader can fail to appreciate as the chief gifts of the author : one who evidently had at once the power of work and the sense of selection in perfect order. The loss of so admirable a critic, so wise and altogether competent a workman, is a loss to be regretted till it can be replaced—a

* Gilchrist's " Life of Blake."

date we are not likely to see in our days. At least his work is in no danger of following him. This good that he did is likely to live after him ; no part of it likely to be interred in his grave. For the book, unfinished, was yet not incomplete, when the writer's work was broken short off. All or nearly all the biographical part had been ably carried through to a good end. It remained for other hands to do the editing ; to piece together the loose notes left, and to supply all that was requisite or graceful in the way of remark or explanation. With what excellent care and taste this has been done, no one can miss of seeing. Of the critical and editorial part there will be time to speak further in its own place. All, in effect, which could be done for a book thus left suddenly and sadly to itself, has been done as well as possible ; no tenderness of labour grudged, no power and skill spared to supply or sustain it. So that we now have it in a fair and sufficient form, and can look with reasonable hope for this first critical Life of Blake and selected edition of his Works to make its way and hold its place among the precious records and possessions of Englishmen.

What has been once well done need not be tried at again and done worse. No second writer need now recapitulate the less significant details of Blake's life : space and skill wanting, we can but refer readers to the complete biography. That the great poet and artist was a hosier's son,* born near Golden Square,

* It may be as well set down here as at any further stage of our business, that the date of Blake's birth appears, from good MS.

put to school in the Strand to learn drawing at ten
of one Pars, apprenticed at fourteen to learn engrav-
ing of one Basire; that he lived " smoothly enough "
for two years, and was then set to work on abbey
monuments, "to be out of harm's way," other
apprentices being "disorderly," "mutinous," and
given to "wrangling;" these facts and more, all of
value and weight in their way, Mr. Gilchrist has
given at full in his second and third chapters, adding
just enough critical comment to set the facts off and
give them their proper relief and significance.   His
labours among Gothic monuments, and the especial
style of his training as an engraver, left their marks
on the man afterwards.   Two things here put on
record are worthy of recollection : that he began
seeing visions at "eight or ten;" and that he took
objections to Ryland (a better known engraver than
Basire), when taken to be apprenticed to him, on a
singular ground : " the man's face looks as if he will
live to be hanged:" which the man was, ten years
later.   But the first real point in Blake's life worth
marking as of especial interest is the publication of
his " Poetical Sketches ;" which come in date before

authority, to have been the 20th of November (1757), not the
28th; that he was the second of five children, not four; James,
the hosier in Broad Street, being his junior, not, as the biography
states, his senior by a year and a half.   The eldest son was John,
a favourite child who came to small good, enlisted, and died it
seems in comparative youth; of him Mr. Gilchrist evidently had
not heard.   In some verses of the Felpham period (written in
1801, printed in vol. ii. p. 189 of the " Life and Selections ")
Blake makes mention, hitherto unexplained, of "my brother John
the evil one," which may now be comprehensible enough.

any of his paintings or illustrative work, and are quite as much matters of art as these. Though never printed till 1783, the latest written appears to belong to 1777, or thereabouts.

Here, at a time when the very notion of poetry, as we now understand it, and as it was understood in older times, had totally died and decayed out of the minds of men ; when we not only had no poetry, a thing which was bearable, but had verse in plenty, a thing which was not in the least bearable ; a man, hardly twenty years old yet, turns up suddenly with work in that line already done, not simply better than any man could do then ; better than all except the greatest have done since : better too than some still ranked among the greatest ever managed to do. With such a poet to bring forward it was needless to fall back upon Wordsworth for excuse or Southey for patronage. The one man of genius alive during any part of Blake's own life who has ever spoken of this poet with anything like a rational admiration is Charles Lamb, the most supremely competent judge and exquisite critic of lyrical and dramatic art that we have ever had. All other extant notices down to our own day, even when well-meaning and not offensive, are to the best of our knowledge and belief utterly futile, incapable and valueless : burdened more or less with chatter about "madness" and such-like, obscured in some degree by mere dullness and pitiable assumption.

There is something too rough and hard, too faint and formless, in any critical language yet devised, to

pay tribute with the proper grace and sufficiency to the
best works of the lyrical art.   One can say, indeed,
that some of these earliest songs of Blake's have the
scent and sound of Elizabethan times upon them ;
that the song of forsaken love—" My silks and fine
array "—is sweet enough to recall the lyrics of Beau-
mont and Fletcher, and strong enough to hold its
own even beside such as that one of Aspatia—" Lay
a garland on my hearse "—which was cut (so to
speak) out of the same yew ; that Webster might
have signed the *Mad Song*, which falls short only
(as indeed do all other things of the sort) of the two
great Dirges in that poet's two chief plays ; that
certain verses among those headed *To Spring*,
and *To the Evening Star*, are worthy even of
Tennyson for tender supremacy of style and noble
purity of perfection ; but when we have to drop com-
parison and cease looking back or forward for verses
to match with these, we shall hardly find words to
suit our sense of their beauty.   We speak of the
best among them only ; for, small as the pamphlet is
(seventy pages long, with title-page and prefatory
leaf), it contains a good deal of chaff and bran besides
the pure grain and sifted honeymeal.   But these
best things are as wonderful as any work of Blake's.
They have a fragrance of sound, a melody of colour,
in a time when the best verses produced had merely
the arid perfume of powder, the twang of dry wood
and adjusted strings ; when here the painting was laid
on in patches, and there the music meted out by pre-
cedent; colour and sound never mixed together into

the perfect scheme of poetry. The texture of these songs has the softness of flowers; the touch of them has nothing metallic or mechanical, such as one feels in much excellent and elaborate verse of this day as well as of that. The sound of many verses of Blake's cleaves to the sense long after conscious thought of the meaning has passed from one: a sound like running of water or ringing of bells in a long lull of the wind. Like all very good lyrical verse, they grow in pleasurable effect upon the memory the longer it holds them—increase in relish the longer they dwell upon the taste. These, for example, sound singularly plain, however sweet, on a first hearing; but in time, to a reader fit to appreciate the peculiar properties and merits of a lyric, they come to seem as perfect as well can be:

> "Thou the golden fruit dost bear,
> I am clad in flowers fair;
> Thy sweet boughs perfume the air,
> And the turtle buildeth there.
> There she sits and feeds her young:
> Sweet I hear her mournful song;
> And thy lovely leaves among,
> There is love, I hear his tongue."

The two songs *To Memory*, and *To the Muses* are perhaps nearer being faultless than any others in the book. This last especially should never be omitted in any professedly complete selection of the best English lyrics. So beautiful indeed is its structure and choice of language that its author's earlier and later vagaries and erratic indulgences in the most lax or bombastic habits of

speech become hopelessly inexplicable. These un-
lucky tendencies do however break out in the same
book which contains such excellent samples of
poetical sense and taste ; giving terrible promise of
faults that were afterwards to grow rank and run
riot over much of the poet's work. But even from
his worst things here, not reprinted in the present
edition, one may gather such lines as these :

> " My lord was like a flower upon the brows
> Of lusty May : ah life as frail as flower !
> My lord was like a star in highest heaven,
> Drawn down to earth by spells and wickedness ;
> My lord was like the opening eye of day ;
> But he is darkened ; like the summer moon
> Clouded ; fall'n like the stately tree, cut down :
> The breath of heaven dwelt among his leaves."

Verses not to be despised, when one remembers that
the boy who wrote them (evidently in his earlier
teens) was living in full eighteenth century. But
for the most part the blank verse in this small book
is in a state of incredible chaos, ominous in tone of
the future " Prophetic Books," if without promise
of their singular and profound power or menace of
their impenetrable mistiness, the obscurity of con-
fused wind and cloud. One is thankful to see here
some pains taken in righting these deformed limbs
and planing off those monstrous knots, by one not
less qualified to decide on such minor points of
execution than on the gravest matters of art ;
especially as some amongst these blank verse poems
contain things of quite original and incomparable
grandeur. Nothing at once more noble and more

sweet in style was ever written, than part of this
To the Evening Star :

> " Smile on our loves ; and while thou drawest round
> The sky's blue curtains, scatter silver dew
> On every flower that closes its sweet eyes
> In timely sleep. Let thy west wind sleep on
> The lake : *speak silence with thy glimmering eyes,*
> *And wash the dusk with silver.*"

The two lines, or half lines, which make the
glory of this extract resemble perfectly, for vigorous
grace and that subtle strength of interpretation
which transfigures the external nature it explains,
the living leader of English poets. Even he has
hardly ever given a study of landscape more large
and delicate, an effect of verse more exquisite and
sonorous. Of the *Spring* we have already said
something ; but for that poem nothing short of
transcription would be adequate. The *Autumn*
too, should hardly have been rejected : it contains
lines of perfect power and great beauty, though
not quite up to the mark of *Spring* or *Summer*.
From another poem, certainly not worthier of the
place it has been refused, we have extracted two
lines worth remembering for their terseness and
weight of scorn, recalling certain grave touches of
satire in Blake's later work :

> " For ignorance is folly's leasing nurse,
> And love of folly needs none other's curse."

All that is worth recollection in the little play of
"Edward the Third" has been here reproduced with
a judicious care in adjusting and rejecting. Blake

had probably never seen the praiseworthy but somewhat verbose historical drama on the same subject, generously bestowed upon Shakespeare by critics of that German acuteness which can accept as poetry the most meritorious powers of rhetoric. His own disjointed and stumbling fragment, deficient as it is in shape or plan or local colour, has far more of the sound and savour of Shakespeare's style in detached lines : more indeed than has ever been caught up by any poet except one to whom his editor has seized the chance of paying tribute in passing—the author of *Joseph and his Brethren* ; a poem which, for strength of manner and freshness of treatment, may certainly recall Blake or any other obscurely original reformer in art ; although we may not admit the resemblance claimed for it on spiritual grounds to the works of Blake, in whose eyes the views taken by the later poet of the mysteries inherent in matters of faith or morality, and generally of the spiritual side of things, would, to our thinking, probably have appeared shallow and untrue by the side of his own mystic personal creed. In dramatic passion, in dramatic character, and in dramatic language, Mr. Wells' great play is no doubt far ahead, not of Blake's work only, but of most other men's : in actual conception of things that lie beyond these, it keeps within the range of common thought and accepted theory ; falling therefore far short, in its somewhat over frequent passages of didactic and religious reflection, of much less original thinkers than Blake.

One other thing we may observe of these
"Sketches;" that they contain, though only in the
pieces rejected from our present collection, sad in-
dications of the inexplicable influence which an early
reading of the detestable pseudo-Ossian seems to
have exercised on Blake. How or why such lank
and lamentable counterfeits of the poetical style did
ever gain this luckless influence—one, too, which in
after years was to do far worse harm than it has
done here—it is not easy to guess. Contemporary
vice of taste, imperfect or on some points totally
deficient education, may explain much and more
than might be supposed, even with regard to the
strongest untrained intellect ; but on the other hand,
the songs in this same volume give evidence of so
rare a gift of poetical judgment, such exquisite
natural sense and art, in a time which could not
so much as blunder except by precedent and
machinery, that such depravity of error as is implied
by admiration and imitation of such an one as Mac-
pherson remains inconceivable. Similar puzzles will,
however, recur to the student of Blake's art ; but
will not, if he be in any way worthy of the study,
be permitted for a minute to impair his sense of
its incomparable merits. Incomparable, we say ad-
visedly : for there is no case on record of a man's
being quite so far in advance of his time, in every-
thing that belongs to the imaginative side of art, as
Blake was from the first in advance of his.

In 1782 Blake married, it seems after a year or
two of engaged life. His wife Catherine Boucher

deserves remembrance as about the most perfect wife on record. In all things but affection, her husband must have been as hard to live with as the most erratic artist or poet who ever mistook his way into marriage. Over the stormy or slippery passages in their earlier life Mr. Gilchrist has passed perhaps too lightly. No doubt Blake's aberrations were mainly matters of speech or writing; it is however said, truly or falsely, that once in a patriarchal mood he did propose to add a second wife to their small and shifting household, and was much perplexed at meeting on one hand with tears and on all hands with remonstrances. For any clandestine excursions or furtive eccentricities he had probably too much of childish candour and impulse; and this one hopeful and plausible design he seems to have sacrificed with a good grace, on finding it really objectionable to the run of erring men. As to the rest, Mrs. Blake's belief in him was full and profound enough to endure some amount of trial. Practically he was always, as far as we know, regular, laborious, immaculate to an exception; and in their old age she worked after him and for him, revered and helped and obeyed him, with an exquisite goodness.

For the next eighteen years we have no continuous or available record under Blake's own hand of his manner of life; and of course must not expect as yet any help from those who can still, or could lately, remember the man himself in later days. He laboured with passionate steadiness of energy, at work sometimes valueless and sometimes invaluable; made, retained, and lost friends of a varying quality. Even to the lamentable taskwork of bad comic engravings for dead and putrescent "Wit's Magazines" his biographer has tracked him and taken note of his doings. The one thing he did get published—his poem, or apology for a poem, called "The French Revolution" (the first of seven projected books)—is, as far as I know, the only original work of its author worth little or even nothing; consisting mainly of mere wind and splutter. The six other books, if extant, ought nevertheless to be looked up, as they can hardly be without some personal interest or empirical value, even if no better in workmanship than this first book. During these years however he produced much of his greatest work; among other things, the "Songs of Innocence and Experience," and the "Prophetic Books" from *Thel* to *Ahania;* of all which we shall have to speak in due time and order. The notes on Reynolds and Lavater, from which we have here many extracts given, we must hope to see some day printed in full. Their vivid and vigorous style is often a model in its kind; and the matter, however violent and eccentric at times, always clear, noble, and thoughtful; remarkable especially for the eagerness of approbation lavished on the meanest of impulsive or fanciful men, and the fervour of scorn excited by the best works and the best intentions of others. The watery wisdom and the bland absurdity of Lavater's axioms meet with singular tolerance

c

from the future author of the " Proverbs of Hell ; "
the considerate regulations and suggestions of
Reynolds' " Discourses " meet with no tolerance at
all from the future illustrator of Job and Dante.   In
all these rough notes, even we may say in those on
Bacon's Essays, there is always a bushel of good
grain to an ounce of chaff.   What is erroneous or
what seems perverse lies for the most part only on
the surface ; what is falsely applied is often truly
said ; what is unjustly worded is often justly con-
ceived.   A man insensible to the perfect manner and
noble matter of Bacon, while tolerant of the lisping
and slavering imbecilities of Lavater, seems at first
sight past hope or help ; but subtract the names
or alter the symbols given, and much of Blake's
commentary will seem, as it is, partially true and
memorable even in its actual form, wholly true and
memorable in its implied meaning.   Again, partly
through ingrained humour, partly through the rough
shifts of his imperfect and tentative education, Blake
was much given to a certain perverse and defiant
habit of expression, meant rather to scare and offend
than to allure and attract the common run of readers
or critics.   In his old age we hear that he would
at times try the ironic method upon objectionable
reasoners ; not, we should imagine, with much
dexterity or subtlety.

The small accidents and obscure fluctuations of
luck during these eighteen years of laborious town
life, the changes of residence and acquaintance, the
method and result of the day's work done, have been

traced with much care and exhibited in a direct
distinct manner by the biographer. Nothing can be
more clear and sufficient than the brief notices of
Blake's favourite brother and pupil, in character
seemingly a weaker and somewhat violent *replica* of
his elder, not without noble and amiable qualities ;
of his relations with Fuseli and Flaxman, with John-
son the bookseller, and others, whose names are
now fished up from the quiet comfort of obscurity,
and made more or less memorable for good or evil
through their connexion with one who was then
himself among the obscurest of men. His alliance
with Paine and the ultra-democrats then working or
talking in London is the most curious episode of these
years. His republican passion was like Shelley's,
a matter of fierce dogmatic faith and rapid assump-
tion. Looking at any sketch of his head and face
one may see the truth of his assertion that he was
born a democrat of the imaginative type. The faith
which accepts and the passion which pursues an
idea of justice not wholly attainable looks out of the
tender and restless eyes, moulds the eager mobile-
seeming lips. Infinite impatience, as of a great
preacher or apostle—intense tremulous vitality, as
of a great orator—seem to me to give his face the
look of one who can do all things but hesitate. We
need no evidence to bid us believe with what fervour
of spirit and singleness of emotion he loved the name
and followed the likeness of freedom, whatever new
name or changed likeness men might put upon her.
Liberty and religion, taken in a large and subtle

sense of the words, were alike credible and adorable
to him ; and in nothing else could he find matter for
belief or worship.   His forehead, largest (as he said)
just over the eyes, shows an eager steadiness of
passionate expression.   Shut off any single feature,
and it will seem singular how little the face changes
or loses by the exclusion.   With all this, it is curious
to read how the author of *Urisen* and *Ahania*
saved from probable hanging the author of the
Rights of Man and *Age of Reason*.   Blake had as
perfect a gift of ready and steady courage as any
man : was not quicker to catch fire than he was
safe to stand his ground.   The swift quiet resolution
and fearless instant sense of the right thing to do
which he showed at all times of need are worth
notice in a man of such fine and nervous habit of
mind and body.

In the year after Paine's escape from England, his
deliverer published a book which would probably
have been something of a chokepear for the *con-
ventionnel*.   This set of seventeen drawings was
Blake's first series of original designs, not meant
to serve as merely illustrative work.   Two of the
"Prophetic Books," and the "Songs of Innocence,"
had already been engraved; but there the designs
were supplementary to the text; here such text as
there was served only to set out the designs ; and
even these "Keys" to the "Gates of Paradise,"
somewhat of the rustiest as they are, were not
supplied in every copy.   The book is itself not
unavailable as a key to much of Blake's fitful and

tempestuous philosophy; and it would have been better to re-engrave the series in full than to give random selections twisted out of their places and made less intelligible than they were at first by the headlong process of inversion and convulsion to which they have here been subjected.

The frontispiece gives a symbol of man's birth into the fleshly and mutable house of life, powerless and painless as yet, but encircled by the likeness and oppressed by the mystery of material existence. The pre-existent spirit here wellnigh disappears under stifling folds of vegetable leaf and animal incrustation of overgrowing husk. It lies dumb and dull, almost as a thing itself begotten of the perishable body, conceived in bondage and brought forth with grief. The curled and clinging caterpillar, emblem of motherhood, adheres and impends over it, as the lapping leaves of flesh unclose and release the human fruit of corporeal generation. With mysterious travail and anguish of mysterious division, the child is born as a thing out of sleep; the original perfect manhood being cast in effect into a heavy slumber, and the female or reflective element called into creation. This tenet recurs constantly in the turbulent and fluctuating evangel of Blake; that the feminine element exists by itself for a time only, and as the shadow of the male; thus Space is the wife of Time, and was created of him in the beginning that the things of lower life might have air to breathe and a place to hide their heads; her moral aspect is Pity. She suffers through the lapse of

obscure and painful centuries with the sufferings of
her children ; she is oppressed with all their oppres-
sions ; she is plagued with all the plagues of transient
life and inevitable death.   At sight of her so brought
forth, a wonder in heaven, all the most ancient gods
or dæmons of pre-material life were terrified and
amazed, touched with awe and softened with passion ;
yet endured not to look upon her, a thing alien from
the things of their eternal life ; for as space is
impredicable of the divine world, so is pity impredi-
cable of the dæmonic nature. (See the *First Book
of Urizen.*) For of all the minor immortal and un-
created spirits Time only is the friend of man ; and
for man's sake has given him Space to dwell in, as
under the shadow and within the arms of a great
compassionate mother, who has mercy upon all her
children, tenderness for all good and evil things.
Only through his help and through her pity can flesh
or spirit endure life for a little, under the iron law of
the maker and the oppressor of man. Alone among
the other co-equal and co-eternal dæmons of his race,
the Creator is brought into contact and collision with
Space and Time ; against him alone they struggle in
Promethean agony of conflict to deliver the children
of men ; and against them is the Creator compelled
to fight, that he may reach and oppress those whose
weakness is defended by all the warring hands ot
Time, sheltered by all the gracious wings of Space.

In the first plate of the "Gates of Paradise," the
woman finds the child under a tree, sprung of the
earth like a mandrake, which he who plucks up and

hears groan must go mad or die ; grown under the
tree of physical life, which is rooted in death, and
the leaf of it is poisonous, and it bears as fruit
the wisdom of the serpent, moral reason or rational
truth, which invents the names of virtue and vice,
and divides moral life into good and evil. Out of
earth is rent violently forth the child of dust and
clay, naked, wide-eyed, shrieking ; the woman bends
down to gather him as a flower, half blind with
fierce surprise and eagerness, half smiling with
foolish love and pitiful pleasure ; with one hand she
holds other children, small and new-blown also as
flowers, huddled in the lap of her garment ; with the
other she plucks him up by the hair, regardless of
his deadly shriek and convulsed arms, heedless that
this uprooting of the mandrake is the seal of her
own death also. Then follow symbols of the four
created elements from which the corporeal man is
made ; the water, blind and mutable as doting age,
emblem of ignorant doubt and moral jealousy ; the
heavy melancholy earth, grievous to life, oppressive
of the spirit, type of all sorrows and tyrannies that
are brought forth upon it, saddest of all the elements,
tightest as a curb and painfullest as a load upon
the soul : then the air wherein man is naked, the
fire wherein man is blind ; ashamed and afraid of
his own nature and its nakedness, surrounded with
similitudes of severance and strife : overhung by
rocks, rained upon by all the storms of heaven,
lighted by unfriendly stars, with clouds spread under
him and over ; "a dark hermaphrodite," enlightened

by the light within him, which is darkness—the light
of reason and morality; evil and good, who was
neither good nor evil in the eternal life before this
generated existence; male and female, who from of
old was neither female nor male, but perfect man with-
out division of flesh, until the setting of sex against
sex by the malignity of animal creation.   Round the
new-created man revolves the flaming sword of
Law, burning and dividing in the hand of the angel,
servant of the cruelty of God, who drives into exile
and debars from paradise the fallen spiritual man
upon earth.   Round the woman (a double type
perhaps at once of the female nature and the
" rational truth " or law of good and evil) roar and
freeze the winds and snows of prohibition, blinding,
congealing, confusing ; and in that tempest of things
spiritual the shell of material things hardens and
thickens, excluding all divine vision and obscuring
all final truth with solid-seeming walls of separation.
But death in the end shall enlighten all the deluded,
shall deliver all the imprisoned ; there, though the
worm weaves, the Saviour also watches ; the new
garments of male and female to be there assumed by
the spirit are so woven that they shall no longer be
as shrouds or swaddling-clothes to hamper the newly
born or consume the newly dead, but free raiment
and fair symbol of the spirit.   For the power of the
creative dæmon, which began with birth, must end
with death ; upon the perfect and eternal man he
had not power till he had created the earthly life to
bring man into subjection ; and shall not have power

upon him again any more when he is once resumed by death. Where the Creator's power ends, there begins the Saviour's power; where oppression loses strength to divide, mercy gains strength to reunite. For the Creator is at most God of this world only, and belongs to the life which he creates; the God of this world is a thing of this world, but the Saviour or perfect man is of eternity, belonging to the spiritual life which was before birth and shall be after death.

In these first six plates is the kernel of the book; round these the subsequent symbols revolve, and toward these converge. The seventh we may assume to be an emblem of desire as it is upon earth, blind and wild, glad and sad, destroying the pleasures it catches hold of, losing those it lets go. One Love, a moth-like spirit, lies crushed at the feet of the boy who pursues another, flinging his cap towards it as though to trap a butterfly; startled with the laugh of triumphant capture even at his lips, as the wingless flying thing eludes him and soars beyond the enclosure of summer leaves and stems toward upper air and cloud. To the original sketch was appended this quotation from Spenser, "The Faerie Queene," Book 2, Canto 2, v. 2:

> "Ah luckless babe, born under cruel star,
> And in dead parents' baleful ashes bred;
> Full little weenest thou what sorrows are
> Left thee for portion of thy livelyhed."

Again, Youth, with the bow of battle lifted in his right hand, turns his back upon Age, and leaves him lamenting in vain remonstrance and piteous

reclamation : the fruit of vain-glory and vain teach-
ing, ending in rebellion and division of spirit, when
the beliefs and doctrines of a man turn against him
and he becomes at variance with himself and with
his own issue of body or of soul.   In the ninth plate,
men strive to set a ladder against the moon and
climb by it through the deepest darkness of night ;
a white segment of narrow light just shows the
sharp tongue of precipitous land upon which they
are gathered together in vain counsel and effort.
This was originally a satirical sketch of "amateurs
and connoisseurs," emblematic merely of their way
of studying art, analyzing all great things done with
ready rule and line, and scaling with ladders of logic
the heaven of invention ; here it reappears enlarged
and exalted into a general type of blind belief and
presumptuous reason, indicative also of the helpless
hunger after spiritual things ingrained in those made
subject to things material ; the effusion and elucta-
tion of spirits sitting in prison towards the truth
which should make them free.   In the tenth plate,
the half-submerged face and outstretched arm of a
man drowning in a trough of tumbling sea show
just above the foam, against the glaring and windy
clouds whose blown drift excludes the sky.   Perhaps
the noble study of sea registered in the Catalogue
as No. 128 of the second list was a sketch for this
design of man sinking under the waves of time.   Of
the two this sketch is the finer ; a greater effect of
tempest was never given by the work of any hand
than in this weltering and savage space of sea, with

the aimless clash of its breakers and blind turbu-
lence of water veined and wrinkled with storm,
enridged and cloven into drifting array of battle,
with no lesser life visible upon it of man or vessel,
fish or gull : no land beyond it conceivable, no
heaven above it credible. This drawing, which has
been reproduced by photography, might have found
a place here or later in the book. In the eleventh
plate, emblematic of religious restraint and the
severities of artificial holiness, an old man, spec-
tacled and strait-mouthed, clips with his shears the
plumes of a winged boy, who writhes vainly in a
passionate attempt at self-release, his arm hiding his
face, his lithe slight limbs twisting with pain and
fear, his curled head bent upon the curve of his
elbow, his hand straining the air with empty violence
of barren agony; a sun half risen lights up the
expansion of his half-shorn wings and the helpless
labour of his slender body. The twelfth plate con-
tinues this allegory under the type of father and
sons, the vital energy and its desires or passions,
thrust down into prison-houses of ice and snow.
Next, man as he is upon earth attains for once to
the vision of that which he was and shall be ; his
eyes open upon the sight of life beyond the mundane
and mortal elements, and the chains of reason and
religion relax. In the evening he travels towards
the grave ; a figure stepping out swiftly and steadily,
staff in hand, over rough country ground and beside
low thick bushes and underwood, dressed as a man
of Blake's day ; a touch of realism curious in the

midst of such mystical work.   Next in extreme age
he passes through the door of death to find the
worm at her work; and in the last plate of the
series, she is seen sitting, a worm-like woman, with
hooded head and knees drawn up, the adder-like
husk or shell of death at her feet, and behind her
head the huge rotting roots and serpentine nether
fibres of the tree of life and death : shapes of strange
corruption and conversion lie around her, and
between the hollow tree-roots the darkness grows
deep and hard.   " I have said to corruption, thou
art my father ; to the worm, thou art my mother
and my sister."   This is she who is nearest of kin to
man from his birth to his death :

> " Weaving to dreams the sexual strife,
>   And weeping over the web of life."

I have given thus early a rough and tentative
analysis of this set of designs, rather than leave it
to find a place among the poems or prophecies,
because it does in effect belong rather to art than
poetry, the verses being throughout subordinate to
the engravings, and indeed scarcely to be accounted
of as more than inscriptions or appendages.   It may
however be taken as being in a certain sense one of
the prophetic or evangelic series which was after-
wards to stretch to such strange lengths.   In this
engraved symbolic poem of life and death, most of
Blake's chief articles of faith are advanced or im-
plied ; noticeably, for example, that tenet regarding
the creative deity and his relations to time and to

the sons of men. Thus far he can see and no
farther ; for so long and no longer he has power
upon the actions and passions of created and
transient life. Him let no Christians worship, nor
the law of his covenant ; the written law which its
writer wept at and hid beneath his mercy-seat ; but
instead let them write above the altars of their faith
a law of infinite forgiveness, annihilating in the
measureless embrace of its mercy the separate
existences of good and evil. So speaks Blake in his
prologue ; and in his epilogue thus :

To the Accuser, who is the God of this World.

Truly, my Satan, thou art but a dunce,
And dost not know the garment from the man ;
Every harlot was a virgin once,
Nor canst thou ever change Kate into Nan.
Though thou art worshipped by the names divine
Of Jesus and Jehovah, thou art still
The Son of Morn in weary night's decline ;
The lost traveller's dream under the hill.

Upon the life which is but as a vesture, and as
a vesture shall be changed, he who created it has
power till the end ; appearances and relations he can
alter, and turn a virgin to a harlot ; but not change
one individual life to another, reverse or rescind the
laws of personality. Virtue and vice, chastity and
unchastity, are changeable and perishable ; "they
all shall wax old as doth a garment:" but the
underlying individual life is imperishable and in-
tangible. All qualities proper to human nature
are inventions of the Accuser ; not so the immortal

prenatal nature, which is the essence of every man
severally from eternity.   That lies beyond the
dominion of the God of this world; he is but the
Son of Morning, that having once risen, will set
again ; shining only in the darkness of spiritual
night; his light is but a light seen in dreams before
the dawn by men belated and misled, which shall
pass away and be known no more at the advent of
the perfect day.

All these mystical heresies may seem turbid and
chaotic ; but the legend or subject-matter of the
present book is transparent as water, lucid as flame,
compared to much of Blake's subsequent work.
The designs, even if taken apart from their signifi-
cance, are among his most inventive and interesting.
They were done "for children," because, in Blake's
mind, the wise innocence of children was likeliest to
appreciate and accept the message involved in them;
"for the sexes," that they might be at once en-
lightened to see beyond themselves, and enfranchised
from the bondage of pietism or materialism.   Inter-
preted according to Blake's intention, the book was
a small leaf or chapter of the inspired gospel of
deliverance which he was charged to preach through
the organs of his art ; a gospel not easily to be made
acceptable or comprehensible.

Of the "Prophetic Books" produced about this
time we shall not as yet speak ; nor have we much
to say of the next set of designs, those illustrative of
Young's "Night Thoughts," which were done, as
will be surmised, on commission.   Power, invention,

and a certain share of beauty, these designs of course have ; but less, as it seems to me, of Blake's great qualities and more of his faults or errors than usual. That the text which serves as a peg to hang them on, or a finger-post to point them out, is itself a thing dead and rotten, does not suffice to explain this ; for Blake could do admirable work by way of illustration to the verse of Hayley.

This name brings us to a new and singular division of our present task. During the four important years of Blake's residence at Felpham we can trace his doings and feelings with some fulness and with some confidence. They were probably no busier than other years of his life ; but by a happy accident we hear more concerning the sort of labour done. In August 1800 Blake moved out of London for the first time ; he returned " early in 1804."

Hayley's patronage of Blake is a piece of high comedy perfect in its way. The first act or two were played out with sufficient liking on either side. "Mr. Hayley acts like a prince " towards " his good Blake," not it seems in the direct way of pecuniary gifts or loans, but in such smaller attentions as he could easily show to the husband and wife on their first arrival close at hand. It must be remarked and remembered that throughout this curious and incongruous intercourse there is no question whatever of obligation on Blake's part for any kindness shown beyond the equal offices of friend to friend. It is for " Mr. Hayley's usual brotherly affection " that he expresses such ready gratitude. That the poor man's goodwill was genuine we need not hesitate to allow ; but the fates never indulged in a freak of stranger humour than when it seemed good to their supreme caprice to couple in the same traces for even the shortest stage a man like Hayley with a man like Blake, and bracket the "Triumphs of Temper" with the "Marriage of Heaven and Hell."

England, with a deplorable ingratitude, has apparently forgotten by this time what her Hayley was once like. It requires a certain strength of imagination to realise the assured fact that he was once a "greatest living poet;" retrospection collapses in the effort, and credulity loses heart to believe. Such, however, was in effect his profession ; he had the witness of his age under hand and seal to the fact, that on the death of his friend Cowper the supreme laurels of the age or day had fallen by in-heritance to that poet's accomplished and ingenious biographer. There is something pathetic and almost piteous in his perfect complacency and his perfect futility. A moral country should not have forgotten that to Mr. Hayley, when at work on his chief poem, "it seemed to be a kind of duty incumbent on those who devote themselves to poetry to render a powerful and too often a perverted art as beneficial to life and manners as the limits of composition and the character of modern times will allow." Although the ages, he regretted to reflect, were past, in which poetry was idolized for *miraculous effects*, yet a poem intended to promote the cultivation of good humour, and designed to unite the special graces of Ariosto, of

Dante, and of Pope, might still be of service to society; or, he added with a chaste and noble modesty, "if this may be thought too chimerical and romantic by sober reason, it is at least one of those pleasing and innocent illusions in which a poetical enthusiast may be safely indulged;" who will deny it?

This was the patron to whom Flaxman introduced Blake as an available engraver, and, on occasion, a commendable designer. Hayley was ready enough to cage and exhibit among the flock of tame geese which composed his troop of swans this bird of foreign feather; and until the eagle's beak and claws came into play under sharp provocation, the Felpham coop and farmyard were duly dignified by his presence and behaviour as a "tame villatic fowl." The master bantam-cock of the hen-roost in person fluttered and cackled round him with assiduous if perplexed patronage. But of such alliances nothing could come in the end but that which did come. "Mr. H.," writes Blake in July 1803 to Mr. Butts, his one purchaser (on the scale of a guinea per picture), "approves of my designs as little as he does of my poems. I have been forced to insist on his leaving me, in both, to my own self-will; for I am determined to be no longer pestered with his genteel ignorance and polite disapprobation. His imbecile attempts to depress me only deserve laughter." Let a compassionate amateur of human poultry imagine what confusion must by this time have been reigning in the poor hen-roost and dove-cote of Eartham! Things, however, took some

time in reaching the tragic pitch of these shrill dis-
cords. For months or years they appear to have
run through various scales of very tolerable har-
mony. Blake, in the intervals of incessant engraving
and occasional designing, was led by his good
Hayley into the greenest pastures of literature and
beside the stillest waters of verse; he was solicited
to help in softening and arranging for public inspec-
tion the horrible and pitiful narrative of Cowper's
life; he was prevailed upon to listen while Hayley
" read Klopstock into English to Blake," with what
result one may trust he never knew. For it was
probably under the sting of this infliction that Blake
scratched down in pencil a brief lyrical satire on
the German Milton, which modern humanity would
refuse to read in public if transcribed; although or
because it might be, for grotesque ease and ringing
breadth of melodious extravagance, a scrap saved
from some tattered chorus of Aristophanes, or
caught up by Rabelais as the fragment of a litany
at the shrine of the *Dive Bouteille*. Let any man
judge, from the ragged shred we can afford to show
by way of sample, how a sight or handling of the
stuff would have affected Hayley;

> " The moon at that sight blushed scarlet red,
> The stars threw down their cups and fled,
> And all the devils that were in hell
> Answered with a ninefold yell.
> Klopstock felt the intripled turn,
> And all his bowels began to churn;
> And his bowels turned round three times three,
> And locked in his soul with a ninefold key;
> *   *   *

Then again old Nobodaddy swore
He never had seen such a thing before
Since Noah was shut in the ark,
Since Eve first chose her hell-fire spark,
Since 'twas the fashion to go naked,
Since the old Anything was created;
And   *   *   "

Only in choice Attic or in archaic French could the rest be endured by modern eyes; but Panurge could hardly have improved on the manner of retribution devised for flaccid fluency and devout sentiment always running at the mouth.

For the rest, when out of the shadow of Klopstock or Cowper, Blake had enough serious work on hand. His designs for various ballads of Hayley's, strays of sick verse long since decomposed, were admirable enough to warrant a hope of general admiration. This they failed of; but Blake's head and hands were full of other work. "Miniature," he writes to Mr. Butts, "is become a goddess in my eyes." He did not serve her long; but while his faith in her godhead lasted he seems to have officiated with some ardour in the courts of her temple. He speaks of orders multiplying upon him, of especial praise received for proficiency in this style of work; not, we may suppose, from any who had much authority to praise or dispraise. It is impossible to imagine that Hayley knew a really great work of Blake's when he saw it; a clever comminution of great power must have seemed to him the worthiest use of it; whereas the design and the glory of Blake was to concentrate and elevate his talent: all he did and all he touched with profit has an air and a savour of greatness. In miniature and such things he must probably have worked with half his heart and less than half his native skill or strength of eye and hand.

There is a certain pathos in the changes of tone which come one by one over Blake's correspondence at this time. All at first is sunlit and rose-coloured. "The villagers are not mere rustics; they are polite and modest. Meat is cheaper than in London; but the sweet air and the voices of winds, trees, and birds, and the odours of the happy ground, make it a dwelling for immortals." This intense and eager pleasure in the freshness of things, this sharp relish of beauty in all the senses, which must needs run over and lapse into sudden musical expression, will recall the passages in Shelley's letters where some delight of sound or sight suddenly felt or remembered forces its way into speech, and makes music of the subservient words. "Work will go on here with God-speed. A roller and two harrows lie before my window." This passion for hints and types, common to all men of highly toned nerves and rapid reflectiveness of spirit, was not with Blake a matter of fugitive impulse or casual occasion. In his quietest moods of mind, in his soberest tempers of fancy, he was always at some such work. At this time, too, he was living at a higher strain of the senses than usual. So sudden a change of air and change of world as had come upon him filled his nerves and

brain at every entrance with keen influences of child-
like and sensitive satisfaction.   Witness his first
sweet and singular verses to Flaxman and to Butts
—"such as Felpham produces by me, though not
such as she produces by her eldest son," he remarks,
with some reason ; that eldest son and heir of every
Muse being her good Hayley.   Witness too the
simple and complete pleasure with which he writes
invitations and descriptions, transcribes visions and
experiences.   Probably too in some measure, could
we trace the perfect relation of flesh with spirit and
blood with brain, we should find that this first daily
communion with the sea wrought upon him at once
within and without ; that the sharp sweetness of the
salted air was not without swift and pungent effect ;
that the hourly physical delight lavished upon every
sense by all tunes and odours and changes and
colours of the sea—the delight of every breath or
sound or shadow or whisper passing upon it—may
have served at first to satiate as well as to stimulate,
before the pressure of enjoyment grew too intense
and the sting of enjoyment too keen.   Upon Blake,
of all men, one may conjecture that these influences
of spirit and sense would act with exquisite force.
It is observable that now, and not before, we hear
of visions making manifest to him the spiritual like-
ness of dead men : that the scene of every such
apocalypse was a sea-beach ; the shore of a new
Patmos, prolific as was the first of splendid and
enormous fancies, of dreams begotten and brought

forth in a like atmosphere and habit of mind.* Now
too the illimitable book of divine or dæmonic revela-
tion called "Jerusalem" was dictated by inspiration
of its authors, who "are in eternity :" Blake "dares
not pretend to be any other than the secretary."
Human readers, if such indeed exist beyond the
singular or the dual number, will wish that the
authors had put themselves through a previous
course of surgical or any other training which might
have cured a certain superhuman impediment of
speech, very perplexing to the mundane ear ; a habit
of huge breathless stuttering, as it were a Titanic
stammer, intolerable to organs of flesh. "Allegory,"
the too obedient secretary writes to his friend,
"addressed to the intellectual powers, while it is
altogether hidden from the corporeal understanding,
is my definition of the most sublime poetry." A
better perhaps could not be given ; as far that is as
relates to the "spirit of sense" which is to be clothed
in the beautiful body of verse ; but when once we
have granted the power of conception, the claims of
form are to be first thought of. It is of small moment
how the work thus done may strike the heavy ear
of vulgarity or affect the torpid palate of prurience ;

* Our greatest poet of the later days may be cited as a third
witness. Through the marvellous last book of the *Contemplations*
the breath and sound of the sea is blown upon every verse ; when
he heard as it were the thunder and saw as it were the splendour
of revelation, it was amid the murmur and above the motion of the
Channel ;

près du dolmen qui domine Rozel,
À l'endroit où le cap se prolonge en presqu'île.

against mere indolence or mere misconstruction it is waste of time to contrive precautions or rear defences; but the laws and the dues of art it is never permissible to forget. It is in fact only by innate and irrational perception that we can apprehend and enjoy the supreme works of verse and colour; these, as Blake indicates with a noble accuracy, are not things of the understanding; otherwise, we may add, the whole human world would appreciate them alike or nearly alike, and the high and subtle luxuries of exceptional temperaments would be made the daily bread of the poor and hungry; the *vinum dæmonum* which now the few only can digest safely and relish ardently would be found medicinal instead of poisonous, palatable instead of loathsome, by the run of eaters and drinkers; all specialties of spiritual office would be abolished, and the whole congregation would communicate in both kinds. All the more, meantime, because this "bread of sweet thought and wine of delight" is not broken or shed for all, but for a few only—because the sacramental elements of art and poetry are in no wise given for the sustenance or the salvation of men in general, but reserved mainly for the sublime profit and intense pleasure of an elect body or church—all the more on that account should the ministering official be careful that the paten and chalice be found wanting in no one possible grace of work or perfection of material.

That too much of Blake's written work while at Felpham is wanting in executive quality, and even in decent coherence of verbal dress, is undeniable. The

Pythoness who delivers these stormy and sonorous oracles is at once exposed and hampered as it were by her loose and heavy raiment; the prophetic robe here slips or gapes, there muffles and impedes; is now a tatter that hardly hides the contorted limbs, and now an encumbrance that catches or trips up the reeling feet. Everything now written in the fitful impatient intervals of the day's work bears the stamp of an overheated brain and of nerves too intensely strung. Everything may well appear to confirm the suggestion that, as high latitudes and climates of rarefied air affect the physical structure of inhabitants or travellers, so in this case did the sudden country life, the taste and savour of the sea, touch sharply and irritate deliciously the more susceptible and intricate organs of mind and nature. How far such passive capacity of excitement differs from insanity; how in effect a temperament so sensuous, so receptive, and so passionate, is further off from any risk of turning unsound than hardier natures carrying heavier weight and tougher in the nerves; need scarcely be indicated. For the rest, our concern at present shall still be mainly with the letters of this date; and by their light we may be enabled to see light shed upon many things hitherto hopelessly dark. As no other samples of Blake's correspondence worth mention have been allowed us by the jealousy of fate and divine parsimony, we must be duly grateful and careful in dealing with all we have; gathering the fragments into commodious baskets, and piecing the shreds into available patchwork.

These letters bear upon them the common stamp
of all Blake's doings and writings ; the fiery and
lyrical tone of mind and speech, the passionate single-
ness of aim, the heat and flame of faith in himself,
the violence of mere words, the lust of paradox, the
loud and angry habits of expression which abound in
his critical or didactic work, are not here missing ;
neither are clear indications wanting of his noblest
qualities ; the great love of great things, the great
scorn of small men, the strong tenderness of heart,
the tender strength of spirit, which won for him
honour from all that were honourable. Ready even
in a too fervent manner to accept, to praise, to
believe in worth and return thanks for it, he will have
no man or thing impede or divert him,. either for
love's sake or hate's. Small friends with feeble
counsels to suggest must learn to suppress their
small feelings and graceful regrets, or be cleared out
of his way with all their powers to help or hinder ;
lucky if they get off without some label of epigram
on the forehead or sting of epigram in the flesh.
Upon Hayley, as we may see by collation of Blake's
note-book with his letters, the lash fell at last, after
long toleration of things intolerable, after "great
objections to my doing anything but the mere
drudgery of business," (as for instance engraving
illustrations to Hayley's poems designed by Flax-
man's sister—not by his wife, as stated at p. 171 of
the "Life" by some momentary slip of a most care-
ful pen), "and intimations that if I do not confine
myself to this I shall not live. This," adds Blake,

"has always pursued me. You will understand by
this the source of all my uneasiness. This from
Johnson and Fuseli brought me down here, and this
from Mr. H. will bring me back again." In a
sharper mood than this, he appended to the decent
skirts of Mr. Hayley one of the best burlesque
epigrams in the language :

> "Of Hayley's birth this was the happy lot
> His mother on his father him begot."

With this couplet tied to his tail, the ghost of
Hayley may perhaps run further than his own strength
of wind or speed of foot would naturally have carried
him : with this hook in his nose, he may be led by
"his good Blake" some way towards the temple of
memory.

What is most to be regretted in these letters is
the wonderful tone of assertion respecting the writer's
own pictures and those of the great Italian schools.
This it would be difficult enough to explain, dishonest
to overlook, easy to ridicule, and unprofitable to re-
buke. All that need be said of this singular habit of
Blake's has been said with admirable clearness and
fairness in the prefatory note to the prose selections
in Vol. II. Higher authority than the writer's of
that note no man can have or can require. And as
Blake's artistic heresies are in fact mere accidents—
the illegitimate growth of chance and circumstance
—we may be content to leave them wholly to the
practical judgment and the wise charity of such
artists as are qualified to pass sentence upon the

achievements and the shortcomings of this great artist. Their praise can alone be thoroughly worth having ; their blame can alone be of any significance : and in no other hands than theirs may we safely leave the memory and the glory of a fellow-labourer so illustrious as Blake.

Other points and shades of character not less singular it is essential here to take notice of. These are not matters of accident, like the errors of opinion or perversities of expression which may distort or disfigure the notes and studies on purely artistic matters ; they compose the vital element and working condition of Blake's talent. From the fifth to the tenth letter especially, it becomes evident that the writer was passing through strange struggles of spirit and passionate stages of faith. As early as the fourth letter, dated almost exactly a year later than the first written on his arrival at Felpham, Blake refers in a tone of regret and perplexity to the " abstract folly " which makes him incapable of direct practical work, though not of earnest and continuous labour. This action of the nerves or of the mind he was plainly unable to regulate or modify. It hurries him while yet at work into "lands of abstraction ; " he " takes the world with him in his flight." Distress he knows would make the world heavier to him, which seems now "lighter than a ball of wool rolled by the wind ; " and this distress material philosophies or methodical regulations would " prescribe as a medicinal potion " for a mind impaired or diseased merely by the animal superflux of spirits and child-

like excess of spiritual health. But this medicine
the strange and strong faculty of faith innate in the
man precludes him from taking. Physical distress
"is his mock and scorn ; mental no man can give ;
and if Heaven inflicts it, all such distress is a mercy."
It is not easy, but it is requisite, to realise the per-
petual freshness and fulness of belief, the inalterable
vigour and fervour of spirit with which Blake, heretic
and mystic as he may have been, worshipped and
worked ; by which he was throughout life possessed
and pursued. Above all gods or dæmons of creation
and division, he beheld by faith in a perfect man a
supreme God. "Though I have been very unhappy,
I am so no longer. I am again emerged into the
light of day ; I still (and shall to eternity) embrace
Christianity, and adore Him who is the express
image of God." In the light of his especial faith all
visible things were fused into the intense heat and
sharpened into the keen outline of vision. He walked
and laboured under other heavens, on another earth,
than the earth and the heaven of material life :

> "With a blue sky spread over with wings,
> And a mild sun that mounts and sings ;
> With trees and fields full of fairy elves
> And little devils who fight for themselves ;
> With angels planted in hawthorn bowers,
> And God Himself in the passing hours."

All this was not a mere matter of creed or opinion,
much less of decoration or ornament to his work.
It was, as we said, his element of life, inhaled at
every breath with the common air, mixed into his

veins with their natural blood. It was an element almost painfully tangible and actual; an absolute medium or state of existence, inevitable, inexplicable, insuperable. To him the veil of outer things seemed always to tremble with some breath behind it : seemed at times to be rent in sunder with clamour and sudden lightning. All the void of earth and air seemed to quiver with the passage of sentient wings and palpitate under the pressure of conscious feet. Flowers and weeds, stars and stones, spoke with articulate lips and gazed with living eyes. Hands were stretched towards him from beyond the darkness of material nature, to tempt or to support, to guide or to restrain. His hardest facts were the vaguest allegories of other men. To him all symbolic things were literal, all literal things symbolic. About his path and about his bed, around his ears and under his eyes, an infinite play of spiritual life seethed and swarmed or shone and sang. Spirits imprisoned in the husk and shell of earth consoled or menaced him. Every leaf bore a growth of angels ; the pulse of every minute sounded as the falling foot of God ; under the rank raiment of weeds, in the drifting down of thistles, strange faces frowned and white hair fluttered ; tempters and allies, wraiths of the living and phantoms of the dead, crowded and made populous the winds that blew about him, the fields and hills over which he gazed. Even upon earth his vision was "twofold always ;" singleness of vision he scorned and feared as the sign of mechanical intellect, of talent that walks while the soul sleeps, with the mere activity of a blind somnambulism. It was fourfold in the intervals of keenest inspiration and subtlest rapture ; threefold in the paradise of dreams lying between earth and heaven, lulled by lighter airs and lit by fainter stars ; a land of night and moonlight, spectral and serene. These strange divisions of spirit and world according to some dim and mythologic hierarchy were with Blake matters at once serious and commonplace. The worlds of Beulah and Jerusalem, the existence of Los god of Time and Enitharmon goddess of Space, the fallen manhood of Theotormon, the imprisoned woman-hood of Oothoon, were more to him even than significant names ; to the reader they must needs seem less. This monstrous nomenclature, this jargon of miscreated things in chaos, rose as by nature to his lips, flowed from them as by instinct. Time, an incarnate spirit clothed with fire, stands before him in the sun's likeness ; he is threatened with poverty, tempted to make himself friends of this world ; and makes answer as though to a human tempter :

> " My hands are laboured day and night
> And rest comes never in my sight ;
> My wife has no indulgence given
> Except what comes to her from heaven ;
> We eat little, we drink less ;
> This earth breeds not our happiness."

He beheld, he says, Time and Space as they were eternally, not as they are seen upon earth ; he saw nothing as man sees : his hopes and fears were alien

from all men's ; and upon him and his the light of
prosperous days and the terrors of troubled time had
no power.

> "When I had my defiance given
> The sun stood trembling in heaven ;
> The moon, that glowed remote below,
> Became leprous and white as snow ;
> And every soul of man on the earth
> Felt affliction and sorrow and sickness and dearth."

In all this we may see on one side the reflection
and refraction of outer things, on the other side the
projection of his own mind, the effusion of his
individual nature, throughout the hardest and re-
motest alien matter. Strangely severed from other
men, he was, or he conceived himself, more strangely
interwoven with them. The light of his spiritual
weapons, the sound of his spiritual warfare, was
seen, he believed, and was heard in faint resonance
and far reverberation among men who knew not
what such sights and sounds might mean. If,
worsted in this " mental fight," he should let " his
sword sleep in his hand," or " refuse to do spiritual
acts because of natural fears and natural desires,"
the world would be the poorer for his defection, and
himself "called the base Judas who betrays his
friend." Fear of this rebuke shook and wasted him
day and night ; he was rent in sunder with pangs of
terror and travail. Heaven was full of the dead,
coming to witness against him with blood-shedding
and with shedding of tears :

> " The sun was hot
> With the bows of my mind and with arrows of thought."

In this spirit he wrought at his day's work, seeing everywhere the image of his own mood, the presence of foes and friends. Nothing to him was neutral ; nothing without significance. The labour and strife of soul in which he lived was a thing as earnest as any bodily warfare. Such struggles of spirit in poets or artists have been too often made the subject of public study ; nay, too often the theme of chaotic versifiers. A theme more utterly improper it is of course impossible to devise. It is just that a workman should see all sides of his work, and labour with all his might of mind and dexterity of hand to make it great and perfect ; but to use up the details of the process as crude material for cruder verse—to invite spectators as to the opening of a temple, and show them the unbaked bricks and untempered mortar—to expose with immodest violence and impotent satisfaction the long revolting labours of mental abortion—this no artist will ever attempt, no craftsman ever so perform as to escape ridicule. It is useless for those who can carve no statue worth the chiselling to exhibit instead six feet or nine feet of shapeless plaster or fragmentary stucco, and bid us see what sculptors work with ; no man will accept that in lieu of the statue. Not less futile and not less indecent is it for those who can give expression to no great poem to disgorge masses of raw incoherent verse on the subject of verse-making : to offer, in place of a poem ready wrought out, some chaotic and convulsive story about the way in which a poet works, or does not work.

To Blake the whole thing was too grave for any such exposure of spiritual nudity. In these letters he records the result of his " sore travail ;" in these verses he commemorates the manner of his work "under the direction of messengers from heaven daily and nightly, not without trouble or care ; " but he writes in private and by pure instinct ; he speaks only by the impulse of confidence, in the ardour of faith. What he has to say is said with the simple and abstract rapture of apostles or prophets ; not with the laborious impertinence and vain obtrusion of tortuous analysis. For such heavy play with gossamer and straws his nature was too earnest and his genius too exalted. This is the mood in which he looks over what work he has done or has to do : and in his lips the strange scriptural language used has the sincerity of pure fire. "I see the face of my Heavenly Father ; He lays His hand upon my head, and gives a blessing to all my work. Why should I be troubled ? why should my heart and flesh cry out ? I will go on in the strength of the Lord ; through hell will I sing forth His praises ; that the dragons of the deep may praise Him, and that those who dwell in darkness and in the sea-coasts may be gathered into His kingdom." So did he esteem of art, which indeed is not a light thing ; nor is it wholly unimportant to men that they should have one capable artist more or less among them. How it may fare with artisans (be they never so pretentious) is a matter of sufficiently small moment. One blessing there assuredly was upon

E

all Blake's work; the infinite blessing of life; the fervour of vital blood.

In spite however of all inspiration and of all support, sickness and uncongenial company impeded his hours of labour and corroded his hours of repose. A trial on the infamous charges of sedition and assault, brought by a private soldier whose name of Scholfield was thus made shamefully memorable, succeeded finally in making the country unendurable to him. It must be said here of the hapless Hayley that he behaved well in this time of vexation and danger: coming forward to bail " our friend Blake," and working hard for the defence in a tumultuous and spluttering way: he " would appear in public at the trial, living or dying," and did, with or without leave of doctors, appear and speak up for the accused. Blake's honourable acquittal does not make it less disgraceful that the charge should at all have been entertained. His own courage, readiness of wit, and sincerity of spirit are fully shown in the letter relating this short and sharp episode in his quiet life. Some months later he returned to London once for all, and once for all broke off relations with Felpham: commending, it may be hoped, Hayley to the Muses and Scholfield to the halberts.

Having read these letters, we are not lightly to judge of Blake as of another man. Thoughts and creeds peculiar to his mind found expression in ways and words peculiar to his lips. It was no vain or empty claim that he put forward to especial insight and individual means of labour. If he spoke strangely, he had great things to speak. If he acted strangely, he had great things to do. "Mount Sinai was altogether on a smoke, because the Lord descended on it in fire." Let the tree be judged by its fruit. If the man who wrote thus had nothing to do or to say worth the saying or the doing, it may fairly be said that he was mad or foolish. The involving smoke, here again, implied the latent fire. Where the particles of dust are mere hardened mud, where the cloud is mere condensing fog hatched from the stagnation of a swamp, one may justly complain of the obstruction and the obscurity. There is here indeed too much of mist, but it is at least clear ; the air that breeds it is high, the moisture that feeds it is pure. This man had never lived in the low places of thought. In the words of a living poet,* whose noble verses are worthy to stand thus near Blake's own—

> " He had seen the moon's eclipse
> By the fire from Etna's lips,
> With Orion had he spoken,
> His fast with honey-dew had broken."

His dialect was too much the dialect of a far country ; but it was from a far country that he came, from a lofty station that he spoke. To a poet who has

* W. B. Scott. The few and great words cited above occur, it will be observed, in a poem affording throughout no inapt allegory of Blake's life and works. More accurate and more admirable expression was never given to a theme so pregnant and so great. The whole "fable" may be well applied by students of the matter in hand to the history of Blake's relations with minor men of more turn for success; which, as Victor Hugo has noted in his royal manner, is so often "a rather hideous thing."

given us so much, to an artist who has done great
things to such great purpose, we may give at least
some allowance and some toleration. The distance
is great which divides a fireside taper from the eclipsed
moon on Etna. Rules which are useful or necessary
for household versifiers may well be permitted to
relax or even to dissolve when applied to one who
has attained to see with unblinded eyes and to speak
with adequate words of matters so far above them.

The next point noticeable by us in the story of
Blake's life is his single-handed duel with Cromek
and Stothard ; and of this we need not wish to speak
at much length. The engraver, swift and sharp in
all his dealings—never scrupulous, insolent some-
times, and always cunning—had an easy game to
play, and played it without shame ; not even taking
the trouble to hide his marked cards or to load his
dice in private. In spite or in consequence of this
rapacity and mendacity,* Cromek was evidently of

---

* It appears that some effort, laudable if wholly sincere, and
not condemnable if partly coloured by personal feeling, has been
made to rebut the charges brought against Stothard and Cromek
by the biographer of Blake. What has been written in the text
is of course based upon the assumption that Mr. Gilchrist has given
an account of the matter as full and as fair as it was assuredly his
desire to make it. As junior counsel (so to speak) on behalf of
Blake, I have followed the lead of his biographer ; for me in fact
nothing remained but to revise and restate, with such clearness and
brevity as I could, the case as laid down by him. This, finding
on the face of it nothing incoherent or incredible, I have done ;
whether any man can disprove it remains to be seen. Meantime
we are not left to our own choice in the matter of epithets. There
is but one kind of phrase that will express such things and the
doers of such things. Against Stothard no grave charge has been

some use to Blake. And even for the exercise of
these special talents he is perhaps not to be blamed ;

brought ; none therefore can be refuted. Any reference to sub-
sequent doings or sufferings of his must be unspeakably irrelevant
to the matter in hand. Against Cromek a sufficiently heavy indict-
ment has been laid ; one which cannot be in the least degree
lightened by counter-charges of rash violence on Blake's part or
blind hastiness on Mr. Gilchrist's. One thing alone can avail him
in the way of whitewash. He is charged with theft ; prove that
he did not steal. He is charged with breach of contract ; prove
that his contract was never broken. He is charged with denying
a commission given by him ; prove that he did not deny it. For
no man, it is to be feared, will now believe that Blake, sleeping
or waking, forged the story of the commission or trumped up the
story of the contract. That point of the defence the counsel for
Cromek had best give up with all convenient speed ; had better
indeed not dream at all of entering upon it. Again : he is charged,
as above, with adding to his apparent perfidy a superfetation of
insolence, an accretion or excrescence of insult. Prove that he
did not write the letter published by Mr. Cunningham in 1852.
It is undoubtedly deplorable that any one now living should in any
way have to suffer for the misdoings of a man, whom, were it just
or even possible, one would be willing to overlook and to forget.
But time is logical and equable ; and this is but one among many
inevitable penalties which time is certain to bring upon such
wrong-doers in the end ; penalties, or rather simple results of the
thing done. Had this man either dealt honestly or while dealing
dishonestly been but at the pains to keep clear of Walter Scott and
William Blake, no writer would have had to disturb his memory.
But now, however strong or sincere may be our just sense of pity
for all to whom it may give pain, truth must be spoken ; and the
truth is that, unless the authorities cited can be utterly upset and
broken down by some palpable proof in his favour, Cromek was
what has been stated. Mr. Gilchrist also, in the course of his fair
and lucid narrative, speaks once of " pity." Pity may be good,
but proof is better. Until such proof come, the best that can be
done for Cromek is to let well alone. Less could not have been said
of him than equitable biography has here been compelled to say ;
no more need be said now and for ever, if counsel will have the
wisdom to let sleeping dogs lie. This advice, if they cannot refute

the man did but work with such qualities as he had ;
did but put out to use his natural gifts and capacities.
But that he should have done this at Blake's expense

what is set down without more words, we must give them ; μὴ
κίνει Καμάριναν. The waters are muddy enough without that.
Vague and vain clamour of deprecation or appeal may be plaintive
but is not conclusive. As to any talk of cruelty or indelicacy
shown in digging up the dead misdeeds of dead men, it is simply
pitiable. Were not reason wasted on such reasoners it might be
profitable (which too evidently it is not) to reply that such an
argument cuts right and left at once. Suppress a truth, and you
suggest a lie ; and a lie so suggested is the most "indelicate" of
cruelties possible to inflict on the dead. If, for pity's sake or
contempt's or for any other reason, the biographer had explained
away the charges against Cromek which lay ready to his hand, he
must have left upon the memory of Scott and upon the memory
of Blake the stain of a charge as grave as this : if Cromek was
honest, they were calumniators. To one or two the good name
of a private man may be valuable ; to all men the good name of a
great man must be precious. This difference of value must not be
allowed to weigh with us while considering the evidence ; but the
fact seems to be that no evidence in disproof of the main charges
has been put forward which can be seriously thought worth sifting
for a moment. This then being the sad case, to inveigh against
Blake's biographer is utterly idle and hardly honest. If the stories
are not true, any man's commentary which assumes their truth
must be infinitely unimportant. If the stories are true, no remark
annexed to the narrative can now blacken the accused further.
Those alone who are responsible for the accusation brought can be
convicted of unfairness in bringing it ; Mr. Gilchrist, it must be
repeated, found every one of the charges which we now find in his
book, given under the hand and seal of honourable men. These
he found it, as I do now, necessary to transcribe in a concise form ;
adding, as I have done, any brief remarks he saw fit to make in
the interest of justice and for the sake of explanation. Let there
be no more heard of appeal against this exercise of a patent right,
of invective against this discharge of an evident duty. Disproof is
the one thing that will now avail ; and to anything short of that no
one should again for an instant listen.

is and must remain unpardonable : and therefore he must be left to hang with the head downwards from the memorial gallows to which biography has nailed him ; a warning to all such others to choose their game more warily. A tradesman who, by their own account, swindled Blake and robbed Scott can hardly expect to be allowed safe harbourage under the compassionate shelter of complete oblivion or behind the weather-tight screen of simple contempt. It may be worth while to condense the evidence as to his dealings with Blake and Stothard. One alone of these three comes out clear from the involved net-work of suspicious double-dealing. In the matter of the engravings to Blair, Cromek had entrapped and cheated Blake from the first. In the matter of the drawing from Chaucer, he had gone a step further down the steep slope of peculation. After the pro-posal to employ Schiavonetti, Blake might at once have thrown him over as a self-detected knave. He did not ; and was accordingly plundered again in a less dexterous and a more direct manner. It is fortunate that the shameful little history has at last been tracked through all its scandalous windings by so keen an eye and so sure a hand as Mr. Gilchrist's. Two questions arise at first sight ; did Cromek give Blake a commission for his design of the " Pilgrims " ? did Stothard, when Cromek proposed that he should take up the same subject, know that the proposal was equivalent to the suggestion of a theft ? Both these questions Blake would have answered in the affirmative ; and in his dialect the affirmative mood

was distinct and strong. Further evidence on the
first head can be wanted by no one of decent insight
or of decent candour. That Cromek, with more than
professional impudence, denied the charge, is an
incident in the affair neither strange nor important.
The manner of his denial may be matched for
effrontery with the tone of his insolent letter to Blake
on the subject of the designs to Blair. With the
vulgarities and audacities, the shifts and the doubles
of this shuffling man of prey, no one need again be
troubled. That a visitor caught with the spoons in
his pocket should bluster, stammer, and grin as he
pleads innocence or affects amazement, is natural
and desirable; for every word and gesture, humble
or shameless, incoherent or intrepid, serves to convict
him twice over. Undoubtedly he saw Blake's sketch,
tried to conjure it into his pocket, and failed; un-
doubtedly, finding that the artist would not again
give up his work to be engraved by other hands, he
made such approach to an honest offer as was com-
patible with his character; undoubtedly also he then
made money in his uncleanly way out of the failure
by tossing the subject to another painter as a bait.
No man has a right to express wonder that Blake
refused to hold Stothard blameless. It is nothing
whatever to the purpose that, while Cromek's some-
what villainous share in the speculation was as yet
under cover, Blake may have bestowed on Stothard's
unfinished design his friendly counsel and his frank
applause. After the dealer's perfidy had been again
bared and exposed by his own act, it was, and it is

yet, a stretch of charity to suppose that his associate was not likewise his accomplice. And the manner of Stothard's retort upon Blake, when taxed by him with unfair dealing, was not of a sort qualified to disperse or to allay suspicion. He charged, and he permitted Cromek to charge, the plundered man with the act of plunder. Even though we, who can now read the whole account without admixture of personal feeling, may acquit Stothard of active or actual treachery, as all must gladly do who remember how large a debt is due from all to an artist of such exquisite and pleasurable talent, it is hopeless to make out for him a thoroughly sufficient case. The fellowship of such an one as Cromek leaves upon all who take his part at least the suspicion of a stain. All should hope that Stothard on coming out of the matter could have shown clean hands ; none can doubt that Blake did. That on Stothard's part irritation should have succeeded to surprise, and rancour to irritation, is not wonderful. If he was indeed injured by the fault of Cromek and the misfortune of Blake, it would doubtless have been admirably generous to have controlled the irritation and overcome the rancour ; but in that case the worst that should be said of him is that he did not adopt the noblest course of action possible to him. Admitting this, he is not blameable for choosing to throw in his lot with Cromek ; but we must then suppose not merely that Cromek had abstained from any avowal of his original treachery, but that Stothard was unhappily able to accept in good faith the bare

assertion of Cromek in preference to the bare asser-
tion of Blake. If we believe this, we are bound to
admit no harsher feeling than regret that Cromek
should so have duped and blinded his betters; but
in common fairness we are also bound to restrict the
question within these limits. For Stothard a door
of honourable escape stands open; and all must
desire rather to widen than to narrow the opening.
No one can wish to straiten his chance of acquittal,
or to inquire too curiously whether there be not a
pretext for closing the door that now stands ajar.
But for the rest, it is simply necessary to choose
between Blake's authority and Cromek's; and to
consider this alternative seriously for a moment
would be at once an act of condescension towards
Cromek and of impertinence towards Blake, equally
unjustifiable on either side. It is possible that Blake
was not wronged by Stothard; it is undeniable that
he was wronged through him. It is probable that
Stothard believed himself to be not in the wrong; it
is certain that Blake was in the right.*

About the close of this quarrel, and before the
publication of Blake's designs to Blair as engraved

---

* It is to be regretted that the share taken in this matter by
Flaxman, who defended Stothard from the charge of collusion with
Cromek, appears to have alienated Blake from one of his first
friends. Throughout the MS. so often cited by his biographer,
he couples their names together for attack. In one of his rough
epigrams, formless and pointless for the most part, but not without
value for the sudden broken gleams of light they cast upon Blake's
character and history, he reproaches both sculptor and painter with
benefits conferred by himself and disowned by them: and the
blundering stumbling verses thus jotted down to relieve a minute's

for Cromek by Schiavonetti, a book came out which would have deserved more notice and repaid more interest than has yet been shown it. The graceful design by Blake on its frontispiece is not the only or even the chief attraction of Dr. Malkin's "Memoirs of his Child." The writer indeed treads ponderously and speaks thickly ; but there is extant no picture at fit of private anger are valuable as evidence for his sincere sense of injury.

To F. and S.

"I found them blind : I taught them how to see ;
And now they know neither themselves nor me.
'Tis excellent to turn a thorn to a pin,
A fool to a bolt, a knave to a glass of gin."

Whether or not he had in fact thus utilized his rivals by making the most out of their several qualities, may be questionable. If so, we must say he managed to scratch his own fingers with the pin, to miss his shot with the bolt, and to spill the liquor extracted from the essence of knavery. The following dialogue has equal virulence and somewhat more sureness of aim.

Mr. Stothard to Mr. Cromek.

"For fortune's favour you your riches bring ;
But fortune says she gave you no such thing.
Why should you prove ungrateful to your friends,
Sneaking, and backbiting, and odds-and-ends?"

Mr. Cromek to Mr. Stothard.

"Fortune favours the brave, old proverbs say ;
But not with money; that is not the way :
Turn back, turn back ; you travel all in vain ;
Turn through the iron gate down Sneaking Lane."

For the "iron gate" of money-making the brazen-browed speaker was no unfit porter. The crudity of these rough notes for some unfinished satire is not, let it be remembered, a fair sample of Blake's capacity for epigram ; and it would indeed be unfair to cite them but for their value as to the matter in hand.

once so perfect and so quaint of a purely childlike
talent. Even supreme genius, which usually has a
mind now and then to try, has never given us the
complete and vivid likeness which a child has for
once given of himself. Even Shakespeare, even
Hugo, even Blake, has not done this. The husky
dialect of his father suffices to express something ;
and the portrait is significant and pleasant, repro-
ducing as it does the solid grace and glad gravity
proper to children ; a round and bright figure, with
no look of over-training or disease. But the child's
own scraps and scrawls contain the kernel and jewel
of the book. His small drawings are certainly
firmer, clearer, more inventive than could have been
looked for in a six-year-old artist. Any slight
imitative work in a child implies the energy which
impels invention in a man. His little histories and
geographies are delightful for illogical sequence of
events and absurd coherence of fancy. Only a child
could have invented and combined such unimagin-
able eccentricities of innocence. The language and
system of proper names strongly recall Blake's own
habits of speech. The province of Malleb and the
city of Tumblebob are no unfit abodes for Hand and
Hyle, Kwantok and Kotope. The moral polity of
Allestone is not unlike that which prevails among
the Emanations "who in the aggregate are called
Jerusalem." The pamphlet, condensed and com-
pressed into a form more thoroughly readable,
would be worth republishing.

It seems probable that the verses following were

written by Blake about this time, as Mr. Gilchrist refers the design of the " Last Judgment," executed on commission for Lady Egremont, to the year 1807. They are evidently meant to match the beautiful dedication of the designs to Blair, which were not brought out till the next year. Less excellent in workmanship, they are not less important by way of illustration. The existence of some mythical or symbolic island of Atalantis, where the arts were to be preserved as in paradise, now walled round or washed over by the blind and bitter waters of time, was a favourite vision with Blake. At a first reading some of these verses seemed to refer to the subsequent series of designs from Dante ; but there is no evidence of any such later commission as we must in that case take for granted.

> " The caverns of the grave I've seen,
> And these I showed to England's queen ;
> But now the caves of hell I view,
> Who shall I dare to show them to ?
> What mighty soul in beauty's form
> Shall dauntless view the infernal storm ?
> Egremont's Countess can control
> The flames of hell that round me roll.
> If she refuse, I still go on,
> Till the heavens and earth are gone ;
> Still admired by noble minds,
> Followed by Envy on the winds.
> Re-engraved time after time,
> Ever in their youthful prime,
> My designs unchanged remain ;
> Time may rage, but rage in vain ;
> For above Time's troubled fountains,
> On the great Atlantic mountains,
> In my golden house on high,
> There they shine eternally."

Blake was always looking westward for his
islands of the blest. All transatlantic things appear
to have a singular hold upon his fancy. America
was a land of misty and stormy morning, struck by
the fierce and fugitive fires of intermittent war and
nascent freedom. In a dim confused manner, he seems
to mix up the actual events of history with the form-
less and labouring legends of his own mythology;
or rather to cast circumstances into the crucible of
vision, and extract a strange amalgam of metals unfit
for mortal currency and difficult to bring to any test.

In 1808 the illustrations to Blair's "Grave"
appeared, and found some acceptance; a success on
which the shameful soul of Cromek fed exultingly
and fattened scandalously. The ravenous gamester
had packed his cards from the first with all due care,
and was able now to bluster without fear as he had
before swindled without shame. Twenty pounds of
the profits fell to the share of the designer for some
of the most admirable works extant in that line.
The sweetness and vivid grace of these designs are
as noticeable as the energy and rapidity of imagi-
nation implied by them. Even in Blake's lifetime
their tender and lofty beauty drew down some re-
cognition; and incautious criticism, as it praised
them, forgot that the artist was not dead yet. The
generous oversight was afterwards amply and con-
sistently redeemed. For the moment it was perhaps
not wonderful that even so much excellence should
obtain something of mistrustful admiration. The
noble passion and exaltation of spirit here made

visible burnt its way into notice for a time; and Cromek was allowed to claim applause for his invention of Blake. We will choose two designs only for reference. None who have seen can well forget the glorious violence of reunion between soul and body, meeting with fierce embraces, with glad agony and rage of delight; with breasts yearning and eyes wide, with sweet madness of laughter at their lips; the startled and half-arisen body not less divine already than the descending soul, though the earth clings yet about his knees and feet, and though she comes down as with a clamour of rushing wind and prone impulse of falling water, fresh from the stars and the highest air of heaven. But for perfect beauty nothing of Blake's can be matched against the design of the soul departing; in this drawing the body lies filled as it were and clothed with the supreme sleep of flesh, no man watching by it; with limbs laid out and covered, with eyelids close; and the soul, with tender poise of pausing feet, with painless face and sad pure eyes, looks back as with a serene salutation full of pity, before passing away into the clear air and light left at the end of sunset on heaven and the hills; where outside the opened lattice a soft cold land of rising fields and ridged moorland bears upon it the barren beauty of shadow and sleep, the breath and not the breeze of evening. The sweet and grave grace of this background, with a bright pallor in the sky and an effect upon field and moor of open air without wind, brings with it a sense as of music.

A year later Blake advertised and opened his exhibition ; which he was about as qualified to manage as little Malkin might have been. Between anger, innocence, want of funds and sense of merit, he would assuredly have ruined a better chance than he ever had. With the exception of his *Canterbury Pilgrims*, the choice of pictures and designs for exhibition seems to have been somewhat unhappy.* The admirable power and high dramatic quality of that singular but noble picture, the latent or super-incumbent beauty which corrects and redeems its partial ugliness, the strong imagination and the fanciful justice of the entire work, were invisible to all but such spectators as Charles Lamb ; if indeed there were ever another capable of seeing them to such purpose. Whatever portion of the like merit there may have been in the other works exhibited was still more utterly lost upon the few who saw them at all ; for of these we have scarcely any record beyond Blake's own. One journal alone appears to have noticed the exhibition. An angry allusion of Blake's to some assault of the *Examiner* newspaper upon his works and character has been

* Since writing the lines above I have been told by Mr. Seymour Kirkup that one picture at least among those exhibited at this time was the very noblest of all Blake's works ; *The Ancient Britons*. It appears to have dropped out of sight, but must be still hidden somewhere. Against the judgment of Mr. Kirkup there can be no appeal. The saviour of Giotto, the redeemer of Dante, has power to pronounce on the work of Blake. I allow what I said to stand as I said it at first, only that I may not miss the chance of calling attention to the loss and paying tribute to the critic.

hitherto left unexplained, presumably through a not irrational contempt. That Blake may be cleared from any charge of perversity, a brief account of the quarrel is here appended. Contemptible as are both the journeyman writer and his poor day's work, they have been found worth tracking down on account of the game flown at.

In the thirtieth number of the *Examiner* (August 7th, 1808) there is a review (signed R. H.) of the *Blair's Grave*, sufficiently impudent in manner and incapable in matter to have provoked a milder spirit than Blake's. Fuseli's prefatory note is cited with a tone of dissentient patronage not lightly to be endured ; "none but such a visionary as Mr. Blake or such a frantic (*sic*) as Mr. Fuseli could possibly fancy," and so forth ; then follows some chatter about the failures of great poets, "utter impossibility of representing *Spirit* to the eye" (except by means of italic type), "insipid," "absurd," "all the wise men of the East would not possibly divine," "*small* assistance of the title" (italics again), "how are we to find out?" (might not one reply with Thersites, "Make that demand of thy Maker"?), "how absurd," "more serious censure," "most heterogeneous and serio-fantastic," "most indecent," "appearance of libidinousness," "much to admire, but more to censure," and all the common-places of that pestilent old style which, propped on italics and points of exclamation, halts at every sentence between a titter, a shrug, and a snarl. Schiavonetti also "has done more than justice" to Blake, and

Blair and his engraver are finally bidden to divide the real palm. Who this reviewer was, no man need either know or care ; but all may now understand the point of Blake's allusion. Next year however the real batteries were opened. It is but loathsome labour to shovel out this decomposed rubbish from the catacombs of liberal journalism ; but if thus only we can explain an apparently aimless or misplaced reference on the great artist's part, it may be worth while to throw up a few spadefuls.

This second article bears date September 17th, 1809, No. 90 of the *Examiner*, and is labelled " Mr. Blake's Exhibition." The contributor has already lapsed from simple fatuity into fatuity compound with scurrility. Blake here figures as " an unfortunate lunatic, whose personal inoffensiveness secures him from confinement, and consequently of whom no public notice would have been taken, if he was not " (the man's grammar here goes mad on its own account, but what then ?) " forced on the notice and animadversion of the *Examiner* in having been held up " (the case by this time is fairly desperate) " to public admiration ; " such is the eccentricity of human error. The " Blair " of last year " was a futile endeavour *by* bad drawings to represent immateriality *by* bodily personifications," and so forth ; once again, " the tasteful hand of Schiavonetti," one regrets to remember, was employed to bestow " an exterior charm on deformity and nonsense. Thus encouraged, the poor man " (to wit, Blake) " fancies himself a great master, and has painted a few wretched pictures, some of which are "—any one may finish that for the critic. The catalogue is "a farrago of nonsense, unintelligibleness (*sic*), and egregious vanity." Stothard and the irrepressible Schiavonetti are of course held up in contrast to the "distempered brain" which produced Blake's *Pilgrims*. The picture of *The Ancient Britons* "is a complete caricature ; the colour of the flesh is exactly like hung beef." Here we will pull the man up short and have done with him. He shirks a signature this time ; and whether or no he were the same as last year's critic, those may find out who care.

"Arcadiæ pecuaria rudere dicas ; " would not one say that this mingling bray and howl had issued through the throat and nostril of some one among the roving or browsing cattle of our own daily or weekly literature, startled at smelling some incongruous rose in his half-eaten thistle-heap? Such feeders were always one in voice and one in palate : it were waste of wood and iron to cudgel or to prod them. Even when their clamour becomes too intolerably dissonant we may get out of hearing and solace our vexed ears and spirits with reflection on that axiom of Blake's, which, though savouring in such a case of excessive optimism, we will strive to hope is true :

> "The bleat, the bark, bellow, and roar,
> Are waves that beat on Heaven's shore."

This was not Blake's only connexion or collision with the journals of his day. An adverse notice of

Fuseli had excited him to more direct reprisals than the attack upon himself now did. The *Monthly Magazine* for July 1st, 1806 (vol. xxi. pp. 520, 521), contains the following letter, which is now first unearthed and seems worth saving. It is not without perversities ; neither is it wanting in vigour and fervour of thought.

"To the Editor of the ' Monthly Magazine.'

" Sir,—My indignation was exceedingly moved at reading a criticism in *Bell's Weekly Messenger* (25th May) on the picture of Count Ugolino, by Mr. Fuseli, in the Royal Academy Exhibition ; and your magazine being as extensive in its circulation as that paper, and as it also must from its nature be more permanent, I take the advantageous opportunity to counteract the widely-diffused malice which has for many years, under the pretence of admiration of the arts, been assiduously sown and planted among the English public against true art, such as it existed in the days of Michael Angelo and Raphael. Under pretence of fair criticism and candour, the most wretched taste ever produced has been upheld for many, very many years ; but now, I say, now its end has come. Such an artist as Fuseli is invulnerable, he needs not my defence ; but I should be ashamed not to set my hand and shoulder, and whole strength, against those wretches who, under pretence of criticism, use the dagger and the poison.

" My criticism on this picture is as follows : Mr. Fuseli's Count Ugolino is the father of sons of feeling and dignity, who would not sit looking in their parent's face in the moments of his agony, but would rather retire and die in secret while they suffer him to indulge his passionate and innocent grief, his innocent and venerable madness, and insanity, and fury, and whatever paltry cold-hearted critics cannot, because they dare not, look upon. Fuseli's Count Ugolino is a man of wonder and admiration, of resentment against man and devil, and of humiliation before God : prayer and parental affection fills the figure from head to foot. The child in his arms, whether boy or girl signifies not (but the critic must be a fool who has not read Dante, and who does not know a boy from a girl) ; I say, the child is as beautifully drawn as it is coloured—in both, inimitable; and the effect of the whole is truly sublime, on account of that very colouring which our critic calls black and heavy. The German-flute colour, which was used by the Flemings (they call it burnt bone), has [? so] possessed the eye of certain connoisseurs, that they cannot see appropriate colouring, and are blind to the gloom of a real terror.

"The taste of English amateurs has been too much formed upon pictures imported from Flanders and Holland, consequently our countrymen are easily brow-beat on the subject of painting; and hence it is so common to hear a man say, ' I am no judge of pictures ;' but, O Englishmen ! know that every man ought to be a judge of pictures, and every man is so who has not been con-noisseured out of his senses.

"A gentleman who visited me the other day said, ' I am very much surprised at the dislike which some connoisseurs show on viewing the pictures of Mr. Fuseli ; but the truth is, he is a hundred years beyond the present generation.' Though I am startled at such an assertion, I hope the contemporary taste will shorten the hundred years into as many hours ; for I am sure that any person consulting his own eyes must prefer what is so supereminent ; and I am as sure that any person consulting his own reputation, or the reputation of his country, will refrain from disgracing either by such ill-judged criticisms in future.

"Yours, WM. BLAKE."

This ready championship, erratic and excessive as it may be, is not less characteristic of the man than is that outspoken violence which helped to make his audience often deaf and unfriendly. The letter, as we said, did not happen to turn up in time for insertion in any niche of the Life or Appendix : it will not seem a valueless windfall if read by the light of the Catalogue, the Address, and other notes on art embalmed in the second volume.

No part of Blake's life was nobler in action or is yet worthier of study than the period of neglected labour and unbroken poverty which followed. Much of the work done is now, it appears, irretrievably lost. New friends gathered about him as the old ones died out; for indeed all men capable of seeing the beauty of greatness and goodness were drawn at once to such a man as he was. Violent and petulant as he may have seemed on some rare occasions of public protest, he endured all the secret slights and wants of his latter life with a most high patience, and with serene if not joyous acceptance of his fate. Without brute resignation, nay with keen sense of neglect shown and wrong done, he yet laboured gladly and without ceasing. Sick or well, he was at work; his utmost rest was mere change of labour. To relax the intense nerve or deaden the travailing brain would have been painful and grievous to him. Fervent incessant action was to him as the breath of every moment, the bread of every day. His talk was eager and eloquent; his habits of life were simple and noble, alike above compassion and beyond regret. To all the poor about him—and among the poor he had to live out all his latter days of life—he showed all the supreme charities of courtesy. From one or two things narrated of him, we may all see and be assured that a more perfect and gentle excellence of manner, a more royal civility of spirit, was never found in any man. Fearless, blameless, and laborious, he had also all tender and exquisite qualities of breeding, all courteous and gracious instincts of kindness. As there was nothing base in him, so was there nothing harsh or weak. This old man, whose hand academicians

would not take because he had to fetch his own
porter, had the habit and spirit of the highest train-
ing. He was born a knight and king among men,
and had the great and quiet way of such. To say
that he was not ashamed or afraid of his poverty
seems an expression actually libellous by dint of
inadequacy. Fear and shame of any base kind are
inconceivable of him. The great and sleepless soul
which impelled him to work and to speak could take
no taint and no rest in this world. Conscious as he
was of the glory of his gift and capacity, he was ap-
parently unconscious how noble a thing was his own
life. The work which he was able and compelled to
perform he knew to be great ; that his manner of
living should be what it was, he seems to have
thought but simple. "Few," his biographer has
well said, "are so persistently brave." But his was
the supreme valour which ignorantly assumes and
accepts itself. It was natural to him not to cease
from doing well or complain of faring ill, as it is
natural to a soldier not to turn tail. That he should
do great things for small wages was a condition of
his life. Neither, with all his just and distinct self-
assertion, did he assume any special credit for this.
He did not ask for more of meat and drink, more of
leisure or praise ; he demanded only such recognition
as might have enabled him to do more work and
greater while strength and sight were left in him.
That neglect, and the necessities of mere handiwork
involved by neglect, should thus shorten his time
and impair his capacity for higher labours, he did at

times complain, not without an audible undertone of scornful and passionate rebuke. "Let not that nation," he says once, "where less than nobility is the 'reward,' pretend that Art is encouraged by that nation." There was no angry prurience for fame or gold underlying such complaints.

His famous drawings, burlesque or serious, of visionary heads are interesting chiefly for the evidence they give of Blake's power upon his own mind and nerves, and of the strong and subtle mixture of passion with humour in his temperament. Faith, invention, and irony are here mingled in a rare and curious manner. The narrow leer of stolid servile vigour, the keen smirk of satisfied and brutish achievement, branded upon the grotesque face of the *Man who built the Pyramids*, implies a good satire on workmen of base talent and mean success. Several others, such as *The Accusers* and the celebrated *Ghost of a Flea*, are grotesque almost to grandeur, and full of strength and significance. More important than hundreds of these are the beautiful designs to Virgil—or to Phillips. Reproduced at page 271 of Vol. I. with the utmost care and skill, they have of course lost something by the way ; enough remains, and would remain had less favour been shown them, to give great and keen pleasure. In the first, the remote sweet curve of hill against a sky filled with evening, seen far above the rows of folded sheep, may recall a splendid former design in the *Blair*. In the second, which perhaps has lost more than any in course of transference, the

distance of winding road and deepening gorge,
woods and downs and lighted windy sky, is among
the noblest inventions of imaginative landscape.
Highest of all in poetical quality I should class the
third design. Upon the first two, symbolic as they
are of vision and of pilgrimage, the shadow of peace
is cast like a garment; rest lies upon them as a
covering. In the third, a splendour of sweet and
turbulent moonlight falls across blown bowed hedge-
rows, over the gnarled and labouring branches of a
tough tortuous oak, upon soft ears of laid corn like
long low waves without ripple or roll ; every bruised
blade distinct and patient, every leaf quivering and
straightened out in the hard wind. The stormy
beauty of this design, the noble motion and passion
in all parts of it, are as noticeable as its tender sense
of detail and grace in effect of light. Not a star shows
about the moon ; and the dark hollow half of her
glimmering shell, emptied and eclipsed, is faint upon
the deep air. The fire in her crescent burns high
across the drift of wind. Blake's touch in this
appears to me curiously just and perfect ; the moon
does not seem to quail or flicker as a star would ;
but one may feel and see, as it were, the wind pass-
ing beneath her ; amid the fierce fluctuation of
heaven in the full breath of tempest, blown upon with
all the strength of the night, she stands firm in the
race of winds, where no lesser star can stand ; she
hangs high in clear space, pure of cloud ; but no
likeness of the low-hung labouring moon, no blurred
and blinking planet with edges blotted and soiled in

fitful vapour, would have given so splendid a sense
of storm as this white triumphal light seen above the
wind.   Small and rough as these half-engraved
designs may be, it is difficult to express in words all
that is latent, even all that is evident, in the best of
them.   Poets and painters of Blake's kind can put
enough into the slightest and swiftest work they do
to baffle critics and irritate pretenders.

Friends, as we have said, were not wanting to
Blake in his old age ; to one of them we owe, among
other more direct obligations, an inestimable debt for
the " Illustrations to Job," executed on his commis-
sion. Another worthy of notice here was, until our
own day called forth a better, the best English critic
on art ; himself, as far as we know, admirable alike
as a painter, a writer, and a murderer.   In each pur-
suit, perhaps, there was a certain want of solid worth
and fervour, which at times impeded or impaired the
working of an excellent faculty ; but in each it is
evident there was a noble sense of things fair and fit;
a seemliness and shapeliness of execution, a sensitive
relish of excellence, an exquisite aspiration after
goodness of work, which cannot be overpraised.
With pen, with palette, or with poison, his hand was
never a mere craftsman's.   The visible vulgarities
and deficiencies of his style went hardly deeper than
the surface.   Excess of colour and levity of handling
have not unjustly been charged against him ; he does
not seem to have always used the material on hand,
whether strychnine or mere ink, to the best purpose ;
his work has a certain crudity and violence of tone ;

his articles and his crimes are both too often wanting
in the most delightful qualities of which finished art
is capable; qualities which a more earnest man of
lesser genius might have given them. The main
object in both seems wrong, or at best insufficient;
in the one case he looked less to achievement than
to effect; in the other he aimed rather at money-
getting than at enjoyment; which is the more deplor-
able, as a man so greatly gifted must have been in
every way fitted to apprehend, to relish, and to realize
all noble and subtle pleasure in its more vigorous
forms and in its more delicate sense. What he has
done however is excellent; and we need not inquire
with a captious ingratitude whether another could
have done better: that meaner men have since done
worse, we know and lament. Too often the murderer
is not an artist; and the converse defect is no doubt
yet more unhappily frequent. On all accounts we
may suppose that in days perhaps not remote a philo-
sophic posterity, mindful that the harvest of art has
few reapers worthy of their hire, and well aware that
what is exalted must also be exceptional, will inscribe
with due honour upon the list of men who have de-
served well of mankind the name of Wainwright.
Those who would depreciate his performance as a
simple author must recollect that in accordance with
the modern receipt he " lived his poems;" that the
age prefers deeds to songs; that to do great things
is better than to write; that action is of eternity,
fiction of time; and that these poems were doubtless
the greater for being " inarticulate." Remembering

which things, the sternest critic will not deny that no kaiser or king ever "polished his stanza" to better purpose with more strenuous will.

What concerns us at present is, that there grew up between Blake and Wainwright an intimacy not unpleasing to commemorate. An artist in words, in oils, and in drugs, Wainwright had an exquisite power of recognition, and a really noble relish of all excellence. No good work came in his way but he praised it with all his might. The mixture of keen insight with frank pleasure, innate justice of eye with fresh effusion of enjoyment, gives to his papers on art a special colour or savour which redeems the offences of a tricked and tinselled style. Clearly too he did what he could for Blake in the way of journalism; but a super-editorial thickness of hide and head repelled the light sharp shafts loosed from a bow too relaxed by too unsteady a hand. It is lamentable that the backstroke of a recalcitrant hoof should have broken this bowman's arm when it might have done good service. Help shown to Blake about this time, especially help of the swift efficient nature that Wainwright would have given, might have been infinitely important; it was no light thing to come so near and yet fall short of. Exposition of the beloved "Song of Jerusalem," adequate at least on the side of pure art, would assuredly have given the great old man pleasure beyond words and beyond gold. This too he was not to have. There are men set about the ways of life who seem made only to ful- fil the office of thorns; it is difficult for retrospection

to observe that they have done anything but hurt
and hinder the feet of higher men. Doubtless they
have had their use and taken their pleasure. These
have left no trace; we can still see the scars they
made on the hand and the fragments they rent from
the cloak of a great man as he passed by them. A
little of the honour which he has lately received would
have been to Blake in his life a great and pleasant
thing to attain; praise of his work now leaves an
after-taste of bitterness on the lips which utter it.
His work, not done for wages, hardly repaid with
thanks, we can touch and handle and remark upon
as ability is given us; "nothing can touch him
further." Those who might have done what we
would give much to do left it undone. And even to
men who enjoy such power to do and such wisdom
to choose greatly as were the inheritance of Blake it
is not a thing worth no regret to have been allowed
upon earth no comprehension and no applause. He
had a better part in life than the pleasure that comes
of such things; but these also he might have had.
He would not come down to chaffer for them or stoop
to gather them up from unclean or unsafe ground;
but they might have been laid at his feet freely and
with thanks; which they never were.

Foiled as he had been in his good purpose, the
critic at least won full gratitude from the gentle and
great nature of his friend, who repaid him in a kingly
manner with praise worth gold. One may hope that
a picture painted by Wainwright and commended by
Blake will yet be traced somewhere, in spite of the

singular fate which hung upon so much of their lives,
and which still obscures so much of their work. At
least its subject and quality should be sought out
and remembered. But for the strange collision with
social laws which broke up his life and scattered his
designs, it might also be hoped that some other relics
of Wainwright would be found adrift in manuscript
or otherwise, and a collection of his stray works be
completed and published, with an adequate notice of
his life, well weeded of superfluous lamentations,
duly qualified to put an end to perversion and foolish
fancies, clear of deprecation or distortion, just,
sufficient, and close to the purpose. Few things
would be better worth doing by a competent editor.

Even of the " Inventions to the Book of Job," as
far as I know, no especial notice was taken. Upon
these, the greatest of all Blake's designs, such noble
exposition has now at length been bestowed that
further remark may henceforward well be spared.
This commentary has something of the stately beauty
and vigorous gravity of style which distinguish the

work spoken of. Blake himself, had he undertaken
to write notes on his designs, must have done them
less justice than this. The perfect apprehension and
the perfect representation of the great qualities which
all men, according to their capacity, must here in
some degree perceive, give to these notes a value
beyond that of mere eloquence or of mere sympathy.
The words chosen do not merely render the subject
with fluency and fitness; they attain a choiceness
and exaltation of expression, which give to the

writing much of the character of the designs.
Whether or not from any exceptional aptitude in
the material, these designs are more lucid and
dramatic in effect than perhaps any of Blake's works.
His specialties of belief or sentiment hardly show
in this series at all; except perhaps in the passionate
and penitent character which seems here to supplant
the traditional divine look of patience and power.
The whole work has in it a vibration as of fire;
even the full stars and serene lines of hill are set
in frameworks of fervent sky or throbbing flame.
But for the most part those intense qualities of
sleepless invention which in many of Blake's other
works impel him into fierce aberration and blind
ecstasy, through ways which few can tread and
mists which few can pierce, are now happily diverted
and kept at work upon the exquisite borders and
appendages. In these there is enough of fiery
fancy and tender structure of symbol to employ the
whole wide and vivid imagination of the artist. And
throughout the series there is a largeness and a
loftiness of manner which sustain the composition
at the height of the poem. In the highest flights of
spiritual passion and speculation, in the subtle con-
tention with fate and imperious agony of appeal
against heaven, Blake has matched himself against
his text, and translated its sharp and profound
harmonies into a music of design not less adorable.

Those who have read with any care or com-
prehension the excellent chapters on Blake's per-
sonal life will regret, not it may be without a keen

suppressed sense of vain vexation, that the author did not live to get sight of the letters which have since been found and published. They will at least observe with how much reason the editor of the "Life" has desired us to notice the close and complete confirmation given by that correspondence to the accuracy of these chapters. No tribute more valuable could be devised to the high sincerity, the clear sagacity, the vigorous sense of truth and lucid power of proof, which have left us for the first time an acceptable and endurable portrait of Blake. All earlier attempts were mere masses of blot and scratch, evidently impossible and false on the face of them, and even pitifully conscious that they could not be true, not being human. The bewildered patronage, fear, contempt, goodwill and despair which Blake had excited among those hapless biographers have left in their forlorn failures a certain element of despicable pathos. We have now, thanks to no happier chance, but solely to the strenuous ability and fidelity of a man qualified to study and to speak upon the matter, a trustworthy, perspicuous, and coherent summary of the actual facts of Blake's life, of the manner in which he worked, and of the causes which made his work what it was.

Among these late labours of Blake the "Dante" may take a place of some prominence. The seven published plates, though quite surprisingly various in merit, are worth more notice than has yet been spared them. Three at least, for poetical power and nobility of imaginative detail, are up to the artist's

highest mark. Others have painted the episode of
Francesca with more or less of vigour and beauty ;
once above all an artist to whom any reference here
must be taken as especially apposite has given with
the tenderest perfection of power, first the beauty of
beginning love in the light and air of life on earth,
then the passion of imperishable desire under the
dropping tongues of flame in hell. To the right the
lovers are drawn close, yearning one toward another
with touch of tightened hands and insatiable appeal
of lips ; behind them the bower lattice opens on deep
sunshine and luminous leaves ; to the left, they drift
before the wind of hell, floated along the misty and
straining air, fastened one upon another among the
fires, pale with perpetual division of pain ; and be-
tween them the witnesses stand sadly, as men that
look before and after. Blake has given nothing like
this : of personal beauty and special tenderness his
design has none; it starts from other ground.
Often as the lovers had been painted, here first has
any artist desired to paint the second circle itself.
To most illustrators, as to most readers, and (one
might say) to Dante himself, the rest are swallowed
up in those two supreme martyrs. Here we see,
not one or two, but the very circle of the souls that
sinned by lust, as Dante saw it ; and as Keats after-
wards saw it in the dream embalmed by his sonnet ;
the revolution of infinite sorrowing spirits through
the bitter air and grievous hurricane of hell. Through
strange immense implications of snake-shaped fold
beyond fold, the involved chain of figures that circle

G

and return flickers in wan white outline upon the
dense dark.   Under their feet is no stay as on earth ;·
over their heads is no light as in heaven.   They
have no rest, and no resting-place : they revolve like
circles of curling foam or fire.   The two witnesses,
who alone among all the mobile mass have ground
whereon to set foot, stand apart upon a broken
floor-work of roots and rocks, made rank with the
slime and sprawl of rotten weed and foul flag-leaves
of Lethe.   Detail of drawing or other technical work
is not the strong point of the design; but it does
incomparably well manage to render the sense of the
matter in hand, the endless measured motion, the
painful and fruitless haste as of leaves or smoke
upon the wind, the grey discomforted air and divid-
ing mist.   Blake has thoroughly understood and
given back the physical symbols of this first punish-
ment in Dante ; the whirling motion of his figures
has however more of blind violence and brute speed
than the text seems to indicate : they are dashed and
dragged one upon another like weed or shingle torn
up in the drift of a breaking sea : overthrown or
beaten down, haled or crushed together, as if by
inanimate strength of iron or steam : not moved as
we expect to see them, in sad rapidity of stately
measure and even time of speed.   The flame-like
impulse of idea natural to Blake cannot absolutely
match itself against Dante's divine justice and intense
innate forbearance in detail ; nor so comprehend,
as by dint of reproduction to compete with, that
supreme sense of inward and outward right which
rules and attunes every word of the " Commedia."

Two other drawings in this series are worth remark and praise; the sixth and seventh in order. In the sixth, Dante and Virgil, standing in a niche of rifted rock faced by another cliff up and down which a reptile crowd of spirits swarms and sinks, look down on the grovelling and swine-like flocks of Malebolge; lying tumbled about the loathsome land in hateful heaps of leprous flesh and dishevelled deformity, with limbs contorted, clawing nails, and staring horror of hair and eyes: one figure thrown down in a corner of the crowded cliff-side, her form and face drowned in an overflow of ruined raining tresses. The pure grave folds of the two poets' robes, long and cleanly carved as the straight drapery of a statue, gain chastity of contrast from the swarming surge and monstrous mass of all foulest forms beneath, against the reek of which both witnesses stop their noses with their gowns. Behind and between, huge outlines of dark hill and sharp curves of crag show like stiffened ridges of solid sea, amid heaving and glaring motion of vapour and fire. Slight as the workmanship is of this design also, alien as is perhaps its structure of precipice and mountain from the Dantesque conception of descending circles and narrowing sides, it has a fiery beauty of its own; the background especially, with its climbing or crawling flames, the dark hard strength and sweep of its sterile ridges, seen by fierce fits of reflected light, washed about with surf and froth of tideless fire, and heavily laden with the lurid languor of hell. In the seventh design

G 2

we reach the circle of traitors; the foot of the
passenger strikes against one frost-bound face;
others lie straight, with crowned congealing hair
and beard taken in the tightening rivets of ice.
To the right a swarm of huge and huddled figures
seems gathering with moan or menace behind a veil
of frozen air, a mask of hardening vapour; and
from each side the bitter light of ice or steel falls
grey in cruel refraction. Into the other four designs
we will not enter; some indeed are too savagely
reckless in their ugly and barren violation of form
or law, to be redeemed by even an intenser appre-
hension of symbol and sense; and one at least,
though with noble suggestions dropped about it, is
but half sketched in. In that of the valley of
serpents there is however a splendid excess of
horror and prodigal agony; the ravenous delight
of the closing and laughing mouths, the folded
tension of every scale and ring, the horrible head
caught and crushed with the last shriek between its
teeth and the last strain upon its eyelids, in the
serrated jaws of the erect serpent—all have the
brand of Blake upon them.

These works were the last he was to achieve;
out of the whole Dantesque series, seven designs
alone have ever won their way into such notice as
engraving could earn for them. The latest chapters
of Blake's life are perhaps also the noblest. His
poverty, if that word implies anything of a destitute
or sordid way of living, seems to have grown and
swollen somewhat beyond its actual size in the dim

form of report. Stories have come to hand of late,
which, being seemingly accurate in the main, though
not as yet duly fixed in detail or date, remove any
such ground of fear. They do better ; they bring
proof once again of the noble charity, the tender
exaltation of mind, the swift bounty of hand, which
would have made memorable a man meaner in
talent. Once, it is said, he lent £40 to some friend
in distress, which friend's wife, having laid out most
of her windfall in dress, thought Mrs. Blake might
like to see *that* by way of change for her husband's
money. Once too they received into their lodging
(into which does not yet seem certain) a young
student of art, sick and poor, who died some time
after upon their hands. These things, and such as
these, we know dimly. One or two such deeds,
seen through such dull vague obstruction, in the
midst of so many things forgotten, should be taken
to imply much. How few we know of, it is easy
to say ; how many there must have been, it is not
easy. This also may be remembered, that the man
so liberal when he had little might once have had
much to give, and would not take it at the price.
It is recorded on the authority of a personal friend,
that some proposal had once been made to "engage
Blake as teacher of drawing to the royal family ;"
a proposal declined on his part from no folly or
vulgarity of prepossession, but from a simple and
noble sense of things reasonable and right. For
once, it is also said, some samples of his work were
laid before the king, not then, unluckily, in his

strait-waistcoat ; " Take them away ! " spluttered
the lunatic—not quite as yet " blind, mad, despised,
and dying," as when Byron and Shelley embalmed
him in corrosive rhymes ; not all of these as yet.
But as a great man then alive and yet living* has
well asked—" What mortal ever heard Any good
of George the Third ? " Blake's MSS. contain an
occasional allusion expressive of no ardent reverence
for the person or family of that insane Dagon, so
long left standing as the leaden rather than brazen
idol of hypocrites and dunces. As to the arts, it
was well for Blake to keep clear of the patron of
West. All he ever got from government was the
risk of hanging, or such minor penalty as that
equitable time might have inflicted on seditious
laxity of speech and thought.

In smaller personal matters, Blake was as fear-
less and impulsive as in his conduct of these graver
affairs. Seeing once, somewhere about St. Giles's,
a wife knocked about by some husband or other
violent person, in the open street, a bystander saw
this also—that a small swift figure coming up in full
swing of passion fell with such counter violence of
reckless and raging rebuke upon the poor ruffian,
that he recoiled and collapsed, with ineffectual
cudgel ; persuaded, as the bystander was told on
calling afterwards, that the very devil himself had
flown upon him in defence of the woman ; such
Tartarean overflow of execration and objurgation
had issued from the mouth of her champion. It was

* Written in 1863. Mr. Landor died Sept. 17th, 1864.

the fluent tongue of Blake which had proved too strong for this fellow's arm : the artist, doubtless, not caring to remember the consequences, proverbial even before Molière's time, of such interference with conjugal casualties.

These things, whenever it was that they happened, were now of the past ; as were many labours of many days, to be followed by not many more. Among a few good friends, and not without varieties of changed scene and company, Blake drew daily nearer to death. Of all the records of these his latter years, the most valuable perhaps are those furnished by Mr. Crabb Robinson, whose cautious and vivid transcription of Blake's actual speech is worth more than much vague remark, or than any commentary now possible to give. A certain visible dislike and vexation excited by the mystic violence of Blake's phrases, by the fierce simplicity of his mental bearing, have not been allowed to impair the excellent justice of tone and evident accuracy of report which give to these notes their singular value. In his correspondence, in his conversation, and in his prophecies, Blake was always at unity with himself ; not, it seems to us, actually inconsistent or even illogical in his fitful varieties of speech and expression. His faith was large and his creed intricate ; in the house of his belief there were many mansions. In these notes, for instance, the terms "atheism" and "education" are wrested to peculiar uses ; education must mean not exactly training, but moral tradition and the retailed sophistries of

artificial right and wrong ; atheism, as applicable to
Dante, must mean adherence to the received "God
of this world "—that confusion of the Creator with
the Saviour which was to Blake the main rock of
offence in all religious systems less mystic than his
own ; being indeed, together with "Deism," the
perpetual butt of his prophetic slings and arrows.
All this, however, we must leave now for time to
enlighten in due course as it best may ; meanwhile
some last word has to be said concerning Blake's
life and death.

· To a life so gentle and great, so brave and stain-
less, there could be but one manner of end, come
when and how it might ; a serene and divine death,
full of placid ardour and hope unspotted by fear.
Having lived long without a taint of shame upon
his life, having long laboured without a stain of
falsehood upon his work, it was no hard task for
him to set the seal of a noble death upon that noble
life and labour. He, it might be said, whom the
gods love well need not always die young ; for this
man died old in years at least, having done work
enough for three men's lives of strenuous talent and
spirit. After certain stages of pain and recovery and
relapse, the end came on the second Sunday in
August 1827. A few days before he had made a
last drawing of his wife—faithful to him and loving
almost beyond all recorded faith and love. Forty-
five years she had cloven to him and served him
all the days of her life with all the might of her
heart ; for a space of four years and two months

they were to be divided now. He did not draw her
like, it appears: that which "she had ever been to
him," no man could have drawn. Of her, out of
just reverence and gratitude that such goodness
should have been, we will not say more. All words
are coarse and flat that men can use to praise one
who has so lived.* It has been told more than once
in print—it can never be told without a sense of

---

* Since the lines above were written, I have been informed
by a surviving friend of Blake, celebrated throughout Italy as
over England, in a time nearer our own, as (among other things)
the discoverer of Giotto's fresco in the Chapel of the Podestà, that
after Blake's death a gift of £100 was sent to his widow by the
Princess Sophia, who must not lose the exceptional honour due
to her for a display of sense and liberality so foreign to her blood.
At whose suggestion it was made is not known, and worth knowing.
Mrs. Blake sent back the money with all due thanks, not liking
to take or keep what (as it seemed to her) she could dispense with,
while many to whom no chance or choice was given might have
been kept alive by the gift; and, as readers of the "Life" know,
fell to work in her old age by preference. One complaint only
she was ever known to make during her husband's life, and that
gently. "Mr. Blake" was so little with her, though in the body
they were never separated; for he was incessantly away "in Para-
dise;" which would not seem to have been far off. Mr. Kirkup
also speaks of the courtesy with which, on occasion, Blake would
waive the question of his spiritual life, if the subject seemed at all
incomprehensible or offensive to the friend with him: he would
no more obtrude than suppress his faith, and would practically
accept and act upon the dissent or distaste of his companions
without visible vexation or the rudeness of a thwarted fanatic.
It was in the time of this intimacy (see note at p. 64) that Mr.
Kirkup also saw, what seems long since to have dropped out of
human sight, the picture of *The Ancient Britons;* which, himself
also an artist, he thought and thinks the finest work of the painter :
remembering well the fury and splendour of energy there contrasted
with the serene ardour of simply beautiful courage; the violent life
of the design, and the fierce distance of fluctuating battle.

some strange and sweet meaning—how, as Blake
lay with all the tides of his life setting towards the
deep final sleep, he made and sang new fragments
of verse, the last oblations he was to bring who
had brought so many since his first conscience of
the singular power and passion within himself that
impels a man to such work. Of these songs not a
line has been spared us ; for us, it seems, they were
not made. In effect, they were not his, he said.
At last, after many songs and hours, still in the true
and pure presence of his wife, his death came upon
him in the evening like a sleep.*

* The direct cause of Blake's death, it appears from a MS.
source, " was the mixing of the gall with the blood." It may
be worth remark, that one brief notice at least of Blake's death
made its way into print; the *Literary Gazette* (No. 552; the
Gentleman's Magazine published it in briefer form but nearly
identical words as far as it went) of August 18, 1827, saw fit to
"record the death of a singular and very able man," in an article
contributed mainly by " the kindness of a correspondent," who
speaks as an acquaintance of Blake, and gives this account of his last
days, prefaced by a sufficiently humble reference to the authorities
of Fuseli, Flaxman, and Lawrence. " Pent, with his affectionate
wife, in a close back-room in one of the Strand courts, his bed in
one corner, his meagre dinner in another, a ricketty table holding
his copper-plates in progress, his colours, books (among which his
Bible, a Sessi Velutello's Dante, and Mr. Carey's translation, were
at the top), his large drawings, sketches, and MSS. ; his ankles
frightfully swelled, his chest disordered, old age striding on, his
wants increased, but not his miserable means and appliances ; even
yet was his eye undimmed, the fire of his imagination unquenched,
and the preternatural never-resting activity of his mind unflagging.
He had not merely a calmly resigned, but a cheerful and mirthful
countenance. He took no thought for his life, what he should eat
or what he should drink ; nor yet for his body, what he should put
on; but had a fearless confidence in that Providence which had
given him the vast range of the world for his recreation and delight.

Only such men die so; though the worst have been known to die calmly and the meanest bravely, this pure lyric rapture of spirit and perfect music of sundering soul and body can only be given to these few. Knowing nothing of whence and whither, the how and the when of a man's death we can at least know, and put the knowledge to what uses we may. In this case, if we will, it may help us to much in the way of insight and judgment; it may show us many things that need not be wrought up into many words. For what more is there now to say of the man? Of the work he did we must speak gradually, if we are to speak adequately. Into his life and method of work we have looked, not without care and veneration; and find little to conclude with by way of comment. If to any reader it should not by

Blake died last Monday; died as he had lived, piously, cheerfully, talking calmly, and finally resigning himself to his eternal rest like an infant to its sleep. He has left nothing except some pictures, copper-plates, and his principal work, a series of a hundred large designs from Dante. . . . He was active" (the good correspondent adds, further on) "in mind and body, passing from one occupation to another without an intervening minute of repose. Of an ardent, affectionate, and grateful temper, he was simple in manner and address, and displayed an inbred courteousness of the most agreeable character." Finally, the writer has no doubt that Mrs. Blake's "cause will be taken up by the distributors of those funds which are raised for the relief of distressed artists, and also by the benevolence of private individuals:" for she "is left (we fear, from the accounts which have reached us) in a very forlorn condition, Mr. Blake himself having been much indebted for succour and consolation to his friend Mr. Linnell the painter." The discreet editor, "when further time has been allowed him for inquiry, will probably resume the matter:" but, we may now more safely prophesy, assuredly will not.

this time appear that he was great and good among the chief of good and great men, it will not appear for any oration of ours.   Most funeral speeches also are cheap and inconclusive.   Especially they must be so, or seem so, when delivered over the body of a great man to whom his own generation could not even grant a secure grave.   In 1831 his wife was buried beside him : where they are laid now no man can say : it seems certain only that their graves were violated by hideous official custom, and their bones cast out into some consecrated pit among other nameless relics of poor men.   It might not have hurt them even to foresee this ; but nevertheless the doers of such a thing had better not have done it. Having missed of a durable grave, Blake need not perhaps look for the "weak witness" of any late memorial.   Such things in life were indifferent to him ; and should be more so now.   To be buried among his nearest kin, and to have the English burial service read over him, he did, we are told, express some wish ; and this was done.   The world of men was less by one great man, and was none the wiser ; while he lived he was called mad and kept poor ; after his death much of his work was destroyed ; and in course of time not so much as his grave was left him.   All which to him must matter little, but is yet worth a recollection more fruitful than regret.   The dead only, and not the living, ought, while any trace of his doings remains, to forget what was the work and what were the wages of William Blake.

II

WE must here be allowed space to interpolate a word of the briefest possible comment on the practical side of Blake's character. No man ever lived and laboured in hotter earnest; and the native energy in him had the property of making all his atmosphere of work intense and keen as fire—too sharp and rare in quality of heat to be a good working element for any more temperate intellect. Into every conceivable channel or byway of work he contrived to divert and infuse this overflowing fervour of mind; the least bit of engraving, the poorest scrap or scratch of drawing or writing traceable to his hands, has on it the mark of passionate labour and enjoyment ; but of all this devotion of laborious life, the only upshot visible to most of us consists in a heap of tumbled and tangled relics, verse and prose mainly inexplicable, paintings and engravings mainly unacceptable if not unendurable. And if certain popular theories of the just aims of life, duties of an earnest-minded man, and meritorious nature of practical deeds and material services only, are absolutely correct—in that case the work of this man's life is certainly a sample of deplorable waste and failure. A religion which has for Walhalla some factory of the Titans, some prison fitted with moral cranks and divine treadmills of all the virtues, can have no place among its heroes for the most energetic of mere artists. To him, as to others of his kind, all faith, all virtue, all moral duty or religious necessity, was not so much abrogated or superseded as summed up, included and involved, by the one matter of art. To him, as to other such workmen, it seemed better to do this well and let all the rest drift than to do incomparably well in all other things and dispense with this one. For this was the thing he had to do; and this once well done, he had the assurance of a certain faith that other things could not be wrong with him. As long as two such parties exist among men who think and act, it must always be some pleasure to deal with a man of either party who has no faith or hope in compromise. These middle-men, with some admirable self-sufficient theory of reconciliation between two directly opposite aims and forces, are fit for no great work on either side. If it be in the interest of facts really desirable that "the poor Fine Arts should take themselves away," let it be fairly avowed and preached in a distinct manner. That thesis, so delivered, is comprehensible, and deserves respect. One may add that if art can be destroyed it by all means ought to be. If for example the art of verse is not indispensable and indestructible, the sooner it is put out of the way the better. If anything can be done instead better worth doing than painting or poetry, let that preferable thing be done with all the might and haste that may be attainable. And if to live well be really better than to write or paint well, and a noble action more valuable than the greatest poem or most perfect picture, let us have done at once with the meaner things that stand in the way of the higher. For we cannot on any terms have everything ; and assuredly no chief artist or poet has ever been fit to hold rank among the world's supreme benefactors in the way of doctrine, philanthropy, reform, guidance, or example : what is called the artistic faculty not being by any means the same thing as a general capacity for doing good work, diverted into this one strait or shallow in default of a better outlet. Even were this true for example of a man so imperfect as Burns, it would remain false of a man so perfect as Keats. The great men, on whichever side one finds them, are never found trying to take truce or patch up terms. Savonarola burnt Boccaccio ; Cromwell proscribed Shakespeare. The early Christians were not great at verse or sculpture. Men of immense capacity and energy who do seem to think or assert it possible to serve both masters—a Dante, a Shelley, a Hugo—poets whose work is mixed with and coloured by personal action or suffering for some cause moral or political —these even are no real exceptions. It is not as artists that they do or seem to do this. The work done may be, and in such high cases often must be, of supreme value to art ; but not the moral implied.

Strip the sentiments and re-clothe them in bad verse, what residue will be left of the slightest importance to art? Invert them, retaining the manner or form (supposing this feasible, which it might be), and art has lost nothing. Save the shape, and art will take care of the soul for you : * unless that is all right, she will refuse to run or start at all ; but the shape or style of workmanship each artist is bound to look to, whether or no he may choose to trouble himself about the moral or other bearings of his work. This principle, which makes the manner of doing a thing the essence of the thing done, the purpose or result of it the accident, thus reversing the principle of moral or material duty, must inevitably expose art to the condemnation of the other party—the party of those who (as aforesaid) regard what certain of their leaders call an earnest life or a great acted poem (that is, material virtue or the mere doing and saying of good or instructive deeds and words) as infinitely preferable to any possible feat of art. Opinion is free, and the choice always open ; but if any man leaning on crutches of theory chooses to halt between the two camps, it shall be at his own peril—imminent peril of conviction as one unfit for service on either side. For Puritanism is in this one thing absolutely right about art ; they cannot live

---

* Of course, there can be no question here of bad art : which indeed is a nonentity or contradiction in terms, as to speak of good art is to run into tautology. It is assumed, to begin with, that the artist has something to say or do worth doing or saying in an artistic form.

ground, which made him not simply the chief of
dramatic story, but also the great master of morals,*
would not have failed of foothold or eyesight even
in this cloudy and noisy borderland of vision and of

* The reader who cares to remember that everything here set
down is of immediate importance and necessity for the understand-
ing of the matter in hand (namely, the life of Blake, and the
faith and works which made that life what it was) may as well take
here a word of comment. It will soon be necessary for even the
very hack-writers and ingenious people of ready pens and wits who
now babble about Balzac in English and French as a splendid
specimen of their craft, fertile but faulty, and so forth—to under-
stand that they have nothing to do with Balzac; that he is not of
their craft, nor of any but the common craft of all great men—the
guild of godlike things and people; that a shelf holding "all
Balzac's novels—forty volumes long," is not "cabin-furniture" for
any chance "passenger" to select or reject. Error and deficiency
there may be in his work; but none such as they can be aware of.
Of poetic form, for example, we know that he knew nothing; the
error would be theirs who should think his kind of work the worse
for that. Among men equally great, the distinctive supremacy of
Balzac is this; that whereas the great men who are pure artists
(Shakespeare for instance) work by implication only, and hardly
care about descending to the level of a preacher's or interpreter's
work, he is the only man not of their kind who is great enough to
supply their place in his own way—to be their correlative in
a different class of workmen; being from his personal point of view
simply impeccable and infallible. The pure artist never asserts;
he suggests, and therefore his meaning is totally lost upon moralists
and sciolists—is indeed irreparably wasted upon the run of men who
cannot work out suggestions. Balzac asserts; and Balzac cannot
blunder or lie. So profound and extensive a capacity of moral
apprehension no other prose writer, no man of mere analytic faculty,
ever had or can have. This assuredly, when men become (as they
will have to become) capable of looking beyond the mere clothes
and skin of his work, will be always, as we said, his great especial
praise; that he was, beyond any other man, the master of morals—
the greatest direct expounder of actual moral fact. Once consent
to forget or overlook the mere *entourage* and social habiliment of

I

faith. Even to him too, the supreme student and
interpreter of things, our impulsive prophet with his
plea of mere direct inspiration might have been of
infinite help and use : to such an eye and brain as
his, Blake might have made straight the ways
which Swedenborg had left crooked, set right the
problems which mesmerism had set wrong.   As
however we cannot have this, we must do what
share of interpreter's work falls to our lot as well
as we can.

There are two points in the work of Blake which
first claim notice and explanation ; two points con-
nected, but not inseparable ; his mysticism and his
mythology.   This latter is in fact hardly more in its
relation to the former, than the clothes to the body
or the body to the soul.   To make either comprehen-
sible, it is requisite above all things to get sight of
the man in whom they became incarnate and active
as forces or as opinions.   Now, to those who regard
mysticism with distaste or contempt, as essentially
in itself a vain or noxious thing—a sealed bag or
bladder that can only be full either of wind or of poison
—the man, being above all and beyond all a mystic
in the most subtle yet most literal sense, must remain
obscure and contemptible.   Such readers—if indeed
such men should choose or care to become readers at
all—will be (for one thing) unable to understand that

Balzac's intense and illimitable intellect, you cannot fail of seeing
that he of all men was fittest to grapple with all strange things and
words, and compel them by divine violence of spiritual rape to bring
forth flowers and fruits good for food and available for use.

one may think it worth while to follow out and track
to its root the peculiar faith or fancy of a mystic with-
out being ready to accept his deductions and his
assertions as absolute and durable facts. Servility
of extended hand or passive brain is the last quality
that a mystic of the nobler kind will demand or
desire in his auditors. Councils and synods may
put forth notes issued under their stamp, may exact
of all recipients to play the part of clerks and indorse
their paper with shut eyes: to the mystic such a
way of doing spiritual business would seem the very
frenzy of fatuity; whatever else may be profitable,
that (he would say) is suicidal. And assuredly it is
not to be expected that Blake's mystical creed, when
once made legible and even partially coherent, should
prove likely to win over proselytes. Nor can this be
the wish or the object of a reasonable commentator,
whose desire is merely to do art a good turn in some
small way, by explaining the "faith and works" of
a great artist. It is true that whatever a good poet
or a good painter has thought worth representing by
verse or design must probably be worth considering
before one deliver judgment on it. But the office of
an apostle of some new faith and the business of a
commentator on some new evangel are two sufficiently
diverse things. The present critic has not (happily)
to preach the gospel as delivered by Blake; he has
merely, if possible, to make the text of that gospel a
little more readable. And this must be worth doing,
if it be worth while to touch on Blake's work at all.
What is true of all poets and artists worth judging

is especially true of him ; that critics who attempt to
judge him piecemeal do not in effect judge him at all,
but some one quite different from him, and some one
(to any serious student) probably more inexplicable
than the real man. For what are we to make of a
man whose work deserves crowning one day and
hooting the next? If the "Songs" be so good, are
not those who praise them bound to examine and try
what merit may be latent in the "Prophecies"?—
bound at least to explain as best they may how the
one comes to be worth so much and the other worth
nothing? On this side alone the biography appears
to us emphatically deficient ; here only do we feel
how much was lost, how much impaired by the un-
timely death of the writer. Those who had to com-
plete his work have done their part admirably well ;
but here they have not done enough. We are not
bound to accept Blake's mysticism ; we are bound to
take some account of it. A disciple must take his
master's word for proof of the thing preached. This
it would be folly to expect of a biographer ; even
Boswell falls short of this, having courage on some
points to branch off from the strait pathway of his
teacher and strike into a small speculative track of
his own. But a biographer must be capable of ex-
pounding the evangel (or, if such a word could be,
"dysangel") of his hero, however far he may be
from thinking it worth acceptance. And this, one
must admit, the writers on Blake have upon the whole
failed of doing. Consequently their critical remarks
on such specimens of Blake's more speculative and

subtle work as did find favour in their sight have but a narrow range and a limited value. Some clue to the main character of the artist's habit of mind we may hope already to have put into the reader's hands—some frayed and ravelled "end of the golden string," which with due labour he may "wind up into a ball." To pluck out the heart of Blake's mystery is a task which every man must be left to attempt for himself: for this prophet is cer-tainly not "easier to be played on than a pipe." Keeping fast in hand what clue we have, we may nevertheless succeed in making some further way among the clouds. One thing is too certain; if we insist on having hard ground under foot all the way we shall not get far. The land lying before us, bright with fiery blossom and fruit, musical with blowing branches and falling waters, is not to be seen or travelled in save by help of such light as lies upon dissolving dreams and dividing clouds. By moonrise, to the sound of wind at sunset, one may tread upon the limit of this land and gather as with muffled apprehension some soft remote sense of the singing of its birds and flowering of its fields.

This premised, we may start with a clear con-science. Of Blake's faith we have by this time endea-voured to give the reader some conception—if a faint one, yet at least not a false: of the form assumed by that faith (what we have called the mythology) we need not yet take cognizance. To follow out in full all his artistic and illustrative work, with a view to extract from each separate fruit of it some

core of significance, would be an endless labour : and
we are bound to consider what may be feasible
rather than what, if it were feasible, might be worth
doing. Therefore the purpose of this essay is in the
main to deal with the artist's personal work in pre-
ference to what is merely illustrative and decorative.
Designs, however admirable, made to order for the
text of Blair, of Hayley, or of Young, are in com-
parison with the designer's original and spontaneous
work mere extraneous by-play. These also are if
anything better known than Blake's other labours.
Again, the mass of his surviving designs is so enor-
mous and as yet (except for the inestimable Catalogue
in Vol. 2 of the " Life ") so utterly chaotic and un-
arrangeable that in such an element one can but
work as it were by fits and plunges. Of these designs
there must always be many which not having seen
we cannot judge ; many too on which artists alone
are finally competent to deliver sentence by authority.
Moreover the supreme merits as well as the more
noticeable qualities merely special and personal of
Blake are best seen in his mixed work. Where both
text and design are wholly his own, and the two
forms or sides of his art so coalesce or overlap as to
become inextricably interfused, we have the best
chance of seeing and judging what the workman
essentially was. In such an enterprise, we must be
always duly grateful for any help or chance of help
given us : and for one invaluable thing we have at
starting to give due honour and thanks to the bio-
grapher. He has, one may rationally hope, finally

beaten to powder the rickety and flaccid old theory
of Blake's madness. Any one wishing to moot that
question again will have to answer or otherwise get
over the facts and inferences so excellently set out
in Chap. xxxv. : to refute them we may fairly con-
sider impossible. Here at least no funeral notice or
obsequies will be bestowed on the unburied carcase
of that forlorn fiction. Assuming as a reasonable
ground for our present labour that Blake was superior
to the run of men, we shall spend no minute of time
in trying to prove that he was not inferior. Logic
and sense alike warn us off such barren ground.

Of the editing of the present selections—a matter
evidently of most delicate and infinite labour—we
have here to say this only ; that as far as one can see
it could not have been done better : and indeed that
it could only have been done so well by the rarest of
happy chances. Even with the already published
poems there was enough work to get through ; for
even these had suffered much from the curiously
reckless and helpless neglect of form which was
natural to Blake when his main work was done and
his interest in the matter prematurely wound up.
Those only who have dived after the original copies
can fully appreciate or apprehend with what tender-
ness of justice and subtlety of sense these tumbled
folds have been gathered up and these ragged edges
smoothed off. As much power and labour has gone
to the perfect adjustment of these relics of another
man's work as a meaner man could have dreamed
only of expending on his own. Nor can any one

thoroughly enter into the value and excellence of the
thing here achieved who has not in himself the im-
pulsive instinct of form—the exquisite desire of just
and perfect work. Alike to those who seem to be
above it as to those who are evidently below, such
work must remain always inappreciable and inex-
plicable. To the ingeniously chaotic intellect, with
its admirable aptitude for all such feats of conjectural
cleverness as are worked out merely by strain and
spasm, it will seem an offensive waste of good work.
But to all who relish work for work's sake and art
for art's it will appear, as it is, simply invaluable—
the one thing worth having yet not to be had at any
price or by any means, except when it falls in your
way by divine accident. True however as all this is
of the earlier and easier part of the editor's task, it
is incomparably more true of the arrangement and
selection of poems fit for publishing out of the price-
less but shapeless chaos of unmanageable MSS.
The good work here done and good help here given
it is not possible to over-estimate. Every light slight
touch of mere arrangement has the mark of a great
art consummate in great things—the imprint of a
sure and strong hand, in which the thing to be done
lies safe and gathers faultless form. These great
things too are so small in mere size and separate
place that they can never get praised in due detail.
They are great by dint of the achievement implied
and the forbearance involved. Only a chief among
lyric poets could so have praised the songs of Blake;
only a leader among imaginative painters could so

have judged his designs; only an artist himself
supreme at once in lordship of colour and mastery of
metre could so have spoken of Blake's gifts and feats
in metre and colour. Reading these notes, one can
rest with sufficient pleasure on the conviction that,
wherever else there may be failure in attaining the
right word of judgment or of praise, here certainly
there is none. Here there is more than (what all
critics may have) goodwill and desire to give just
thanks; for here there is authority, and the right to
seem right in delivering sentence.

But these notes, good as they are and altogether
valuable, are the least part of the main work. To
the beauty and nobility of style, the exquisite
strength of sifted English, the keen vision and deep
clearness of expression, which characterize as well
these brief prefaces as the notes on " Job " and that
critical summary in the final chapter of the " Life,"
one need hardly desire men's attention; that splendid
power of just language and gift of grace in detail
stand out at once distinguishable from the surround-
ing work, praiseworthy as that also in the main is;
neither from the matter nor the manner can any
careful critic mistake the exact moment and spot
where the editor of the poems has taken up any part
of the business, laid any finger on the mechanism of
the book. But this work, easier to praise, must
have been also easier to perform than the more
immediate editorial labours which were here found
requisite. With care inappreciable and invaluable
fidelity has the editing throughout been done. The

selection must of necessity have been to a certain degree straitened and limited by many minor and temporary considerations; publishers, tasters, and such-like, must have fingered the work here and there, snuffing at this and nibbling at that as their manner is. For the work and workman have yet their way to make in the judicious reading world; and so long as they have, they are more or less in the lax limp clutch of that "dieu ganache des bourgeois" who sits nodding and ponderously dormant in the dust of publishing offices, ready at any jog of the elbow to snarl and start—a new Pan, feeding on the pastures of a fat and foggy land his Arcadian herds of review or magazine:

ἐντί γε πικρός,
καί οἱ ἀεὶ δριμεῖα χολὰ ποτὶ ῥινὶ κάθηται.

Arcadian virtue and Bœotian brain, under the presidency of such a stertorous and splenetic goat-god, given to be sleepy in broadest noonday, are not the best crucibles for art to be tried in. Then, again, thought had to be taken for the poems themselves; not merely how to expose them in most acceptable form for public acceptance, but how at the same time to give them in the main all possible fulness of fair play. This too by dint of work and patience, still more by dint of pliable sense and taste, has been duly accomplished. Future editions may be, and in effect will have to be, altered and enlarged: it is as well for people to be aware that they have not yet a final edition of Blake; that will

have to be some day completed on a due scale.   But
for the great mass of his lyrical verse all there was
to do has been done here, and the ground-plan taken
of a larger building to come.   These preliminaries
stated, we pass on to a rapid general review of those
two great divisions which may be taken as resuming
for us the ripe poetry of Blake's manhood.   Two divi-
sions, the one already published and partially known,
the other now first brought into light and baptized
with some legible name ; the " Songs of Innocence
and Experience," and the " Ideas of Good and Evil."
Under this latter head we will class for purposes of
readier reference as well the smaller MS. volume of
fairly transcribed verses as the great mass of more
disorderly writing in verse and prose to which the
name above given is attached in a dim broad scrawl
of the pencil evidently meant to serve as general
title, though set down only on the reverse page of
the second MS. leaf.   This latter and larger book,
extending in date at least from 1789 to (August) 1811,
but presumably beyond the later date, is the great
source and treasure-house from which has been
drawn out most of the fresh verse and all of the
fresh prose here given us : and is of course among
the most important relics left of Blake.

     First then for the " Songs of Innocence and Ex-
perience."   These at a first naming recall only that
incomparable charm of form in which they first came
out clothed, and hence vex the souls of men with
regretful comparison.   For here by hard necessity
we miss the lovely and luminous setting of designs,

which makes the "Songs" precious and pleasurable to those who know or care for little else of the master's doing ; the infinite delight of those drawings, sweeter to see than music to hear, where herb and stem break into grace of shape and blossom of form, and the branch-work is full of little flames and flowers, catching as it were from the verse enclosed the fragrant heat and delicate sound they seem to give back ; where colour lapses into light and light assumes feature in colour. If elsewhere the artist's strange strength of thought and hand is more visible, nowhere is there such pure sweetness and singleness of design in his work. All the tremulous and tender splendour of spring is mixed into the written word and coloured draught ; every page has the smell of April. Over all things given, the sleep of flocks and the growth of leaves, the laughter in dividing lips of flowers and the music at the moulded mouth of the flute-player, there is cast a pure fine veil or light, softer than sleep and keener than sunshine. The sweetness of sky and leaf, of grass and water— the bright light life of bird and child and beast—is so to speak kept fresh by some graver sense of faithful and mysterious love, explained and vivified by a conscience and purpose in the artist's hand and mind. Such a fiery outbreak of spring, such an insurrection of fierce floral life and radiant riot of childish power and pleasure, no poet or painter ever gave before : such lustre of green leaves and flushed limbs, kindled cloud and fervent fleece, was never wrought into speech or shape. Nevertheless this decorative work is after all the mere husk and shell of the "Songs." These also, we may notice, have to some extent shared the comparative popularity of the designs which serve as framework to them. They have absolutely achieved the dignity of a reprint; have had a chance before now of swimming for life; whereas most of Blake's offspring have been thrown into Lethe bound hand and foot, without hope of ever striking out in one fair effort. Perhaps on some accounts this preference has been not unreasonable. What was written for children can hardly offend men; and the obscurities and audacities of the prophet would here have been clearly out of place. It is indeed some relief to a neophyte serving in the outer courts of such an intricate and cloudy temple, to come upon this little side-chapel set about with the simplest wreaths and smelling of the fields rather than incense, where all the singing is done by clear children's voices to the briefest and least complex tunes. Not at first without a sense of release does the human mind get quit for a little of the clouds of Urizen, the fires of Orc, and all the Titanic apparatus of prophecy. And these poems are really unequalled in their kind. Such verse was never written for children since verse-writing began. Only in a few of those faultless fragments of childish rhyme which float without name or form upon the memories of men shall we find such a pure clear cadence of verse, such rapid ring and flow of lyric laughter, such sweet and direct choice of the just word and figure, such an impeccable simplicity; nowhere but here such a tender wisdom of holiness, such a light and perfume of innocence. Nothing like this was ever written on that text of the lion and the lamb; no such heaven of sinless animal life was ever conceived so intensely and sweetly.

Night

> " And there the lion's ruddy eyes
>   Shall flow with tears of gold,
> And pitying the tender cries,
>   And walking round the fold,
> Saying *Wrath by His meekness*
> *And by His health sickness*
> *Is driven away*
> *From our immortal day.*
> *And now beside thee, bleating lamb,*
>   *I can lie down and sleep,*
> *Or think on Him who bore thy name,*
>   *Graze after thee, and weep.*"

The leap and fall of the verse is so perfect as to make it a fit garment and covering for the profound tenderness of faith and soft strength of innocent impulse embodied in it. But the whole of this hymn of *Night* is wholly beautiful; being perhaps one of the two poems of loftiest loveliness among all the "Songs of Innocence." The other is that called *The Little Black Boy;* a poem especially exquisite for its noble forbearance from vulgar pathos and achievement of the highest and most poignant sweetness of speech and sense; in which the poet's mysticism is baptized with pure water and taught to speak as from faultless lips of children, to such effect as this.

" And we are put on earth a little space
That we may learn to bear the beams of love ;
And these black bodies and this sunburnt face
Are like a cloud and like a shady grove."

Other poems of a very perfect beauty are those of *The Piper, The Lamb, The Chimney-sweeper,* and *The two-days-old Baby* ; all, for the music in them, more like the notes of birds caught up and given back than the modulated measure of human verse. One cannot say, being so slight and seemingly wrong in metrical form, how they come to be so absolutely right ; but right even in point of verses and words they assuredly are. Add fuller formal completion of rhyme and rhythm to that song of *Infant Joy,* and you have broken up the soft bird-like perfection of clear light sound which gives it beauty ; the little bodily melody of soulless and painless laughter.

Against all articulate authority we do however class several of the " Songs of Experience " higher for the great qualities of verse than anything in the earlier division of these poems. If the " Songs of Innocence " have the shape and smell of leaves or buds, these have in them the light and sound of fire or the sea. Entering among them, a fresher savour and a larger breath strikes one upon the lips and forehead. In the first part we are shown who they are who have or who deserve the gift of spiritual sight : in the second, what things there are for them to see when that gift has been given. Innocence, the quality of beasts and children, has the keenest eyes ; and such eyes alone can discern and interpret the actual mysteries of experience. It is natural that this second part, dealing as it does with such things as underlie the outer forms of the first part, should rise higher and dive deeper in point of mere words. These give the distilled perfume and extracted blood of the veins in the rose-leaf, the sharp, liquid, intense spirit crushed out of the broken kernel in the fruit. The last of the " Songs of Innocence " is a prelude to these poems ; in it the poet summons to judgment the young and single-spirited, that by right of the natural impulse of delight in them they may give sentence against the preachers of convention and assumption ; and in the first poem of the second series he, by the same "voice of the bard," calls upon earth herself, the mother of all these, to arise and become free : since upon her limbs also are bound the fetters, and upon her forehead also has fallen the shadow, of a jealous law : from which nevertheless, by faithful following of instinct and divine liberal impulse, earth and man shall obtain deliverance.

> " Hear the voice of the bard !
>   Who present, past, and future sees :
> Whose ears have heard
> The ancient Word
>   That walked among the silent trees :
> Calling the lapsèd soul
>   And weeping in the evening dew ;
> That might control
> The starry pole
>   And fallen fallen light renew ! "

and work together, or the one under the other. All ages which were great enough to have space for both, to hold room for a fair fighting-field between them, have always accepted and acted upon this evident fact. Take the Renaissance age for one example; you must have Knox or Ronsard, Scotch or French; not both at once; there is no place under reformers for the singing of a "Pléiade." Take the mediæval period in its broadest sense; not to speak of the notably heretical and immoral Albigeois with their exquisite school of heathenish verse, or of that other rebellious gathering under the great emperor Frederick II., a poet and pagan, when eastern arts and ideas began to look up westward at one man's bidding and open out Saracenic prospects in the very face and teeth of the Church—look at home into familiar things, and see by such poems as Chaucer's "Court of Love," absolutely one in tone and handling as it is with the old Albigensian "Aucassin" and all its paganism,* how the poets of

---

* Observe especially in Chaucer's most beautiful of young poems that appalling passage, where, turning the favourite edgetool of religious menace back with point inverted upon those who forged it, the poet represents men and women of religious habit or life as punished in the next world, beholding afar off with jealous regret the salvation and happiness of Venus and all her servants (converse of the Hörsel legend, which shows the religious or anti-Satanic view of the matter; though there too there is some pity or sympathy implied for the pagan side of things, revealing in the tradition the presence and touch of some poet): expressly punished, these monks and nuns, for their continence and holiness of life, and compelled after death to an eternity of fruitless repentance for having wilfully missed of pleasure and made light of indulgence in this

H

the time, with their eager nascent worship of beautiful form and external nature, dealt with established opinion and the incarnate moralities of church or household. It is easy to see why the Church on its own principle found it (as in the Albigensian case) a matter of the gravest necessity to have such schools of art and thought cut down or burnt out. Priest and poet, all those times through, were proverbially on terms of reciprocal biting and striking. That magnificent invention of making " Art the handmaid of Religion " had not been stumbled upon in the darkness of those days. Neither minstrel nor monk

world; which is perfect Albigeois. Compare the famous speech in "Aucassin et Nicolette," where the typical hero weighs in a judicial manner the respective attractions of heaven and hell; deciding of course dead against the former on account of the deplorably bad company kept there; priests, hermits, saints, and such-like, in lieu of knights and ladies, painters and poets. One may remark also, the minute this pagan revival begins to get breathing-room, how there breaks at once into flower a most passionate and tender worship of nature, whether as shown in the bodily beauty of man and woman or in the outside loveliness of leaf and grass; both Chaucer and his anonymous southern colleague being throughout careful to decorate their work with the most delicate and splendid studies of colour and form. Either of the two choice morsels of doctrinal morality cited above would have exquisitely suited the palate of Blake. He in his time, one need not doubt, was considerably worried and gibbered at by " monkeys in houses of brick," moral theorists, and " pantopragmatic " men of all sorts; what can we suppose he would have said or done in an epoch given over to preachers (lay, clerical, and mixed) who assert without fear or shame that you may demand, nay are bound to demand, of a picture or poem what message it has for you, what may be its moral utility or material worth ? " Poetry must conform itself to " &c.; " art must have a mission and meaning appreciable by earnest men in an age of work," and so forth. These be thy gods, O Philistia.

would have caught up the idea with any rapture. As indeed they would have been unwise to do ; for the thing is impossible. Art is not like fire or water, a good servant and bad master; rather the reverse. She will help in nothing, of her own know-ledge or freewill : upon terms of service you will get worse than nothing out of her. Handmaid of religion, exponent of duty, servant of fact, pioneer of morality, she cannot in any way become ; she would be none of these things though you were to bray her in a mortar. All the battering in the world will never hammer her into fitness for such an office as that. It is at her peril, if she tries to do good : one might say, borrowing terms from the other party, "she shall not try that under penalty of death and damnation." Her business is not to do good on other grounds, but to be good on her own : all is well with her while she sticks fast to that. To ask help or furtherance from her in any extraneous good work is exactly as rational as to expect lyrical beauty of form and flow in a logical treatise. The contingent result of having good art about you and living in a time of noble writing or painting may no doubt be this ; that the spirit and mind of men then living will receive on some points a certain exaltation and insight caught from the influence of such forms and colours of verse or painting ; will become for one thing incapable of tolerating bad work, and capable therefore of reasonably relishing the best ; which of course implies and draws with it many other advantages of a sort you may call

moral or spiritual. But if the artist does his work
with an eye to such results or for the sake of bring-
ing about such improvements, he will too probably
fail even of them. Art for art's sake first of all, and
afterwards we may suppose all the rest shall be
added to her (or if not she need hardly be overmuch
concerned); but from the man who falls to artistic
work with a moral purpose, shall be taken away
even that which he has—whatever of capacity for
doing well in either way he may have at starting.
A living critic * of incomparably delicate insight and
subtly good sense, himself "impeccable" as an artist,
calls this "the heresy of instruction" (*l'hérésie de*

* I will not resist the temptation to write a brief word or
comment on this passage. While my words of inadequate and now
of joyless praise were in course of printing, I heard that a mortal
illness had indeed stricken the illustrious poet, the faultless critic,
the fearless artist; that no more of fervent yet of perfect verse, no
more of subtle yet of sensitive comment, will be granted us at the
hands of Charles Baudelaire : that now for ever we must fall back
upon what is left us. It is precious enough. We may see again as
various a power as was his, may feel again as fiery a sympathy, may
hear again as strange a murmur of revelation, as sad a whisper of
knowledge, as mysterious a music of emotion ; we shall never find
so keen, so delicate, so deep an unison of sense and spirit. What
verse he could make, how he loved all fair and felt all strange
things, with what infallible taste he knew at once the limit and the
licence of his art, all may see at a glance. He could give beauty
to the form, expression to the feeling, most horrible and most
obscure to the senses or souls of lesser men. The chances of things
parted us once and again ; the admiration of some years, at last in
part expressed, brought me near him by way of written or trans-
mitted word ; let it be an excuse for the insertion of this note, and
for a desire, if so it must be, to repeat for once the immortal words
which too often return upon our lips ;

"Ergo in perpetuum, frater, ave atque vale

l'enseignement) : one might call it, for the sake of a shorter and more summary name, the great moral heresy. Nothing can be imagined more futile ; nothing so ruinous. Once let art humble herself, plead excuses, try at any compromise with the Puritan principle of doing good, and she is worse than dead. Once let her turn apologetic, and promise or imply that she really will now be "loyal to fact" and useful to men in general (say; by furthering their moral work or improving their moral nature), she is no longer of any human use or value. The one fact for her which is worth taking account of is simply mere excellence of verse or colour, which involves all manner of truth and loyalty necessary to her well-being. That is the important thing ; to have her work supremely well done, and to disregard all contingent consequences. You may extract out of Titian's work or Shakespeare's any moral or immoral inference you please ; it is none of their business to see after that. Good painting or writing, on any terms, is a thing quite sufficiently in accordance with fact and reality for them. Supplant art by all means if you can ; root it out and try to plant in its place something useful or at least safe, which at all events will not impede the noble moral labour and trammel the noble moral life of Puritanism. But in the name of sense and fact itself let us have done with all abject and ludicrous pretence of coupling the two in harness or grafting the one on the other's stock : let us hear no more of the moral mission of earnest art ; let us no longer be pestered with the frantic and flatulent assumptions of quasi-secular clericalism willing to think the best of all sides, and ready even, with consecrating hand, to lend meritorious art and poetry a timely pat or shove. Philistia had far better (always providing it be possible) crush art at once, hang or burn it out of the way, than think of plucking out its eyes and setting it to grind moral corn in the Philistine mills ; which it is certain not to do at all well. Once and again the time has been that there was no art worth speaking of afloat anywhere in the world ; but there never has been or can have been a time when art, or any kind of art worth having, took active service under Puritanism, or indulged for its part in the deleterious appetite of saving souls or helping humanity in general along the way of labour and progress.* Let no artist or poet listen to the bland bark of those porter dogs of the Puritan kingdom even when they fawn and flirt with tongue or tail. *Cave canem.* That Cerberus of the portals of Philistia will swallow your honey-cake to no purpose ; if he does not turn and rend you, his slaver

---

* There are exceptions, we are told from the first, to all rules ; and the sole exception to this one is great enough to do all but establish a rival rule. But, as I have tried already to say, the work—all the work—of Victor Hugo is in its essence artistic, in its accident alone philanthropic or moral. I call this the sole exception, not being aware that the written work of Dante or Shelley did ever tend to alter the material face of things ; though they may have desired that it should, and though their unwritten work may have done so. Accidentally of course a poet's work may tend towards some moral or actual result ; that is beside the question.

as he licks your hand will leave it impotent and palsied for all good work.

Thus much it seemed useful to premise, by way of exposition rather than excursion, so as once for all to indicate beyond chance of mistake the real point of view taken during life by Blake, and necessary to be taken by those who would appreciate his labours and purposes. Error on this point would be ruinous to any student. No one again need be misled by the artist's eager incursions into grounds of faith or principle; his design being merely to readjust all questions of such a kind by the light of art and law of imagination—to reduce all outlying provinces, and bring them under government of his own central empire—the "fourfold spiritual city" of his vision. Power of imaginative work and insight —"the Poetic Genius, as you now call it"—was in his mind, we shall soon have to see, "the first principle" of all things moral or material, " and all the others merely derivative ; " a hazardous theory in its results and corollaries, but one which Blake at all events was always ready to push to its utmost conse-quences and defend at its extreme outworks. Against all pretensions on the part of science or experimental reasoning to assume this post he was especially given to rebel and recalcitrate. Whether or no he were actually prepared to fight science in earnest on its own pitched field—to dispute seriously the con-quest of facts achieved by it—may be questionable ; I for one am inclined to disbelieve this, and to refer much of his verbal pugnacity on such matters to the

strong irregular humour, rough and loose as that of
children, and the half simple half scornful love of
paradox, which were ingrained in the man. For
argument and proof he had the contempt of a
child or an evangelist. Not that he would have
fallen back in preference upon the brute resource of
thaumaturgy ; the coarse and cheap machinery of
material miracle was wholly insufficient and despi-
cable to him. No wonder-monger of the low sort
need here have hoped for a pupil, a colleague, or an
authority. This the biographer has acutely noted,
and taken well into account ; as we must all do
under pain of waste time and dangerous error. Let
this too be taken note of ; that to believe a thing is
not necessarily to heed or respect it ; to despise a
thing is not the same as to disbelieve it. Those who
argue against the reality of the meaner forms of
"spiritualism " in disembodied life, on the ground
apparently that whatever is not of the patent
tangible flesh must be of high imperishable import-
ance, are merely acting on the old ascetic assump-
tion that the body is of its nature base and the soul
of its nature noble, and that between the two there
is a great gulf fixed, neither to be bridged over
nor filled up. Blake, as a mystic of the higher
and subtler kind, would have denied this superior
separate vitality of the spirit ; but far from inferring
thence that the soul must expire with the body,
would have maintained that the essence of the body
must survive with the essence of the soul : accepting
thus (as we may have to observe he did), in its most

absolute and profound sense, the doctrine of the
Resurrection of the Flesh. As a temporary blind
and bar to the soul while dwelling on earth, fit only
(if so permitted) to impede the spiritual vision and
hamper the spiritual feet, he did indeed appear to
contemn the "vegetable" and sensual nature of
man ; but on no ascetic grounds. Admitting once
for all that it was no fit or just judge of things
spiritual, he claimed for the body on its own ground
an equal honour and an equal freedom with the soul ;
denying the river's channel leave to be called the
river—refusing to the senses the licence claimed for
them by materialism to decide by means of bodily
insight or sensation questions removed from the
sphere of sensual evidence—and reserving always
the absolute assurance and certain faith that things
do exist of which the flesh can take no account, but
only the spirit—he would grant to the physical
nature the full right to every form of physical
indulgence : would allow the largest liberty to all
powers and capacities of pleasure proper to the pure
bodily life. In a word, translated into crude
practical language, his creed was about this : as
long as a man believes all things he may do any
thing ; scepticism (not sin) is alone damnable, being
the one thing purely barren and negative ; do what
you will with your body, as long as you refuse it
leave to disprove or deny the life eternally inherent
in your soul. That we believe is what people call or
have called by some such name as "antinomian
mysticism : " do anything but doubt, and you shall

not in the end be utterly lost. Clearly enough it
was Blake's faith ; and one assuredly grounded not
on mere contempt of the body, but on an equal
reverence for spirit and flesh as the two sides or
halves of a completed creature : a faith which will
allow to neither licence to confute or control the
other. The body shall not deny, and the spirit shall
not restrain; the one shall not prescribe doubt
through reasoning ; the other shall not preach salva-
tion through abstinence. A man holding such
tenets sees no necessity to deny that the indulged
soul may be in some men as ignoble as the indulged
body in others may be noble; and that a spirit
ignoble while embodied need not become noble or
noticeable by the process of getting disembodied ;
in other words, that death or change need not be
expected to equalize the unequal by raising or
lowering spirits to one settled level. Much of the
existing evidence as to baser spiritual matters,
Blake, like other men of candid sense and insight,
would we may suppose have accepted—and dropped
with the due contempt into the mass of facts worth
forgetting only, which the experience of every man
must carry till his memory succeeds in letting
go its hold of them. Nothing, he would doubt-
less have said, is worth disputing in disproof of,
which if proved would not be worth giving thanks
for. Let such things be or not be as the fates of
small things please ; but will any one prove or dis-
prove for me the things I hold by warrant of imagi-
native knowledge ? things impossible to discover,

to analyze, to attest, to undervalue, to certify, or to doubt?

This old war—not (as some would foolishly have it defined) a war between facts and fancies, reason and romance, poetry and good sense, but simply between the imagination which apprehends the spirit of a thing and the understanding which dissects the body of a fact—this strife which can never be decided or ended—was for Blake the most important question possible. He for one, madman or no madman, had the sense to see that the one thing utterly futile to attempt was a reconciliation between two sides of life and thought which have no community of work or aim imaginable. This is no question of reconciling contraries. Admit all the implied pretensions of art, they remain simply nothing to science; accept all the actual deductions of science, they simply signify nothing to art. The eternal "Après?" is answer enough for both in turn. "True, then, if you will have it; but what have we to do with your good or bad poetries and paintings?" "Undeniably; but what are we to gain by your deductions and discoveries, right or wrong?" The betrothal of art and science were a thing harder to bring about and more profitless to proclaim than "the marriage of heaven and hell." It were better not to fight, but to part in peace; but better certainly to fight than to temporize, where no reasonable truce can be patched up. Poetry or art based on loyalty to science is exactly as absurd (and no more) as science guided by art or poetry.

Neither in effect can coalesce with the other and retain a right to exist. Neither can or (while in its sober senses) need wish to destroy the other; but they must go on their separate ways, and in this life their ways can by no possibility cross. Neither can or (unless in some fit of fugitive insanity) need wish to become valuable or respectable to the other: each must remain, on its own ground and to its own followers, a thing of value and deserving respect. To art, that is best which is most beautiful; to science, that is best which is most accurate; to morality, that is best which is most virtuous. Change or quibble upon the simple and generally accepted significance of these three words, "beautiful," "accurate," "virtuous," and you may easily (if you please, or think it worth while) demonstrate that the aim of all three is radically one and the same; but if any man be correct in thinking this exercise of the mind worth the expenditure of his time, that time must indeed be worth very little. You can say (but had perhaps better not say) that beauty is the truthfullest, accuracy the most poetic, and virtue the most beautiful of things; but a man of ordinary or decent insight will perceive that you have merely reduced an affair of things to an affair of words— shifted the body of one thing into the clothes or another—and proved actually nothing.

To attest by word or work the identity of things which never can become identical, was no part of Blake's object in life. What work it fell to his lot to do, that, having faith in the fates, he believed the

best work possible, and performed to admiration.
It is in consequence of this belief that, apart from
all conjectural or problematic theory, the work he
did is absolutely good.   Intolerant he was by nature
to a degree noticeable even among freethinkers and
prophets ; but the strange forms assumed by this
intolerance are best explicable by the singular facts
of his training—his perfect ignorance of well-known
ordinary things and imperfect quaint knowledge of
much that lay well out of the usual way.   He
retained always an excellent arrogance and a wholly
laudable self-reliance ; being incapable of weak-
eyed doubts or any shuffling modesty.   His great
tenderness had a lining ot contempt—his fiery self-
assertion a kernel of loyalty.   No one, it is evident,
had ever a more intense and noble enjoyment of
good or great works in other men—took sharper or
deeper delight in the sense of a loyal admiration :
being of his nature noble, fearless, and fond of all
things good ; a man made for believing.   This royal
temper of mind goes properly with a keen relish of
what excellence or greatness a man may have in
himself.   Those must be readiest to feel and to
express unalloyed and lofty pleasure in the great
powers and deeds of a neighbour, who, while
standing clear alike of reptile modesty and pre-
tentious presumption, perceive and know in them-
selves such qualities as give them a right to admire
and a right to applaud.   If a man thinks meanly of
himself, he can hardly in reason think much of his
judgment ; if he depreciates the value of his own

work, he depreciates also the value of his praise. Those are loyallest who have most of a just self-esteem; and their applause is best worth having. It is scarcely conceivable that a man should take delight in the real greatness or merit of his own work for so pitiful and barren a reason as merely that it *is* his own; should be unable to pass with a fresh and equal enjoyment from the study and relish of his own capacities and achievements to the study and relish of another man's. A timid jealousy, easily startled into shrieks of hysterical malice and disloyal spite, is (wherever you may fall in with it) the property of base men and mean artists who, at sight of some person or thing greater than themselves, are struck sharply by unconscious self-contempt, and at once, whether they know it or not, lose heart or faith in their own applauded work. To recognize their equal, even their better when he does come, must be the greatest delight of great men. "All the gods," says a French essayist, "delight in worship: is one lesser for the other's godhead? Divine things give divine thanks for companionship; the stars sang not one at once, but all together." Like all men great enough to enjoy greatness, Blake was born with the gift of admiration; and in his rapid and fervent nature it struck root and broke into flower at the least glimpse or chance of favourable weather. Therefore, if on no other ground, we may allow him his curious outbreaks of passionate dispraise and scorn against all such as seemed to stand in the way of his art.

Again, as we have noted, he had a faith of his own, made out of art for art's sake, and worked by means of art; and whatever made against this faith was as hateful to him as any heresy to any pietist. In a rough and rapid way he chose to mass and sum up under some one or two types, comprehensible at first sight to few besides himself, the main elements of opposition which he conceived to exist. Thus for instance the names of Locke and Newton, of Bacon and Voltaire, recur with the most singular significance in his writings, as emblems or incarnate symbols of the principles opposite to his own : and when the clue is once laid hold of, and the ear once accustomed to the curious habit of direct mythical metaphor or figure peculiar to Blake—his custom of getting whole classes of men or opinions embodied, for purposes of swift irregular attack, in some one representative individual—much is at once clear and amenable to critical reason which seemed before mere tempestuous incoherence and clamour of bodiless rhetoric. There is also a certain half-serious perversity and wilful personal humour in the choice and use of these representative names, which must be taken into account by a startled reader unless he wishes to run off at a false tangent. After all, it is perhaps impossible for any one not specially qualified by nature for sympathy with such a man's kind of work, to escape going wrong in his estimate of Blake ; to such excesses of paradox did the poet-painter push his favourite points, and in such singular attire did he bring forward his most

serious opinions.   But at least the principal and most
evident chances of error may as well be indicated,
by way of warning off the over-hasty critic from
shoals on which otherwise he is all but certain to run.

It is a thing especially worth regretting that
Balzac, in his Swedenborgian researches, could not
have fallen in with Blake's "prophetic" works.
Passed through the crucible of that supreme intellect
—submitted to the test of that supple practical sense,
that laborious apprehension, so delicate and so pas-
sionate at once, of all forms of thought or energy,
which were the great latent gifts of the deepest and
widest mind that ever worked within the limits of
inventive prose—the strange floating forces of Blake's
instinctive and imaginative work might have been
explained and made applicable to direct ends in a
way we cannot now hope for.   The incomparable
power of condensing apparent vapour into tangible
and malleable form, of helping us to handle air
and measure mist, which is so instantly perceptible
whenever Balzac begins to open up any intricate
point of physical or moral speculation, would here
have been beyond price.   He alone who could push
analysis to the verge of creation, and with his
marvellous clearness of eye and strength of hand
turn discovery almost to invention; he who was
not "a prose Shakespeare" merely, but rather
perhaps a Shakespeare complete in all but the lyrical
faculty; he alone could have brought a scale to
weigh this water, a sieve to winnow this wind.
That wonderful wisdom, never at fault on its own

If they will hear the Word, earth and the dwellers upon earth shall be made again as little children; shall regain the strong simplicity of eye and hand proper to the pure and single of heart; and for them inspiration shall do the work of innocence; let them but once abjure the doctrine by which comes sin and the law by which comes prohibition. Therefore must the appeal be made; that the blind may see and the deaf hear, and the unity of body and spirit be made manifest in perfect freedom: and that to the innocent even the liberty of "sin" may be conceded. For if the soul suffer by the body's doing, are not both degraded? and if the body be oppressed for the soul's sake, are not both the losers?

> "O Earth, O Earth, return!
>   Arise from out the dewy grass!
> Night is worn,
> And the morn
>   Rises from the slumberous mass.
> Turn away no more;
>   Why wilt thou turn away?
> The starry shore,
> The watery floor,
>   Are given thee till the break of day."

For so long, during the night of law and oppression of material form, the divine evidences hidden under sky and sea are left her; even "till the break of day." Will she not get quit of this spiritual bondage to the heavy body of things, to the encumbrance of deaf clay and blind vegetation, before the light comes that shall redeem and reveal?

K

But the earth, being yet in subjection to the creator
of men, the jealous God who divided nature against
herself—father of woman and man, legislator of sex
and race—makes blind and bitter answer as in sleep,
" her locks covered with grey despair."

> " Prisoned on this watery shore,
>   Starry Jealousy does keep my den ;
> Cold and hoar,
> Weeping o'er,
>   I hear the father of the ancient men."

Thus, in the poet's mind, Nature and Religion
are the two fetters of life, one on the right wrist,
the other on the left ; an obscure material force on
this hand, and on that a mournful imperious law :
the law of divine jealousy, the government of a God
who weeps over his creature and subject with un-
profitable tears, and rules by forbidding and dividing :
the "Urizen" of the "Prophetic Books," clothed with
the coldness and the grief of remote sky and jealous
cloud.   Here as always, the cry is as much for light
as for licence, the appeal not more against pro-
hibition than against obscurity.

> " Can the sower sow by night,
>   Or the ploughman in darkness plough ? "

In the "Songs of Innocence" there is no such glory
of metre or sonorous beauty of lyrical work as here.
No possible effect of verse can be finer in a great
brief way than that given in the second and last
stanzas of the first part of this poem.   It recalls

within one's ear the long relapse of recoiling water
and wash of the refluent wave; in the third and
fourth lines sinking suppressed as with equal pulses
and soft sobbing noise of ebb, to climb again in the
fifth line with a rapid clamour of ripples and strong
ensuing strain of weightier sound, lifted with the
lift of the running and ringing sea.

Here also is that most famous of Blake's lyrics,
The Tiger; a poem beyond praise for its fervent
beauty and vigour of music. It appears by the
MS. that this was written with some pains; the
cancels and various readings bear marks of frequent
rehandling. One of the latter is worth transcription
for its own excellence and also in proof of the artist's
real care for details, which his rapid instinctive way
of work has induced some to disbelieve in.

> " Burnt in distant deeps or skies
>   The cruel fire of thine eyes?
>   Could heart descend or wings aspire? *
>   What the hand dare seize the fire?"

---

* Could God bring down his heart to the making of a thing so
deadly and strong? or could any lesser dæmonic force of nature
take to itself wings and fly high enough to assume power equal to
such a creation? Could spiritual force so far descend or material
force so far aspire? Or, when the very stars, and all the armed
children of heaven, the "helmed cherubim" that guide and the
"sworded seraphim" that guard their several planets, wept for
pity and fear at sight of this new force of monstrous matter seen in
the deepest night as a fire of menace to man—

> " Did he smile his work to see?
>   Did he who made the lamb make thee?"

We may add another cancelled reading to show how delicately
the poem has been perfected; although by an oversight of the

K 2

Nor has Blake left us anything of more profound
and perfect value than *The Human Abstract;* a
little mythical vision of the growth of error ; through
soft sophistries of pity and faith, subtle humility
of abstinence and fear, under which the pure simple
nature lies corrupted and strangled ; through selfish
loves which prepare a way for cruelty, and cruelty
that works by spiritual abasement and awe.

> " Soon spreads the dismal shade
> Of Mystery over his head ;
> And the caterpillar and fly
> Feed on the Mystery.

---

writer's most copies hitherto have retained some trace of the rough
first draught, neglecting in one line a change necessary to save the
sense as well as to complete the sentence.

> " And when thy heart began to beat,
> What dread hand and what dread feet
>
> Could fetch it from the furnace deep
> And in thy horrid ribs dare steep?
> In what clay and in what mould
> Were thine eyes of fury rolled ? "

Having cancelled this stanza or sketched ghost of a stanza, Blake
in his hurry of rejection did not at once remember to alter the last
line of the preceding one ; leaving thus a stone of some size and
slipperiness for editorial feet to trip upon, until the recovery of that
nobler reading—

> " What dread hand *framed thy* dread feet ? "

Nor was this little "rock of offence" cleared from the channel
of the poem even by the editor of 1827, who was yet not afraid of
laying hand upon the text. So grave a flaw in so short and so
great a lyric was well worth the pains of removing and is yet worth
the pains of accounting for ; on which ground this note must be of
value to all who take in verse with eye and ear instead of touching
it merely with eyelash and finger-tip in the manner of sand-blind
students.

And it bears the fruit of Deceit,
Ruddy and sweet to eat ;
And the raven his nest has made
In the thickest shade."

Under the shadow of this tree of mystery,* rooted
in artificial belief, all the meaner kind of devouring
things take shelter and eat of the fruit of its branches ;
the sweet poison of false faith, painted on its outer
husk with the likeness of all things noble and desir-
able ; and in the deepest implication of barren branch
and deadly leaf, the bird of death, with priests for
worshippers ("the priests of the raven of dawn,"
loud of lip and hoarse of throat until the light of day
have risen), finds house and resting-place. Only in
the "miscreative brain" of fallen men can such a
thing strike its tortuous root and bring forth its
fatal flower ; nowhere else in all nature can the
tyrants of divided matter and moral law, "Gods of
the earth and sea," find soil that will bear such
fruit.

Nowhere has Blake set forth his spiritual creed
more clearly and earnestly than in the last of the
"Songs of Experience." "Tirzah," in his mythology,
represents the mere separate and human nature,
mother of the perishing body and daughter of the

---

* Compare the passage in *Ahania* where the growth of it is
defined ; rooted in the rock of separation, watered with the tears of
a jealous God, shot up from sparks and fallen germs of material
seed ; being after all a growth of mere error, and vegetable (not
spiritual) life ; the topmost stem of it made into a cross whereon to
nail the dead redeemer and friend of men.

"religion" which occupies itself with laying down
laws for the flesh ; which, while pretending (and that
in all good faith) to despise the body and bring it
into subjection as with control of bit and bridle,
does implicitly overrate its power upon the soul for
evil or good, and thus falls foul of fact on all sides
by assuming that spirit and flesh are twain, and that
things pleasant and good for the one can properly
be loathsome or poisonous to the other. This
"religion" or "moral law," the inexplicable pro-
phet has chosen to baptize under the singular type
of "Rahab"—the "harlot virgin-mother," impure
by dint of chastity and forbearance from such things
as are pure to the pure of heart : for in this creed
the one thing unclean is the belief in uncleanness,
the one thing forbidden is to believe in the existence
of forbidden things. Of this mystical mother and
her daughter we shall have to take some further
account when once fairly afloat on those windy
waters of prophecy through which all who would
know Blake to any purpose must be content to steer
with such pilotage as they can get. For the present
it will be enough to note how eager and how direct
is the appeal here made against any rule or reasoning
based on reference to the mere sexual and external
nature of man—the nature made for ephemeral life
and speedy death, kept alive "to work and weep"
only through that mercy which "changed death into
sleep ; " how intense the reliance on redemption
from such a law by the grace of imaginative insight
and spiritual freedom, typified in "the death of

Jesus." * Nor are any of these poems finer in structure or nobler in metrical form.

This present edition of the "Songs of Experience" is richer by one of Blake's most admirable poems of childhood—a division of his work always of especial value for its fresh and sweet strength of feeling and of words. In this newly recovered _Cradle Song_ are perhaps the two loveliest lines of his writing:

> " Sleep, sleep: in thy sleep
> Little sorrows sit and weep." †

---

* Compare again in the _Vision of the Last Judgment_ (v. 2, p. 163), that definition of the "Divine body of the Saviour, the true Vine of Eternity," as " the Human Imagination, who appeared to me as coming to judgment among his saints, and throwing off the Temporal that the Eternal might be established." The whole of that subtle and eloquent rhapsody is about the best commentary attainable on Blake's mystical writings and designs. It is impossible to overstate the debt of gratitude due from all students of Blake to the transcriber and editor of the _Vision_, whose indefatigable sense and patient taste have made it legible for all. To have extracted it piecemeal from the chaos of notes jotted down by Blake in the most inconceivable way, would have been a praiseworthy labour enough; but without addition or omission to have constructed these abortive fragments into a whole so available and so admirable, is a labour beyond praise.

† This exquisite verse did not fall into its place by chance; the poem has been more than once revised. Its opening stanza stood originally thus:

> " Sleep, sleep; in thy sleep
> Thou wilt every secret keep;
> Sleep, sleep, beauty bright,
> Thou shalt taste the joys of night."

Before recasting the whole, Blake altered the second line into—

> " Canst thou any secret keep?"

The gist of the song is this; the speaker, watching a girl newly-

Before parting from this chief lyrical work of the poet's, we may notice (rather for its convenience as an explanation than its merit as a piece of verse) this projected *Motto to the Songs of Innocence and of Experience*, which editors have left hitherto in manuscript:

> " The good are attracted by men's perceptions,
>   And think not for themselves
> Till Experience teaches them how to catch
>   And to cage the Fairies and Elves.

---

born, compares her innocuous infancy with the power that through beauty will one day be hers, her blameless wiles and undeveloped desires with the strong and subtle qualities now dormant which the years will assuredly awaken within her; seeing as it were the whole woman asleep in the child, he smells future fruit in the unblown bud. On retouching his work, Blake thus wound up the moral and tune of this song in a stanza forming by its rhymes an exact antiphonal complement to the end of the first *Cradle Song*.

> " When thy little heart does wake,
>   Then the dreadful lightnings break
>   From thy cheek and from thine eye,
>   O'er the youthful harvests nigh;
>   Infant wiles and infant smiles
>   Heaven and earth of peace beguiles."

The epithet "infant" has supplanted that of "female," which was perhaps better: as to the grammatical licence, Blake followed in that the Elizabethan fashion which made the rule of sound predominate over all others. The song, if it loses simplicity, seems to gain significance by this expansion of the dim original idea; and beauty by expression of the peril latent in a life whose smiles as yet breed no strife between friends, kindle no fire among the unripe shocks of growing corn; but whose words shall hereafter be as very swords, and her eyes as lightning; *teterrima belli causa*.

> And then the Knave begins to snarl,
>   And the Hypocrite to howl ;
> And all his * good friends show their private ends,
>   And the Eagle is known from the Owl."

Experience must do the work of innocence as soon as conscience begins to take the place of instinct, reflection of perception ; but the moment experience begins upon this work, men raise against her the conventional clamour of envy and stupidity. She teaches how to entrap and retain such fugitive delights as children and animals enjoy without seeking to catch or cage them ; but this teaching the world calls sin, and the law of material religion condemns : the face of " Tirzah " is set against it, in the " shame and pride " of sex.

> " Thou, mother of my mortal part,
>   With cruelty didst mould my heart,
> And with false self-deceiving fears
>   Didst bind my nostrils, eyes, and ears."

And thus those who live in subjection to the senses would in their turn bring the senses into subjection ; unable to see beyond the body, they

---

* " His," the good man's : this lax piece of grammar (shifting from singular to plural and back again without much tangible provocation) is not infrequent with Blake, and would hardly be worth righting if that were feasible. A remarkable instance is but too patent in the final " chorus " of the " Marriage of Heaven and Hell." Such rough licence is given or taken by old poets ; and Blake's English is always beautiful enough to be pardonable where it slips or halts : especially as its errors are always those of a rapid lyrical style, never of a tortuous or verbose ingenuity : it stammers and slips occasionally, but never goes into convulsions like that of some later versifiers.

find it worth while to refuse the body its right to freedom.

In these hurried notes on the "Songs" an effort has been made to get that done which is most absolutely necessary—not that which might have been most facile or most delightful. Analytic remark has been bestowed on those poems only which really cannot dispense with it in the eyes of most men. Many others need no herald or interpreter, demand no usher or outrider: some of these are among Blake's best, some again almost among his worst.*

* Such we must consider, for instance, the second *Little Boy Lost*, which looks at first more of a riddle and less worth solution than the haziest section of the "Prophetic Books." A cancelled reading taken from the rough copy in the "Ideas" will at all events make one stanza more amenable to reason :

> " I love myself; so does the bird
> That picks up crumbs around the door."

Blake was rather given to erase a comparatively reasonable reading and substitute something which cannot be confidently deciphered by the most daring self-reliance of audacious ingenuity, until the reader has found some means of pitching his fancy for a moment in the ordinary key of the prophet's. This uncomfortable little poem is in effect merely an allegoric or fabulous appeal against the oppression of formulas (or family "textualism" of the blind and unctuous sort) which refuse to single and simple insight, to the outspoken innocence of a child's laughing or confused analysis, a right to exist on any terms: just as the companion poem is an appeal, so vague as to fall decidedly flat, against the externals of moral fashion. Both, but especially the *Girl*, have some executive merit: not overmuch. To the surprising final query, "Are such things done on Albion's shore?" one is provoked to respond, " On the whole, not, as far as we can see; " but the "Albion" of Blake's verse is never this weaving and spinning country of our working days ; it is rather some inscrutable remote land of Titanic visions, moated with silent white mist instead of solid and sonorous surf,

Poems in which a doctrine or subject once before
nobly stated and illustrated is re-asserted in a shal-
lower way and exemplified in a feebler form,* require
at our hands no written or spoken signs of either
assent or dissent. Such poems, as the editor has

and peopled with vague pre-Adamite giants symbolic of more than
we can safely define or conceive. An inkling of the meaning may,
if anything can, be extracted from some parts of the *Jerusalem* ;
but probably no one will try.

* With more time and room to work in, we might have noticed
in these less dramatic and seemingly less original poems of the
second series which take up from the opposite point of view matters
already handled to such splendid effect in the "Songs of Innocence,"
a depth and warmth of moral quality worth remark ; infinite tender-
ness of heart and fiery pity for all that suffer wrong ; something of
Hugo's or Shelley's passionate compassion for those who lie open
to "all the oppression that is done under the sun ;" something of
the anguish and labour, the fever-heat of sleepless mercy and love
incurable which is common to those two great poets. The second
Holy Thursday is doubtless far enough below the high level of the
first ; but the second *Chimney-sweeper* as certainly has a full share
of this passionate grace of pain and pity. Blake's love of children
never wrung out into his work a more pungent pathos or keener
taste of tears than in the last verse of this poem. It stood thus in
the first draught :

" And because I am happy and dance and sing
    They think they have done me no injury,
    And are gone to praise God and his priest and king,
    Who wrap themselves up in our misery."

The quiet tremulous anger of that, its childish sorrow and con-
tempt, are no less true than subtle in effect. It recalls another
floating fragment of verse on social wrongs which shall be rescued
from the chaos of the "Ideas : "

" There souls of men are bought and sold,
    And milk-fed infancy, for gold ;
    And youths to slaughter-houses led,
    And maidens, for a bit of bread."

well indicated, have places here among their betters :
none of them, it may be added, without some shell
of outward beauty or seed of inward value. The
simpler poems claim only praise ; and of this they
cannot fail from any reader whose good word is in
the least worth having. Those of a subtler kind
(often, as must now be clear enough, the best worth
study) claim more than this if they are to have fair
play. It is pleasant enough to commend and to
enjoy the palpable excellence of Blake's work ; but
another thing is simply and thoroughly requisite—to
understand what the workman was after. First get
well hold of the mystic, and you will then at once
get a better view and comprehension of the painter
and poet. And if through fear of tedium or offence
a student refuses to be at such pains, he will find
himself, while following Blake's trace as poet or
painter, brought up sharply within a very short
tether. "It is easy," says Blake himself in the
Jerusalem, "to acknowledge a man to be great and
good while we derogate from him in the trifles and
small articles of that goodness; those alone are his
friends who admire his minute powers."

Looking into the larger MS. volume of notes we
seem to gain at once a clearer insight into the
writer's daily habit of life and tone of thought, and a
power of judging more justly the sort of work left us
by way of result. Here, as by fits and flashes, one
is enabled to look in upon that strange small house-
hold, so silent and simple on the outside, so content
to live in the poorest domestic way, without any

show of eccentric indulgence or erratic aspiration;
husband and wife to all appearance the commonest
citizens alive, satisfied with each other and with
their minute obscure world and straitened limits of
living. No typical churchwarden or clerk of the
parish could rub on in a more taciturn modest
manner, or seem able to make himself happy with
smaller things. It may be as well for us to hear his
own account of the matter:

PRAYER

I

" I rose up at the dawn of day;
  ' Get thee away; get thee away!
  Pray'st thou for riches? away, away!
  This is the throne of Mammon grey.'

II

Said I, ' This sure is very odd;
I took it to be the throne of God;
For everything besides I have;
It is only for riches that *I* can crave.

III

' I have mental joys and mental health,
And mental friends and mental wealth;
I've a wife I love and that loves me;
I've all but riches bodily;

IV

' Then, if for riches I must not pray,
God knows I little of prayers need say;
So, as a church is known by its steeple,
If I pray, it must be for other people.

V

' I am in God's presence night and day,
And he never turns his face away ;
The accuser of sins by my side does stand,
And he holds my money-bag in his hand ;

VI

' For my worldly things God makes him pay,
And he'd pay for more if to him I would pray ;
And so you may do the worst you can do,
Be assured, Mr. Devil, I won't pray to you.

VII

' He says, if I do not worship him for a God,*
I shall eat coarser food and go worse shod ;
So, as I don't value such things as these,
You must do, Mr. Devil—just as God please.' "

One cannot doubt that to a man of this temper
his life was endurable enough. Faith in God and
goodwill towards men came naturally to him, being
a mystic ; on the one side he had all he wanted, and
on the other he wanted nothing. The praise and
discipleship of men might no doubt have added a
kind of pleasure to his way of life, but they could
neither give nor take away what he most desired to
have ; and this he never failed of having. His wife,
of whose " goodness " to him he has himself borne
ample witness, was company enough for all days.

* This verse is of course to be read as one made up of rough but
regular anapæsts ; the heavier accents falling consequently upon
every third syllable—that is, upon the words *if, not*, and *him*. The
next line is almost as rough, and seems indeed to slip into the solid
English iambic ; but may also be set right by giving full attention
to accent.

And indeed, by all the evidence left us, it appears
that this goodness of hers was beyond example.
Another woman of the better sort might have had
equal patience with his habit of speech and life,
equal faith in his great capacity and character; but
hardly in another woman could such a man have
found an equal strength and sweetness of trust, an
equal ardour of belief and tenderness, an equal
submission of soul and body for love's sake;—
submission so perfect and so beautiful in the manner
of it, that the idea of sacrifice or a separate will
seems almost impossible. A man living with such
a wife might well believe in some immediate divine
presence and in visible faces like the face of an
angel. We have not now of course much chance of
knowing at all what manner of angel she was; but
the few things we do know of her, no form of words
can fitly express. To praise such people is merely
to waste words in saying that divine things are
praiseworthy. No doubt, if we knew how to praise
them, they would deserve that we should try.*

* A strange and rather beautiful, if grotesque, evidence of the
unity of faith and feeling to which Blake and his wife had come by
dint of living and thinking so long together, is given by one of the
stray notes in this same book: which we transcribe at full on
account of its great biographical value as a study of character.
Space might have been found for it in the " Life," if only to prove
once again how curiously the nature and spiritual habits of a great
man leave their mark or dye upon the mind nearest to his own.

"SOUTH MOLTON STREET.
" *Sunday, August,* 1807.—My wife was told by a spirit to
look for her fortune by opening by chance a book which she had

The notes bearing in any way upon this daily life of Blake's are few and exceptional. In the mass of floating verse and prose there is absolutely no hint

in her hand; it was Bysshe's 'Art of Poetry.' She opened the following :

> ' I saw 'em kindle with desire,
> While with soft sighs they blew the fire ;
> Saw the approaches of their joy,
> He growing more fierce and she less coy ;
> Saw how they mingled melting rays,
> Exchanging love a thousand ways.
> Kind was the force on every side ;
> Her new desire she could not hide,
> Nor would the shepherd be denied.
> The blessed minute he pursued,
> Till she, transported in his arms,
> Yields to the conqueror all her charms.
> His panting breast to hers now joined,
> They feast on raptures unconfined,
> Vast and luxuriant ; such as prove
> The immortality of love.
> For who but a Divinity
> Could mingle souls to that degree
> And melt them into ecstasy ?
> Now like the Phœnix both expire,
> While from the ashes of their fire
> Springs up a new and soft desire.
> Like charmers, thrice they did invoke
> The God, and thrice new vigour took.'—*Behn.*

"I was so well 'pleased with her luck that I thought I would try my own, and opened the following :

> ' As when the winds their airy quarrel try,
> Jostling from every quarter of the sky,
> This way and that the mountain oak they bear,
> His boughs they scatter and his branches tear ;
> With leaves and falling mast they spread the ground ;
> The hollow valleys echo to the sound ;

of order whatever, save that, at one end of the
MS., some short poems are transcribed in a slightly
more coherent form. Among these and the other

> Unmoved, the royal plant their fury mocks,
> Or, shaken, clings more closely to the rocks:
> For as he shoots his towering head on high,
> So deep in earth his fixed foundations lie.'
>
> *Dryden's Virgil.*"

Nothing is ever so cynical as innocence, whether it be a child's
or a mystic's. As a poet, Blake had some reason to be "well
pleased" with his wife's curious windfall; for those verses of the
illustrious Aphra's have some real energy and beauty of form,
visible to those who care to make allowance, first for the con-
ventional English of the time, and secondly for the naked violence
of manner natural to that she-satyr, whose really great lyrical gifts
are hopelessly overlaid and encrusted by the rough repulsive husk
of her incredible style of speech. Even "Astræa" must however
have fair play and fair praise; and the simple truth is that, when
writing her best, this "unmentionable" poetess has a vigorous
grace and a noble sense of metre to be found in no other song-
writer of her time. One song, fished up by Mr. Dyce out of the
weltering sewerage of Aphra's unreadable and unutterable plays,
has a splendid quality of verse, and even some degree of sentiment
not wholly porcine. Take four lines as a sample, and Blake's
implied approval will hardly seem unjustifiable:

> " From thy bright eyes he took those fires
>   Which round about in sport he hurled;
> But 'twas from mine he took desires
>   Enough to undo the amorous world."

The strong and subtle cadence of that magnificent fourth verse gives
evidence of so delicate an ear and such dexterous power of hand
as no other poet between the Restoration date and Blake's own time
has left proof of in serious or tragic song. Great as is Dryden's
lyrical work in more ways than one, its main quality is mere strength
of intellect and solidity of handling—the forcible and imperial
manner of his satires; and in pure literal song-writing, which
(rather than any 'ode' or such-like mixed poem) may be taken as
the absolute and final test of a poet's lyrical nature, he never came

L

lyrics, strewn as from a liberal but too lax hand about the chaotic leaves of his note-book, are many of Blake's best things. Some of the slight and scrawled designs, as noted in the Catalogue (pp. 242, 243), have also a merit and a power of their own; but it is with the poet's lyrical work that we have to do at this point of our present notes; and here we may most fitly wind up what remains to be said on that matter.

The inexhaustible equable gift of Blake for the writing of short sweet songs is perceptible at every turn we take in this labyrinth of lovely words, of strong and soft designs. Considering how wide is the range of date from the earliest of these songs to the latest, they seem more excellently remote than ever from the day's verse and the day's habit. They reach in point of time from the season of Mason to the season of Moore; and never in any interval of work by any chance influence do these poems at their weakest lapse into likeness or tolerance of the accepted models. From the era of plaster to the era of pinchbeck, Blake kept straight ahead of the times. To the pseudo-Hellenic casts of the one school or the pseudo-Hibernian tunes of the other he was admirably deaf and blind. While a grazing public straightened its bovine neck and steadied its flicker-

near this mark. François Villon and Aphra Behn, the two most inexpressibly non-respectable of male or female Bohemians and poets, were alike in this as well; that the supreme gift of each, in a time sufficiently barren of lyrical merit, was the gift of writing admirable songs; and this, after all, has perhaps borne better fruit for us than any gift of moral excellence.

ing eyelids to look up betweenwhiles, with the day's
damp fodder drooping half-chewed from its relaxed
jaw, at some dim sick planet of the Mason system,
there was a poet, alive if obscure, who had eyes to
behold

> " the chambers of the East,
> The chambers of the sun, that now
> From ancient melody have ceased ; "

who had ears to hear and lips to reveal the music
and the splendour and the secret of the high places
of verse. Again, in a changed century, when the
reading and warbling world was fain to drop its
daily tear and stretch its daily throat at the bidding
of some Irish melodist—when the " female will" of
"Albion" thought fit to inhale with wide and
thankful nostril the rancid flavour of rotten dance-
roses and mouldy musk, to feed "in a feminine
delusion" upon the sodden offal of perfumed dog's-
meat, and take it for the very eucharist of Apollo—
then too, while this worship of ape or beetle went so
noisily on, the same poet could let fall from lavish
hand or melodious mouth such grains of solid gold
and flakes of perfect honey as this :

> " Silent, silent night,
> Quench the holy light
> Of thy torches bright ;
>
> For possessed of day,
> Thousand spirits stray,
> That sweet joys betray.
>
> Why should love be sweet,
> Usèd with deceit,
> Nor with sorrows meet?"

L 2

Verse more nearly faultless and of a more difficult perfection was never accomplished. The sweet facility of being right, proper to great lyrical poets, was always an especial quality of Blake's. To go the right way and do the right thing, was in the nature of his metrical gift—a faculty mixed into the very flesh and blood of his verse.

There is in all these straying songs the freshness of clear wind and purity of blowing rain: here a perfume as of dew or grass against the sun, there a keener smell of sprinkled shingle and brine-bleached sand; some growth or breath everywhere of blade or herb leaping into life under the green wet light of spring; some colour of shapely cloud or mound of moulded wave. The verse pauses and musters and falls always as a wave does, with the same patience of gathering form, and rounded glory of springing curve, and sharp sweet flash of dishevelled and flickering foam as it curls over, showing the sun through its soft heaving side in veins of gold that inscribe and jewels of green that inlay the quivering and sundering skirt or veil of thinner water, throwing upon the tremulous space of narrowing sea in front, like a reflection of lifted and vibrating hair, the windy shadow of its shaken spray. The actual page seems to take life, to assume sound and colour, under the hands that turn it and the lips that read; we feel the falling of dew and have sight of the rising of stars. For the very sound of Blake's verse is no less remote from the sound of common things and days on earth than is the sense or the sentiment of it.

" O what land is the land of dreams?
   What are its mountains and what are its streams?
   —O father, I saw my mother there,
   Among the lilies by waters fair.

. . . .

—Dear child, I also by pleasant streams
   Have wandered all night in the land of dreams;
   But though calm and warm the waters wide
   I could not get to the other side."

We may say of Blake that he never got back from that other side—only came and stood sometimes, as Chapman said of Marlowe in his great plain fashion of verse, "up to the chin in that Pierian flood," and so sang half-way across the water.

Nothing in the "Songs of Innocence" is more beautiful as a study of childish music than the little poem from which we have quoted; written in a metre which many expert persons have made hideous, and few could at any time manage as Blake did— a scheme in which the soft and loose iambics lapse into sudden irregular sound of full anapæsts, not without increase of grace and impulsive tenderness in the verse. Given a certain attainable average of intellect and culture, these points of workmanship, by dint of the infinite gifts or the infinite wants they imply, become the swiftest and surest means of testing a verse-writer's perfection of power, and what quality there may be in him to warrant his loftiest claim. By these you see whether a man can sing, as by his drawing and colouring whether he can paint. Another specimen of indefinable sweetness

and significance we may take in this symbolic little
piece of song ;

> " I walked abroad on a sunny day;
> I wooed the soft snow with me to play.
> She played and she melted in all her prime ;
> And the winter called it a dreadful crime." *

Against the "winter" of ascetic law and moral pre-
scription Blake never slackens in his fiery animosity ;
never did a bright hot wind of March make such war
upon the cruel inertness of February.   In his obscure
way he was always hurrying into the van of some
forlorn hope of ethics.   Even Shelley, who as we
said was no less ready to serve in the same camp all
his life long, never shot keener or hotter shafts of
lyrical speech into the enemy's impregnable ground.
Both poets seem to have tried about alike, and with
equally questionable results, at a regular blockade of
the steep central fortress of " Urizen ; " both after
a little personal practice fell back, not quite un-
scarred, upon light skirmishing and the irregular
work of chance guerilla campaigns.   Moral custom,
" that twice-battered god of Palestine " round which
all Philistia rallies (specially strong in her British
brigade), seemed to suffer little from all their slings
and arrows.   Being mere artists, they were perhaps
at root too innocent to do as much harm as they

---

* Another version of this line, with less of pungent and brilliant
effect, has yet a touch of sound in it worth preserving : some may
even prefer it in point of simple lyrical sweetness :

> " She played and she melted in all her prime :
> Ah ! that sweet love should be thought a crime."

desired, or to desire as much harm as they might have done. Blake indeed never proposed to push matters quite to such a verge as the other was content to stand on during his "Laon and Cythna" period ; from that inconceivable edge of theory or sensation he would probably have drawn back with some haste. But such sudden cries of melodious revolt as this were not rare on his part.*

> " Abstinence sows sand all over
>   The ruddy limbs and flaming hair,
> But desire gratified
>   Plants fruits of life and beauty there."

Assuredly he never made a more supremely noble and enjoyable effect of verse than that ; the cadence of the first two lines is something hardly to be matched anywhere : the verse (to resume our old simile for a moment) turns over and falls in with the sudden weight and luminous motion of a strong long roller coming in with the wind. So again, lying sad and sick under his marriage myrtle, even in a full rain of fragrant and brilliant blossoms that fall round him to waste, he must needs ask and answer the fatal final question.

> " Why should I be bound to thee,
>   O my lovely myrtle-tree ?
> Love, free love, cannot be bound
>   To any tree that grows on ground."

---

* On closer inspection of Blake's rapid autograph I suspect that in the second line those who please may read " the ruddy limbs and flowering hair," or perhaps " flowery ; " but the type of flame is more familiar to Blake. Compare further on *A Song of Liberty*.

Mixed with this fervour of desire for more perfect freedom, there appears at times an excess of pity (like Chaucer's in his early poems) for the women and men living under the law, trammelled in soul or body. For example, the poem called *Infant Sorrow*, in the "Songs of Experience," ran at first to a greater length and through stranger places than it now overflows into ; and is worth giving here in its original form as extracted by cautious picking and sifting from a heap of tumbled readings.

I

" My mother groaned, my father wept ;
Into the dangerous world I leapt,
Helpless, naked, piping loud,
Like a fiend hid in a cloud.

II

Struggling in my father's hands,
Striving against my swaddling bands,
Bound and weary, I thought best
To sulk upon my mother's breast.

III

When I saw that rage was vain
And to sulk would nothing gain,
Twining many a trick and wile
I began to soothe and smile.

IV

And I grew * day after day,
Till upon the ground I lay ;
And I grew * night after night,
Seeking only for delight.

---

* Other readings are "soothed" and "smiled"—readings adopted after the insertion of the preceding stanza. As the subject

V

And I saw before me shine
Clusters of the wandering vine;
And many a lovely flower and tree
Stretched their blossoms out to me.

VI

But many a priest * with holy look,
In their hands a holy book,
Pronouncèd curses on his head
Who the fruit or blossoms shed.

VII

I beheld the priests by night;
They embraced the blossoms bright;
I beheld the priests by day;
Underneath the vines they lay.

---

is a child not yet grown to standing and walking age, these readings
are perhaps better, though less simple in sound, than the one
I have retained.

   * Here and throughout to the end, duly altering metre and
grammar with a quite laudable care, Blake has substituted "my
father" for "the priests;" not I think to the improvement of the
poem, though probably with an eye to making the end cohere
rather more closely with the beginning. This and *The Myrtle*
are shoots of the same stock, and differ only in the second grafting.
In the last-named poem the father's office was originally thus;

> "Oft my myrtle sighed in vain
> To behold my heavy chain:
> Oft my father saw us sigh,
> And laughed at our simplicity."

Here too Blake had at first written, "Oft the priest beheld us
sigh;" he afterwards cancelled the whole passage, perhaps on first
remarking the rather too grotesque confusion of a symbolic myrtle
with a literal wife; and the last stanza in either form is identical.
The simple subtle grace of both poems, and the singular care of
revision bestowed on them, are equally worth notice.

VIII

Like to serpents in the night,
They embraced my blossoms bright ;
Like to holy men by day,
Underneath my vines they lay.

IX

So I smote them, and their gore
Stained the roots my myrtle bore ;
But the time of youth is fled,
And grey hairs are on my head."

Now not even the spilt blood of those who forbid
and betray shall quicken the dried root or flush the
faded leaf of love ; the myrtle being past all comfort of
soft rain or helpful sun.   So in *The Rose-Tree* (vol. ii.
p. 60), when for the sake of a barren material fidelity
to his "rose" of marriage, he has passed over the
offered flower "such as May never bore," the rose
herself "turns away with jealousy," and gives him
thorns for thanks : nothing left of it for hand or lip
but collapsed blossom and implacable edges of brier.
Blake might have kept in mind the end of his actual
wild vine (vol. i. p. 100 of the "Life"), which ran all
to leaf and never brought a grape worth eating, for
fault of pruning-hooks and vine-dressers.

In all this there is a certain unmistakeable inno-
cence which accounts for the practical modesty and
peaceable forbearance of the man's way of living.
The material shape of his speculations never goes
beyond a sort of boyish defiant complaint, a half-
humorous revolt of the will.   Inconstancy with him
is not rooted in satiety, but in the freshness of pure
pleasure ; he would never cast off the old to put on

the new. The chain once broken, against which between sleeping and waking he chafes and wrestles, he would lie for most hours of the day with content enough in the old shade of wedded rose or myrtle tree. Nor in leaping or reaching after the new flower would he wilfully bruise or break the least bud of the old. His desire is towards the freedom of the dawn of things—not towards the "dark secret hour" that walks under coverings of cloud.

> " Are not the joys of morning sweeter
> Than the joys of night ? "

The sinless likeness of his seeming "sins"—mere fancies as it appears they mostly were, mere soft light aspirations of theory without body or flesh on them—has something of the innocent immodesty of a birds' or babies' paradise—of a fools' paradise, too, translated into the practice and language of the untheoretic world. Shelley's "Epipsychidion" scarcely preaches a more bodiless evangel of bodily liberty. That famous and exquisitely written passage beginning, "True love in this differs from gold and clay," delivers in more daringly definite words the exact message of Blake's belief.

Nowhere has the note of pity been more strongly and sweetly struck than in those lovely opening verses of the *Garden of Love* which must here be read once again :

> " I laid me down upon a bank
> Where Love lay sleeping :
> I heard among the rushes dank
> Weeping, weeping.

Then I went to the heath and the wild,
To the thistles and thorns of the waste ;
And they told me how they were beguiled,
Driven out, and compelled to be chaste."

The sharp and subtle change of metre here and at
the end of the poem has an audacity of beauty and
a justice of impulse proper only to the leaders of
lyrical verse : unfit alike for definition and for imita-
tion, if any copyist were to try his hand at it. The
next song we transcribe from the "Ideas" is lighter
in tone than usual, and admirable for humorous
imagination ; a light of laughter shines and sounds
through the words.

THE WILL AND THE WAY

" I asked a thief to steal me a peach ;
    He turned up his eyes ;
I asked a lithe lady to lie her down
    Holy and meek, she cries.

As soon as I went
    An angel came ;
He winked at the thief
    And smiled at the dame ;

And without one word spoke
    Had a peach from the tree ;
And 'twixt earnest and joke
    Enjoyed the lady." *

A much better and more solid version of the same
fancy than the one given in the "Selections" under

---

* Those who insist on the tight lacing of grammatical stays
upon the "painèd loveliness" of a muse's over-pliant body may
use if they please Blake's own amended reading ; in which other-

the head of *Love's Secret*; which is rather weakly
and lax in manner. Our present poem has on the
other hand an exquisite "lithe" grace of limb and
suppleness of step, suiting deliciously with the "light
high laugh" in its tone: while for sweet and rapid
daring, for angelically puerile impudence as it were,
it may be matched against any song of its fantastic
sort.

Less complete in a small way, but worth taking
some care of, is this carol of a fairy, emblem of a
man's light hard tyranny of will, calling upon the
birds in the harness of Venus and the shafts in the
hand of her son for help in setting up the kingdom
of established and legal love: but caught himself in
the very setting of his net.

THE MARRIAGE RING

" ' Come hither, my sparrows,
    My little arrows.
    If a tear or a smile
    Will a man beguile,
    If an amorous delay
    Clouds a sunshiny day,
    If the step of a foot
    Smites the heart to its root,
    'Tis the marriage ring
    Makes each fairy a king.'

---

wise the main salt of the poem is considerably diluted as by tepid
water: the angel (one might say) has his sting blunted and the best
quill of his pinion pulled out.

" And without one word said
    Had a peach from the tree ;
    And still as a maid," &c.

So a fairy sang.
From the leaves I sprang;
He leaped from his spray
To flee away:
But in my hat caught,
He soon shall be taught,
Let him laugh, let him cry,
He's my butterfly:
For I've pulled out the sting
Of the marriage ring."

It is not so easy to turn wasps to butterflies in the
world of average things; but, as far as verses go,
there are few of more supple sweetness than some of
these. They recall the light lapse of measure found
in the beautiful older germs of nursery rhyme; * and
the seeming retributive triumph of married lovers

* We may find place here for another fairy song, quaint in
shape and faint in colour, but with the signet of Blake upon it;
copied from a loose scrap of paper on the back of which is a pen-
cilled sketch of Hercules throttling the serpents, whose twisted
limbs make a sort of spiral cradle around and above the child's
triumphant figure: an attendant, naked, falls back in terror with
sharp recoil of drawn-up limbs; Alcmena and Amphitryon watch
the struggle in silence, he grasping her hand.

"A fairy leapt upon my knee
Singing and dancing merrily;
I said, 'Thou thing of patches, rings,
Pins, necklaces, and such-like things,
Disgracer of the female form,
Thou paltry gilded poisonous worm!'
Weeping, he fell upon my thigh,
And thus in tears did soft reply:
'Knowest thou not, O fairies' lord,
How much by us contemned, abhorred,
Whatever hides the female form
That cannot bear the mortal storm?

over unmarried, of wedlock over courtship, could
not well be more gracefully translated than in the
" Fairy's " call to his winged and feathered " arrows "
—the lover's swift birds of prey, not without beak
and claw. " If they do for a minute or so darken
our days, dupe our fancies, prevail upon our nerves
and blood, once well married we are kings of them
at least." Pull out that sting of jealous reflective
egotism, and your tamed " fairy "—the love that is
in a man once set right—has no point or poison left
it, but only rapid grace of wing and natural charm
of colour.

Throughout the " Ideas " one or two other favourite
points of faith and feeling are incessantly thrown
out in new fugitive forms ; such as the last (re-
jected) stanza of *Cupid*, which, though the song
may well dispense with it and even gain by such a
loss in the qualities of shape or sound, must be saved
if only as a specimen of the persistent way in which
Blake assumed the Greek and Roman habits of mind
or art to be typical of " war " and restraint ; an iron
frame of mind good to fight in and not good for love
to grow under.

Therefore in pity still we give
Our lives to make the female live ;
And what would turn into disease
We turn to what will joy and please.' "

Even so dim and slight a sketch as this may be of worth as
indicating Blake's views of the apparent and the substantial form of
things, the primary and the derivative life ; also as a sample of his
roughest and readiest work.

" 'Twas the Greek love of war
That turned Love into a boy *
And woman into a statue of stone ;
And away fled every joy."

More frequent and more delightful is the recur-
rence of such loving views of love as that taken
in the last lines of *William Bond*; a poem full of
strange and soft hints, of mist that allures and music
that lulls; typical in the main of the embodied
struggle between selfish and sacrificial passion, be-
tween the immediate impulse that brings at least the
direct profit of delight, and the law of religious or
rational submission that reaps mere loss and late
regret after a life of blind prudence and sorrowful
forbearance—the "black cloud" of sickness, malady
of spirit and body inflicted by the church-keeping
"angels of Providence" who have driven away the
loving train of spirits that live by innate impulse:
not the bulk of Caliban but the soul of Angelo being
the deadliest direct enemy of Ariel.   "Providence"
divine or human, prepense moral or spiritual "fore-
sight," was a thing in the excellence of which our
prophet of divine instinct and inspired flesh could not
consistently believe.   His evangel could   dispense

* Lest the kingdom of love left under the type of a woman
should be over powerful for a nation of hard fighters and reasoners,
such as Blake conceived the "ancients" to be.   Compare for his
general style of fancies on classic matters the prologue to "Milton"
and the "Sibylline Leaves" on Homer and Virgil.   To his half-
trained apprehension Rome seemed mere violence and Greece mere
philosophy.

with that, in favour of such faith in good things as
came naturally to him.

> " I thought Love lived in the hot sunshine,
>   But oh, he lives in the moony light ;
> I thought to find Love in the heat of day,
>   But sweet Love is the comforter of night.

> " Seek Love in the pity of others' woe,
>   In the gentle relief of another's care ;
> In the darkness of night and the winter's snow,
>   In the naked and outcast, seek Love there."

The infinite and most tender beauty of such
words is but one among many evidences how
thoroughly and delicately the lawless fervour and
passionate liberty of desire were tempered in Blake
by an exquisite goodness, of sense rather than of
thought, which as it were made the pain or pleasure,
the well-being or the suffering, of another press
naturally and sharply on his own nerves of feeling.
Deeply as his thought and fancy had struck into
strange paths and veins of spiritual life, he had
never found or felt out any way to the debateable
land where simple and tender pleasures become
complex and cruel, and the roses gathered are redder
at root than in leaf.

Another poem, slight of texture and dim of
feature, but full of a cloudy beauty, is *The Angel :*
a new allegory of love, blindly rejected or blindly
accepted as a thing of course ; foiled and made
profitless in either case : then lost, with all the
sorrow it brings and all the comfort it gives : and
the ways are barred against it by armed mistrust

M

and jealousy, and its place knows it no more : but
this immunity from the joys and sorrows of love is
bought at the bitter price of untimely age. (I offer
these somewhat verbose and wiredrawn attempts at
commentary, only where the poem seems at once to
require analysis and to admit such as I give ; how
difficult it is to make such notes clear and full, yet not
to stumble into confusion or slide into prolixity, those
can estimate who will try their hand at such work.)

Frequent slips and hitches of grammar, it may
be added, are common to Blake's rough studies
and finished writings, and are therefore not always
things to be weeded out.   Little learning and much
reading of old books made him more really inaccu-
rate than were their writers, whose apparent liberties
he might perhaps have pleaded in defence of his own
hardly defensible licences.

None of these poems are worthier, for the delight
they give, of the selected praise and most thankful
study than *The Two Songs* and *The Golden Net :* a
pair of perfect things, their feet taken in the deep
places of thought, and their heads made lovely with
the open light of lyric speech.   Between the former
of these * and *The Human Abstract* there is a certain

---

* Let the reader take another instance of the culture given to
these songs—a gift which has happily been bequeathed by Blake
to his editor.   This one was at first divided into five equal stanzas ;
the last two running thus :

> " ' And pity no more would be
> If all were happy as we ; '
> At his curse the sun went down,
> And the heavens gave a frown.

difference : here, the moral point of the poem is, that innocence is wholly ignorant, and sees no deeper than the shell of form ; experience is mainly malignant, and sees the root of evil and seed of pain under the leaf of good and blossom of pleasant things : * there, the vision is the poet's own, and deals with that evil neither actually nor seemingly inherent in the system or scheme of created nature, but watered into life by the error and fed into luxuriance by the act of " the human brain " alone ; two widely unlike themes for verse. As to execution, here doubtless there is more of that swift fresh quality peculiar to Blake's simpler style ; but the *Abstract* again has more weight of verse and magnificence of symbol.

Akin to *The Golden Net* is the form and manner of *Broken Love ;* which, whatever taste may lie in

> Down poured the heavy rain
> Over the new-reaped grain ;
> And Misery's increase
> Is Mercy, Pity, Peace."

Thus one might say is the curse confuted ; for if, as the " grievous devil " will have it, the root of the sweetest goodness is in material evil, then may the other side answer that even by his own showing the flower or " increase " from that root is not evil, but good : a soft final point of comfort missed by the change which gives otherwise fresher colour to this poem.

* But as above shown the vision of the wise man or poet is wider than both ; sees beyond the angel's blind innocent enjoyment to a deeper faith than his simple nature can grasp or include ; sees also past the truth of the devil's sad ingenious " analytics " to the broader sense of things, seen by which, " Good and Evil are no more."

M 2

the actual kernel of it, is visibly one of the poet's noblest studies of language. The grandeur of the growing metre and heat of passionate pulses felt through the throbbing body of its verse can escape no ear. In our notes on "Jerusalem" we shall have, like the "devil" of *The Two Songs*, to look at it from the inverse side and pass upon it a more laborious and less thankworthy comment.

Of the longest and gravest poem in the "Ideas of Good and Evil" we are bound to take some careful account. This is *The Everlasting Gospel*, a semi-dramatic exposition of faith on the writer's part; full of subtleties and paradoxes which might well straighten the stiffest hairs of orthodoxy and bewilder the sharpest brain of speculation. Blake has here stated once for all the why and the how of his Christian faith; for Christian he averred that it was, and we may let his word pass for it. Readers must be recommended for the present to look at these things as much as possible from what we will call their artistic or poetic side, and bring no pulpit logic to get chopped or minced on the altar of this prophet's vision. His worst heresy, they may be assured, "will not bite." In effect one may hope (or fear, as the case may be) that there is much less of heresy underlying these daring forms of speech than seems to overlay their outer skirt: schism or division of body rather than of spirit from less wilful and outspoken forms of faith.

Let the student of this "Gospel" of inverted belief and intensified paradox lay hold of and cling

fast to the clue given by the " Vision of the Last
Judgment." There for one thing the prophet has
laid down this rule: " Moral virtues do not exist ;
they are allegories and dissimulations." For "moral
allegory " we are therefore not to look here ; we are
in the house of pure vision, outside of which alle-
gory halts blindly across the shifting sand of moral
qualities, her right hand leaning on the staff of
virtue, her left hand propped on the crutch of vice.
Conscious unimpulsive "virtue," measured by the
praise or judged by the laws of men, was to Blake
always Pharisaic: a legal God none other than a
magnified and divine Pharisee. Thus far have other
(even European) mystics often enough pushed their
inference ; but this time the mystic was a poet ; and
therefore always, where it was possible, prone to
prefer tangible form and given to beat out into
human shape even the most indefinite features of his
vision. Assuming Christ as the direct and absolute
divine type (divine in the essential not in the clerical
sense—divine to the spiritual not the technical
reason) he was therefore obliged to set to work
and strip that type of the incongruous garment of
" moral virtues," cast over it by the law of religious
form: to prove, as he elsewhere said, that Christ
"was all virtue," not by the possession of these
" allegoric " qualities called human virtues or ab-
stinence from those others called human sins or
vices: such abstinence or such possession cannot
conceivably suffice for the final type of goodness or
absolute incarnation of a thing unalterably divine.

Virtues are no more predicable of the perfect virtue than vices of the perfect vice. As the supreme sin cannot be said to commit human faults, so neither can the supreme holiness obey the principles of human sanctity. " Deistical virtue " is as the embroidery on the ephod of Caiaphas or the stain left upon the water by the purified hands of Pilate. It is the property of "the heathen schools ;" a bitted and bridled virtue, led by the nose and tied by the neck ; made of men's hands and subject to men's laws. Can you make a God worth worship out of that? To say that God is wise, chaste, humble, philanthropic, gentle, or just ; in one word, that he s " good " after the human sense ; is to lower your image of God not less than if you had predicated of him the exactly reverse qualities, by reason of which these exist, even as they by reason of these. How much of all this Blake had fished up out of his studies of Behmen, Swedenborg, or such others, his present critic has not the means of deciding ; but is assured of one thing ; that where others dealt by inductive rule and law, Blake dealt by assumptive preaching and intuition ; that he found form of his own for the body of thought, and body of his own for the spirit of speculation, supplied by others ; playing Prometheus to their Epimetheus, doing poet's or evangelist's work where they did philosophic business ; not fumbling in the box of Pandora for things flown or fugitive, but bringing from extreme heaven the immediate fire in the hollow of his reed or pen.

Such is the radical "idea " of the poem ; and as

to details, we are to remember that "modesty" with Blake means a timid and tacit prurience, and "humility" a mistrustful and mendacious cowardice: he puts these terms to such uses in his swift fierce way, just as, in his detestation of deism and its "impersonal God," he must needs embody his vision of a deity or more perfect humanity in the personal Christian type: a purely poetical tendency, which if justly apprehended will serve to account for the wildest bodily forms in which he drew forth his visions from the mould of prophecy.

Thus much by way of prologue may suffice for the moral side of this "Gospel;" the mythological or technically religious side is not much easier to deal with, and indeed cannot well be made out except by such misty light as may be won from the "Prophetic Books." It seems evident that Blake, at least for purposes of evangelism, was content to regard the "Creator" of the mere bodily man as one with the "legal" or "Pharisaic" God of the churches: even as the "mother of his mortal part" —of the flesh taken for the moment simply, and separated (for reasoning purposes) from the inseparable spirit—is "Tirzah." This vision of a creator divided against his own creation and having to be subdued by his own creatures will appear more directly and demand more distinct remark when we come to deal with its symbolic form in the great myth of "Urizen;" where also it will be possible to follow it out with less likelihood of offensive misconstruction. One is compelled here to desire from

those who care to follow Blake at all, the keenest
ardour of attention possible ; they will blunder help-
lessly if they once fail to connect this present minute
of his work with the past and the future of it : if
they once let slip the thinnest thread of analogy, the
whole prophetic or evangelic web collapses for them
into a chaos of gossamer, a tangle of unclean and
flaccid fibres, the ravelled woof of an insane and
impotent Arachne, who should be retransmuted with
all haste into a palpable spider by the spell of reason.
Here, as in all swift "inspired" writing, there are
on the outside infinite and indefinable anomalies,
contradictions, incompatibilities enough of all sorts ;
open for any Paine or Paley to impugn or to defend.
But let no one dream that there is here either mad-
ness or mendacity : the heart or sense thus hidden
away is sound enough for a mystic.

The greatest passage of this poem is also the
simplest ; that division which deals with the virtue
of "chastity," and uses for its text the story of
"the woman taken in adultery :" who is identified
with Mary Magdalene. We give it here in full ;
hoping it may now be comprehensible to all who
care to understand, and may bear fruit of its noble
and almost faultless verse for all but those who
prefer to take the sterility of their fig-tree on trust
rather than be at the pains of lifting a single leaf.

> " Was Jesus *chaste ?* or did he
> Give any lessons of chastity ?
> The morning blushed fiery red ;
> Mary was found in adulterous bed.

Earth groaned beneath, and heaven above
Trembled at discovery of love.
Jesus was sitting in Moses' chair;
They brought the trembling woman there.
Moses commands she be stoned to death:
What was the sound of Jesus' breath?
He laid his hand on Moses' law;
The ancient heavens, in silent awe,
Writ with curses from pole to pole,
All away began to roll;
The earth trembling and naked lay
In secret bed of mortal clay—
On Sinai felt the hand Divine
Pulling * back the bloody shrine—
And she heard the breath of God
As she heard by Eden's flood:
' Good and Evil are no more;
Sinai's trumpets, cease to roar;
Cease, finger of God, to write
The heavens are not clean in thy sight.
Thou art good, and thou alone;
Nor may the sinner cast one stone.
To be good only, is to be
A God, or else a Pharisee.
Thou Angel of the Presence Divine,
That didst create this body of mine,
Wherefore hast thou writ these laws
And created hell's dark jaws?
My Presence I will take from thee;
A cold leper thou shalt be.
Though thou wast so pure and bright
That heaven was impure in thy sight,
Though thine oath turned heaven pale,
Though thy covenant built hell's gaol,
Though thou didst all to chaos roll
With the serpent for its soul,
Still the breath Divine does move—
And the breath Divine is love.

* Query " Putting "? This whole poem is jotted down in a
close rough handwriting, not often easy to follow with confidence.

Mary, fear not.   Let me see
The seven devils that torment thee.
Hide not from my sight thy sin,
That forgiveness thou mayst win.
Hath no man condemnèd thee?'
'No man, Lord.'   'Then what is he
Who shall accuse thee?   Come ye forth,
Fallen fiends of heavenly birth
That have forgot your ancient love
And driven away my trembling dove;
You shall bow before her feet;
You shall lick the dust for meat;
And though you cannot love, but hate,
Shall be beggars at love's gate.
—What was thy love?   Let me see 't;
Was it love or dark deceit?'
'Love too long from me has fled;
'Twas dark deceit, to earn my bread;
'Twas covet, or 'twas custom, or
Some trifle not worth caring for:
That they may call a shame and sin
Love's temple that God dwelleth in,
And hide in secret hidden shrine
The naked human form divine,
And render that a lawless thing
On which the soul expands her wing.
But this, O Lord, this was my sin—
When first I let these devils in,
In dark pretence to chastity
Blaspheming love, blaspheming thee.
Thence rose secret adulteries,
And thence did covet also rise.
My sin thou hast forgiven me;
Canst thou forgive my blasphemy?
Canst thou return to this dark hell
And in my burning bosom dwell?
And canst thou die that I may live?
And canst thou pity and forgive?'"

In no second poem shall we find such a sustained
passage as that; such light of thought and thunder

of verse ; such sudden splendour of fire seen across
a strange land and among waste places beyond the
receded landmarks of the day or above the glimmer-
ing lintels of the night. The passionate glory of its
rapid and profound music fills the sense with too
deep and sharp a delight to leave breathing-space
for any thought of analytic or apologetic work. But
the spirit of the verse is not less great than the body
of it is beautiful. " Divide from the divine glory the
softness and warmth of human colour—subtract from
the divine the human presence—subdue all refraction
to the white absolute light—and that light is no
longer as the sun's is, warm with sweet heat of life
and liberal of good gifts ; but foul with overmuch
purity, sick with disease of excellence, unclean
through exceeding cleanness, like the skin of a leper
'as white as snow.'" For the divine nature is not
greater than the human ; (they are one from eternity,
sundered by the separative creation or fall, severed
into type and antitype by bodily generation, but to
be made one again when life and death shall both
have died ;) not greater than the human nature, but
greater than the qualities which the human nature
assumes upon earth. God is man, and man God ;
as neither of himself the greater, so neither of him-
self the less : but as God is the unfallen part of man,
man the fallen part of God, God must needs be (not
more than man, but assuredly) more than the qualities
of man. Thus the mystic can consistently deny that
man's moral goodness or badness can be predicable
of God, while at the same time he affirms man's

intrinsic divinity and God's intrinsic humanity.
Man can only possess abstract qualities—"allegoric
virtues"—by reason of that side of his nature which
he has *not* in common with God : God, not partaking
of the "generative nature," cannot partake of
qualities which exist only by right of that nature.
The other "God"* or "Angel of the Presence"
who created the sexual and separate body of man
did but cleave in twain the "divine humanity," which
becoming reunited shall redeem man without price
and without covenant and without law; he mean-
time, the Creator,† is a divine demon, liable to
error, subduable by and through this very created
nature of his invention, which he for the present
imprisons and torments. *His* law is the law of
Moses, which according to the Manichean heresy
Christ came to reverse as diabolic. This singular

* In the line "A God or else a Pharisee," Blake with a pencil-
scratch has turned "a God" to "a devil;" as if the words were
admittedly or admissibly interchangeable! A prophet so wonder-
fully loose-tongued may well be the despair of his faithfullest com-
mentators : but as it happens the pencil-scratch should here be of
some help and significance to us: following this small clue, we
may come to distinguish the God of his belief from this demon-god
of the created "mundane shell"—the God of Pharisaic religion
and moral law.

† The creator by division, father of men and women, fashioner
of evil and good ; literally in the deepest sense "the God of this
world," who "does not know the garment from the man ;" cannot
see beyond the two halves which he has made by violence of sepa-
ration ; would have the body perishable, yet the qualities of the
bodily life permanent: thus inverting order and reversing fact.
Parallel passages might be brought in by the dozen on all hands,
after a little dipping into mystic books; but I want to make no
more room here for all this than is matter of bare necessity.

(and presumably "Pantheistic") creed of Blake's has a sort of Asiatic flavour about it, but seems harder and more personal in its mythology than an eastern philosopher's; has also a distinct western type and Christian touch in it; being wrought as it were of Persian lotus-leaves hardened into the consistency of English oak-timber. The most wonderful part of his belief or theory is this: "That after Christ's death he became Jehovah:"* which may mean simply that through Christ the law of liberty came to supplant the bondage of law, so that where Jehovah was Christ is; or may typify the change of evangel into law, of full-grown Christianity into a fresh type of "Judaism," of the Gospel or good news of freedom into the Church or dogmatic body of faith; or may imply that the two forces, after

* We shall see this presently. I conceive however that Blake, to save time and contract the space of his preaching, uses the consecrated Hebrew name to design now the giver of the Mosaic law, now that other and opposite Divinity which after the "body of clay" had been "devoured" was the residue or disembodied victorious spirit of the human Saviour. Mysticism need not of necessity be either inaccurate or incoherent: neither need it give offence by its forms and expressions of faith: but a mystic is but human after all, and with the best intentions may slip somewhere, especially a mystic so little in *training* as Blake, and so much of a poet or artist; who is not accustomed to any careful feeling of his way among words, except with an eye to the perfection of their bodily beauty. Indeed, as appears by Mr. Crabb Robinson's notes of his conversation, Blake affirmed that according to scripture itself the world was created by "the Elohim," not by Jehovah; whose covenant he elsewhere asserted was simply "forgiveness of sins." Thus even according to this heretical creed the God of the Jews would seem to be ranged on the same side with Christ against "the God of this world.'

that supreme sacrifice, coalesced and became one, all absolute Deity, being absorbed into the Divine Humanity; or, as a practical public would suggest, may mean or typify nothing. It is certain that Blake appears so far to have accepted the " Catholic tradition" as to regard this death or sacrifice as tending somehow not merely to the redemption of man (which would be no more than the sequel or outcome of his mystic faith in the salvation of man by man, the deliverance or redemption of the accident through the essence), but also to the union of the divine crucified man with the creative governing power. Somehow; but the prophet must explain for himself the exact means. We are now fairly up to the ears in mysticism, and cannot afford to strike out at random, for fear of being carried right off our feet by the ground-swell and drifted into waters where swimming will be yet tougher work.

The belief in " holy insurrection " must be almost as old as the oldest religions or philosophies afloat or articulate. In the most various creeds this feature of faith stands out sharply with a sort of tangible human appeal. Earlier heretics than the author of " Jerusalem " have taken this to be the radical significance of Christianity; a divine revolt against divine law; an evidence that man must become as God only by resistance to God—"the God of this world;" that if Prometheus cannot, Zeus will not deliver us: and that man, if saved at all, must indeed be saved "so as by fire"—by ardour of rebellion and strenuous battle against the God of

nature: who as of old must yet feed upon his
children, and will no longer take stone for flesh
though never so well wrapped up; who must have
the organ of destruction and division, by which
alone he lives * and has ability to beget, cut off from

---

* Compare this fragment of a paraphrase or "excursus" on
a lay sermon by a modern pagan philosopher of more material
tendencies; but given to such tragic indulgence in huge Titanic
dithyrambs. "Nature averse to crime? I tell you, nature lives
and breathes by it; hungers at all her pores for bloodshed, aches in
all her nerves for the help of sin, yearns with all her heart for the
furtherance of cruelty. Nature forbid that thing or this? Nay, the
best or worst of you will never go so far as she would have you; no
criminal will come up to the measure of her crimes, no destruction
seem to her destructive enough. We, when we would do evil, can
disorganise a little matter, shed a little blood, quench a little breath
at the door, of a perishable body; this we can do, and can call it
crime. Unnatural is it? Good friend, it is by criminal things and
deeds unnatural that nature works and moves and has her being;
what subsides through inert virtue, she quickens through active
crime; out of death she kindles life; she uses the dust of man to
strike her light upon; she feeds with fresh blood the innumerable
insatiable mouths suckled at her milkless breast; she takes the
pain of the whole world to sharpen the sense of vital pleasure in
her limitless veins: she stabs and poisons, crushes and corrodes,
yet cannot live and sin fast enough for the cruelty of her great
desire. Behold, the ages of men are dead at her feet; the blood of
the world is on her hands; and her desire is continually toward
evil, that she may see the end of things which she hath made.
Friends, if we would be one with nature, let us continually do evil
with our might. But what evil is here for us to do, where the
whole body of things is evil? The day's spider kills the day's fly,
and calls it a crime? Nay, could we thwart nature, then might
crime become possible and sin an actual thing. Could but a man
do this; could he cross the courses of the stars, and put back the
times of the sea; could he change the ways of the world and find
out the house of life to destroy it; could he go into heaven to defile
it and into hell to deliver it from subjection; could he draw down
the sun to consume the earth, and bid the moon shed poison or fire

him with the sharpest edge of flint that rebellious
hands can whet. In these galliambics of Blake's we
see the flint of Atys whetted for such work; made
ready against the priests of Nature and her God,
though by an alien hand that will cast no incense
upon the altar of Cybele; no Phrygian's, who would
spend his own blood to moisten and brighten the
high places of her worship: but one ready, with
what fire he can get, to burn down the groves and
melt down the cymbals of Dindymus.

Returning now to the residue of the immediate
matter in hand, we may duly notice in this excursive
and all but shapeless poem many of Blake's strong
points put forth with all his strength: curiously
crossed and intermixed with rough skirmishing
attacks on the opposite faction, clerical or sceptical,
by way of interlude. "You would have Christ act
according to what you call a rational or a philan-

upon the air; could he kill the fruit in the seed and corrode the
child's mouth with the mother's milk; then had he sinned and done
evil against nature. Nay, and not then: for nature would fain have
it so, that she might create a world of new things; for she is weary
of the ancient life: her eyes are sick of seeing and her ears are
heavy with hearing; with the lust of creation she is burnt up, and
rent in twain with travail until she bring forth change; she would
fain create afresh, and cannot, except it be by destroying: in all
her energies she is athirst for mortal food, and with all her forces
she labours in desire of death. And what are the worst sins we
can do—we who live for a day and die in a night? a few murders,
a few "——we need not run over the not so wholly insignificant
roll-call; but it is curious to observe how the mystical evangelist
and the material humourist meet in the reading of mere nature and
join hands in their interpretation of the laws ruling the outer body
of life: a vision of ghastly glory, without pity or help possible.

thropic habit of mind—set the actual God to reason, to elevate, to convince or convert after the fashion in which you would set about it? redeem, not the spiritual man by inspiration of his spirit, but the bodily man by application of his arguments? make him as ' Bacon and Newton ' " (Blake's usual types of the mere understanding)?

> " For thus the Gospel St. Isaac confutes :
> 'God can only be known by his attributes ;
> And as to the indwelling of the Holy Ghost
> Or of Christ and the Father, it's all a boast
> And pride and vanity of imagination
> That did wrong to follow this world's fashion.'
> To teach doubt and experiment
> Certainly was not what Christ meant."

Certainly also no doggrel can be rougher, looser, heavier-weighted about the wrists and ankles, than this ; which indeed it was perhaps hardly fair to transcribe ; for take out the one great excerpt already given, and the whole poem is a mass of huddled notes jotted down in a series of hints, on stray sides and corners of leaves, crammed into holes and byways out of sight or reach. So perfect a poet is not to be judged by the scrawls and sketches of his note-book ; but as we cannot have his revision of the present piece of work, and are not here to make any revision of our own, we must either let drop the chance of insight thus afforded, or make shift with the rough and ragged remnants allowed us by the sparing fingers of a close-handed fate. And this chance of insight is not to be lightly let go, if we mean to look at all into Blake's creed and mind. " Experiment " to the

N

mystic seems not insufficient merely, but irrational. "Reason says *miracle;* Newton says *doubt;*" as Blake in another place expounds to such disciples as he may get. On this point also his "Vision of Christ" is other than the Christian public's.

> " Thine is the friend of all mankind ;
> Mine speaks in parables to the blind."

His Christ cared no more to convince "the blind" by plain speech than to save "the world"—the form or flesh of the world, not that imperishable body or complement of the soul which if a man "keep under and bring into subjection" he transgresses against himself; but the mere "sexual" shell which only exists (as we said) by error and by division and by right of temporal appearance.

Keeping in mind the utter roughness and formal incompletion of these notes—which in effect are the mere broken shell or bruised husk of a poem yet unfledged and unembodied—we may put to some present use the ensuing crude and loose fragments.

> " What was he doing all that time
> From twelve years old to manly prime?
> Was he then idle, or the less
> About his Father's business ?
> If he had been Antichrist aping * Jesus,
> He'd have done anything to please us;

---

* Blake|had first written "the creeping," then cancelled "the" and interlined the word "Antichrist": I have no doubt intending some such alteration as that in the text of "creeping" to "aping"; but as far as we can now know the day for rewriting his fair copy never came.

Gone sneaking into synagogues
And not used the elders and priests like dogs;
But humble as a lamb or ass
Obeyed himself to Caiaphas.
God wants not man to humble himself.
That is the trick of the ancient Elf.
This is the race that Jesus ran:
Humble to God, haughty to man;
Cursing the rulers before the people
Even to the temple's highest steeple;
And when he humbled himself to God,
Then descended the cruel rod."

(This noticeable heresy is elsewhere insisted on. Its root seems to be in that doctrine that nothing is divine which is not human—has not in it the essence of complete manhood, clear of accident or attribute; servility therefore to a divine ruler is one with servility to a human ruler. More orthodox men have registered as fervent a protest against the degradation involved in base forms of worship; but this singular mythological form seems peculiar to Blake, who was bent on finding in the sacred text warrant or illustration for all his creed.)

" 'If thou humblest thyself thou humblest me:
Thou also dwell'st in eternity.
Thou art a man; God is no more;
Thine own humanity learn to adore,
For that is my spirit of life.
Awake: arise to spiritual strife;
And thy revenge abroad display
In terror at the Last Judgment Day.' "

(Another special point of faith. " Redemption by forgiveness of sins? yes: but the power of redeeming or forgiving must come by strife. A gospel is no

mere spiritual essence of boiled milk and rose-water.
There are the energies of nature to fight and beat—
unforgivable enemies, embodied in Melitus or Annas,
Caiaphas or Lycon. Sin is pardonable; but these
things, in the body or out of it, are not pardonable.
Revenge also is divine ; whatever you may think or
say while in the body, there is a part of nature not
forgivable, an element in the world not redeemable,
which in the end must be cast out and tormented."
To the priests of Pharisaic morals or Satanic religion
—those who crucify the great " human " nature and
"scourge sin instead of forgiving it "—to these the
Redeemer must be the tormentor.)

> " ' God's mercy and long-suffering
> Are but the sinner to justice to bring.
> Thou on the cross for them shalt pray—
> And take revenge at the last day.'
> Jesus replied, and thunders hurled :
> ' I never will pray for the world.
> Once I did so when I prayed in the garden ;
> I wished to take with me a bodily pardon.' "

These few lines, interpolated by way of comfort-
able exposition, are more likely to increase the
offence and perplexity : but assuredly no irreverent
brutality of paradox was here in the man's mind.
Even the " divine humanity " of his quasi-Pantheistic
worship must give up (he says) the desire of redeem-
ing the unredeemable " world "—the quality subject
to law and technical religion. No " bodily pardon "
for that, whatever the divine pity may have hoped,
while as yet full-grown in love only, not in know-

·ledge—seraphic fire without cherubic light ; before, that is, it had perfect insight into the brute nature or sham body of things.   That must be put off—changed as a vesture—by the risen and reunited body and soul.   What is it that has to be saved ?   What is it that can be ?

> " Can that which was of woman born
>   In the absence of the morn,
>   While the soul fell into sleep .
>   And (? heard) archangels round it weep,
>   Shooting out against the light
>   Fibres of a deadly night,
>   Reasoning upon its own dark fiction,
>   In doubt which is self-contradiction,"

can that reason itself into redemption ?   The absolute body and essential soul, as we have said, are with all their energies, passive and active powers and pleasures, natural properties and liberties, of an imperishable and vital holiness ; but their appended qualities, their form and law, their morals and philosophies, their reason and religion, these are perishable and damnable.   The "holy reasoning power," in whose "holiness is closed the abomination of desolation," must be annihilated.   "Rational Truth, root of Evil and Good," must be plucked up and burnt with fire.   You cannot, save in an empirical sense, walk by sight and not by faith : you cannot "walk by faith and not by sight," for there is no sight except faith.   (Compare generally the "Gates of Paradise," for illustrations of all these intricate and intense conceptions.)   Doubt then, being one of the perishable qualities which depend on externals,

is mere impotence and error: now let us hear
further:

> " Humility is only doubt
> And does the sun and moon blot out,
> Roofing over with thorns and stems
> The buried soul and all its gems.
> This life's dim window of the soul
> Distorts the heavens from pole to pole
> And leads you to believe a lie
> When you see with, not through, the eye,
> That was born in a night, to perish in a night,
> When the soul slept in the beams of light."

Part of this reappears with no less vigour of
evangelic assertion in the *Auguries of Innocence*, but
stripped of the repellent haze of mythological form.
That poem, full as it is of delicate power and clear
sweetness of thought, does not however reproduce in
full the emblematic beauty of our last extract: nor
does it throw so much light of a fitful flame-like
sort upon or over the subtlest profundities of Blake's
faith.

Elsewhere, reverting with fresh spirit to the
same charge, he demands (or his spectre for him—
" This was spoken by my spectre to Voltaire, Bacon,
&c."):

> " Did Jesus teach doubt? or did he
> Give any lessons of philosophy?
> Charge visionaries with deceiving?
> Or call men wise for not believing?"

Unhappily the respective answers from Verulam
and Cirey have not been registered by a too con-
temptuous prophet; they would have been worth
reading.

The dogma of " Christian humility " is totally indigestible to Blake ; he batters upon it with the heaviest artillery of his " gospel."

> " Was Jesus humble? or did he
> Give any proofs of humility?
> Boast of high things with humble tone,
> And give with charity a stone?"

Again ;

> " When the rich learned Pharisee
> Came to consult him secretly,
> Upon his heart with iron pen
> He wrote 'Ye must be born again.'
> He was too proud to take a bribe :
> He spoke with authority, not like a Scribe."

Nor can the love of enemies be accepted literally as an endurable doctrine ; for " he who loves his enemies hates his friends," in the mind of the too ardent and candid poet, who proceeds to insist that the divine teacher " must mean the mere *love* of civility " (*amour de convenance*) ; " and so he must mean concerning humility : " for the willing acceptance of death cannot humiliate, and is therefore no test of " humility "* in Blake's sense ; self-sacrifice in effect implies an " honest triumphant pride."

* There are (says the mystic) two forms of " humility : " detestable both, and condemnable.   By one, the extrinsic form, a man cringes and submits, doubts himself and gives in to others ; becomes in effect impotent, a sceptic and a coward ; by the other or intrinsic form, he conceives too meanly of his own soul, and comes to believe himself less than God—ot course, to a pure Pantheist, the one radical and ruinous error which throws up on all sides a crop of lies and misconceptions, rank and ready ; as base a thing to believe as an act of bodily " humility " were base to do : consequently any

(Here of course the writer drops for a moment the religious view and divine meaning of the Passion, and looks towards Calvary from the simply human side as it appeared to casual bystanders ; for here he

mere external worship is by this law heathenish, heretical and idolatrous. This heathenish or idolatrous heresy of spiritual humility comes merely of too much reliance on the reasoning power ; man is undivine as to his mere understanding, and by using that as an eye instead of an eyeglass "distorts" all which he does not obliterate. "Pride of reason" is a foolish thing for any clerical defender of the "faith" to impugn; such pride is essentially humility. To be proud of having an empty eye-socket implies that you would be ashamed of having eyesight ; then you are proud on the wrong side, and humble there exactly where humility is a mere blundering suicide's cut at his own throat; if you are *not* of your nature heavenly, how shall any alien celestial quality be sewn or stuck on to you? in whose cast clothes will you crawl into heaven by rational or religious cross-roads? "Imputed righteousness" will not much help your case; if you "impute" a wrong quality to any imaginable substance, does your imputation change the substance? What it had not before, it has not now ; your tongue has not the power of turning truth to a lie or a lie to truth ; the fact gives your assertion a straight blow in the face. The mystic who says that man is God has some logical cause for pride ; but the sceptic has no more than the cleric—he who asserts that reason, which is finite, can be final, is essentially as "humble" as he who admits that he can be "saved" by accepting as a gift some "imputed" goodness which is not in any sense his. For reason—the "spectre" of the "Jerusalem"—is no matter for pride ; if you make out that to be the best faculty about you, you give proof of the stupidest modesty and hatefullest humility. Look across the lower animal reason, and over the dim lying limit of tangible and changeable flesh ; and be humble if you can or dare, then; for if what you apprehend of yourself beyond is not God, there is none—except in that sad sense of a dæmon or natural force, strong only to create and to divide and to destroy and to govern by reason or religion the material scheme of things. *Extra hominem nulla salus.* "God is no more than man ; *because* man is no less than God :' there is Blake's Pantheistic Iliad in a nutshell.

has only to deal with what he conceives to be errors
in the human conception of Christ's human character.
"You the orthodox, and you the reasoners, assert
through the mouths of your churches or philosophies
that purely human virtues are actually predicable of
Christ, and appeal for evidence to his life and death.
Well and good ; we will, to gain ground for argu-
ment with you, forget that the Passion is not, and
admit that it is, what you would call a purely human
transaction. Are then these virtues predicable of
it even as such?") A good man who incurs risk
of death by his goodness, is too "proud" to ab-
jure that goodness and live ; here is none of that
you call "humility." Such a man need not have
died ; "Caiaphas would forgive" if one "died with
Christian ease asking pardon" after your "humble"
fashion :

> " He had only to say that God was the devil
> And the devil was God, like a Christian civil ;
> Mild Christian regrets to the devil confess
> For affronting him thrice in the wilderness ; "

and such an one might have become a very Cæsar's
minion, or Cæsar himself. Though of course mainly
made up of violent quibbling and perversities of
passionate humour, which falls to work in this
vehement way upon words as some personal relief
(a relief easily conceivable in Blake's case by any
student of his life), all this has also its value in help-
ing us to measure according to what light we may
have in us the stronger and weaker, the worse and
better, the graver and lighter sides of the man. It

belongs evidently to the period when he painted por-
traits of the dead and transcribed "Jerusalem" from
spiritual dictation. "This," he lets us know by way
of prelude or opening note, "is what Joseph of
Arimathæa said to my Fairy," or natural spiritual
part by which he conversed with spirits. Next in his
defiant doggrel he calls on "Pliny and Trajan"—
heathen learning and heathen power or goodness—
to "come before Joseph of Arimathæa" and "listen
patient." "What, are you here?" he asks as if in
the direct surprise of vision. (I will not give these
roughest notes in the perfection of their pure doggrel.
As verse, serious or humorous, they are irreclaimable
and intolerable; what empirical value they may have
must be wrung out of them with all haste.)

We may now as well look into a later division of
the poem, where Christ is tempted of Satan to obey.

> " 'John for disobedience bled;
> But you can turn the stones to bread.
> God's high king and God's high priest
> Shall plant their glories in your breast
> If Caiaphas you will obey,
> If Herod you with bloody prey
> Feed with the sacrifice * and be
> Obedient, fall down, worship me.'
> Thunder and lightning broke around
> And Jesus' voice in thunder's sound;
> ' Thus I seize the spiritual prey;
> Ye smiters with disease, make way.
> I come your King and God to seize;
> Is God a smiter with disease?'"

---

* An ugly specimen of ready-writing; meaning of course "with
the sacrifice of bloody prey:" but doubtless even Blake would not

This divine revolt and deliverance of the spiritual human "prey" out of the hands of law and fangs of religion is made matter of accusation against him by the "unredeemable part of the world" of which we spoke—using here as its mouthpiece the "shadowy man" or phantasmal shell of man, which "rolled away" when the times were full "from the limbs of Jesus, to make them his prey:"

> "Crying 'Crucify this cause of distress
> Who don't keep the secrets of holiness.
> All mental powers by diseases we bind:
> But he heals the deaf and the dumb and he blind,
> Whom God has afflicted for secret ends;
> He comforts and heals and calls them friends.'"

But Christ, instead of becoming a prey to it, himself makes his prey of this unclean shadow or ghastly ghost of the bodily life now divided from him—this pestilent nature in bondage to the dæmonic deity, which thought to consume *him* by dint of death:

> "An ever-devouring appetite
> Glittering with festering venoms bright;"*

puts it off and devours it in three nights; even as now also he feeds upon it to consume it; being made

---

have let this stand, though we cannot safely alter it: and the passage did upon the whole appear worth citing.

* This is so like Blake's style of design that one can scarcely help fancying he must somewhere have translated it into colours perhaps more comprehensible than his words: have given somewhere in painter's types the likeness of that bodily appetite, serpentine food of the serpent, a lithe and strenuous body of clay, fair with luminous flakes of eruptive poison, foul with cold and coloured

perfect in pride, that he may overcome the body by
spiritual and " galling pride : " eat what " never was
made for man to eat," the body of dust and clay, the
meal's meat of the old serpent : as "the white parts
or lights." of a plate are "eaten away with aqua-
fortis or other acid, leaving prominent " the spiritual
"outline" (" Life," v. 1, ch. ix. p. 89). This symbol,
taken from Blake's own artistic work of engraving—
from the process through which we have with us the
" Songs " and " Prophecies "—will give with some

scales as the scales of a leper in grain ; with green pallor of strain-
ing mouth and blood-like expansion of fiery throat ; teeth and claws
convulsed with the painful lust of pain, eyelids cloven in sunder
with a dull flame of desire, the visible venom of its breath shot
sharp against the face and eyes of the divine human soul : he, dis-
embodied yet incarnate in the eternal body, stripped of accidental
and clothed with essential flesh, naked of attribute that he may be
girdled with substance, wrestling silent with fair great limbs, but
with calm hair and brows blanched as in fire, with light of lordship
in the "sunclear joyful eyes" that already absorb and devour by
sweet strength of radiance the relapsing reluctant bulk of body, that
foulest ravenous birth begotten of accident or error upon time ;
eyes beautiful with the after-light of ancient tears, that shall not
weep again for ever: "for the former things are passed away : "
and by that light of theirs shall all men see light. Behind these two,
an intense and tremulous night stricken through with stars and fire ;
and overhead the dividing roof and underfoot the sundering floor-
work of the grave ; a waste place beyond, full of risen bones that
gather flesh and springing roots that strike out or catch at light
flying flames of life. Decidedly the design must exist somewhere ;
and presumably in "Golgonooza." We have the artist's prophetic
authority for believing that his works written and painted before
he came upon earth do in effect fill whole chambers in heaven,
and are "the delight and study of archangels :" an apocalyptic
fact not unnaturally unacceptable and inconceivable to the cleverest
of Scotch stonemasons.

precision the exact point indicated, and might have
been allowed of by himself, as not unacceptable or
inapposite.

This final absorption of the destructible body,
consumption of "the serpent's meat," is but the
upshot of a life of divine rebellion and "spiritual
war," not of barren physical qualities and temporal
virtues :

> " The God of this world raged in vain ;
> He bound old Satan in his chain :
> Throughout the land he took his course,
> And traced diseases to their source :
> He cursed the Scribe and Pharisee,
> Trampling down hypocrisy."

His wrath was made as it were a chariot of fire ;
at the wheels of it was dragged the God of this
world, overthrown and howling aloud :

> " Where'er his chariot took its way
> Those gates of death let in the day ; "

every chain and bar broken down from them, and
the staples of the doors loosed ; his voice was heard
from Zion above the clamour of axle and wheel,

> " And in his hand the scourge shone bright ;
> He scourged the merchant Canaanite
> From out the temple of his mind,
> And in his body tight does bind
> Satan and all his hellish crew ;
> And thus with wrath he did subdue
> The serpent bulk of nature's dross
> Till he had nailed it to the cross.
> He put on sin in the Virgin's womb,
> And put it off on the cross and tomb
> To be worshipped by the Church of Rome : "

not to speak of other churches.   One may notice
how to the Pantheist the Catholic's worship is a
worship of sin, even as his own is to the Catholic.
"You adore as divine the fallen nature and sinful
energies of man : " " you, again, the cast-off body
wherein Satan and sin were shut up, that he who
assumed it might crucify them."   Sin or false faith
or " hypocrisy " was scourged out of the mind into
the body, and the separate animal body then delivered
over to death with the sins thereof—all the sins of
the world garnered up in it to be purged away with
fire : and of this body you make your God.   The ex-
pressed gird at the " Church of Rome " is an inter-
polation ; at first Blake had merely written " And on
the cross he sealed its doom " in place of our two
last-quoted lines.   Akin to this view of the " body
of sin " is his curious heresy of the Conception ; re-
minding one of that Christian sect which would needs
worship Judas as the necessary gateway of salvation :
for without his sin how could redemption have come
about ?

> " Was Jesus born of a virgin pure
> With narrow soul and looks demure?
> If he intended to take on sin,
> His mother should an harlot (have) been :
> Just such a one as Magdalen,
> With seven devils in her pen.
> Or were Jew virgins still more cursed,
> And more sucking devils nursed ? "

(This ingenious solution, worthy of any mediæval
heresiarch of the wilder sort in a time of leprosy, is
also an afterthought.   From the sudden anti-Judaic

rapture of grotesque faith or humour into which
Blake suddenly dips hereabouts, one might imagine
he had been lately bitten or stung by some dealer or
other such dangerous craftsman of the Hebrew kind ;
for that any mortal Jew—or for that matter any con-
ceivable Gentile—would have credited him to the
amount of a penny sterling, no one will imagine.
Let the reader meanwhile endure him a little further,
suppressing if he is wise any comment on Blake's
"insanity" or "blasphemous doggrel ;" for he should
now at least understand that this literal violence of
manner, these light or grave audacities of mere form,
imply no offensive purpose or significance, except
insomuch as offence is inseparable from any strange
kind of earnestly heretical belief. Neither is Blake
here busied in fetching milk to feed his babes and
sucklings. This he could do incomparably well on
occasion, with such milk as a nursing-goddess gave
to the son of Metaneira ; but here he carves meat for
men—of a strange quality, tough and crude : but not
without savour or sustenance if eaten with the right
sauce and prefaced with a proper grace.)

> " Or what was it that he took on
> That he might bring salvation ?
> A body subject to be tempted,
> From neither pain nor grief exempted,
> Or such a body as could not feel
> The passions that with sinners deal ?
> Yes : but they say he never fell.
> Ask Caiaphas : for he can tell."

Here follow as given by Caiaphas the old charges
of Sabbath-breach, blasphemy and strange doctrine ;

given again almost word for word, but with a nobler
frame of context, in the "Marriage of Heaven and
Hell," where, and not here, we will prefer to read
them.   One charge will be allowed to pass as new
coin, having Blake's image and superscription in lieu
of Cæsar's.

> " He turned the devils into swine
>   That he might tempt the Jews to dine;
>   Since when, a pig has got a look
>   That for a Jew may be mistook.
>   ' Obey your parents '?   What says he?
>   ' Woman, what have I to do with thee?
>   No earthly parents I confess:
>   I am doing my Father's business.'
>   He scorned earth's parents, scorned earth's God,
>   And mocked the one and the other's rod
>   His seventy disciples sent *
>   Against religion and government,"

---

* Compare Hugo's admirable poem in the *Châtiments* (vii. 11.
pp. 319–321)—" Paroles d'un conservateur à propos d'un perturba-
teur : "—where, speaking through the mouth of " Elizab, a scribe,"
the chief poet of our time gives in his great swift manner a dramatic
summary of the view taken by priests and elders of Christ.   It is
worth looking to trace out how nearly the same historical points
of objection are selected and the same lines of inference struck
into by the two poets; one aiming straight at present politics, one
indirectly at mystic doctrine.

> " Cet homme était de ceux qui n'ont rien de sacré,
>   Il ne respectait rien de tout ce qu'on respecte.
>   Pour leur inoculer sa doctrine suspecte,
>   Il allait ramassant dans les plus méchants lieux
>   Des bouviers, des pêcheurs, des drôles bilieux,
>   D'immondes va-nu-pieds n'ayant ni sou ni maille :
>   Il faisait son cénacle avec cette canaille.
>   *   *   *   *   *

and caused his followers to die by the sword of
justice as rebels and blasphemers of this world's God
and his law : overturned " the tent of secret sins and
its God," with all the cords of his weaving, prisons
of his building and snares of his setting ; overthrew
the "bloody shrine of war;" the holy place of the
God of battles, whose cruel light and fire of wrath
was poured forth upon the world till it reached
" from star to star ; " thus casting down all things of
"church and state as by law established," camps
and shrines, temples and prisons,

> " Halls of justice, hating vice,
> Where the devil combs his lice."

Upon all these, to the great grief of Caiaphas and
the grievous detriment of the God of this world, he
sent "not peace but a sword:" lived as a vagrant
upon other men's labour, kept company by preference
with publicans and harlots.

> " And from the adulteress turned away
> God's righteous law, that lost its prey."

L'honnête homme indigné rentrait dans sa maison
Quand ce jongleur passait avec cette séquelle.
 * * * * *

Il traînait à sa suite une espèce de fille.
Il allait pérorant, ébranlant la famille,
Et la religion et la société.
Il sapait la morale et la propriété.
 * * * * *

       Quant aux prêtres,
Il les déchirait ; bref, il blasphémait.   Cela
Dans la rue.   Il contait toutes ces horreurs-là
Aux premiers gueux venus, sans cape et sans semelles.
Il fallait en finir, les lois étaient formelles,
On l'a crucifié."

So we end as we began, at that great practical point of revolt: and finally, with deep fervour of satisfaction, and the sense of a really undeniable achievement, the new evangelist jots down this couplet by way of epilogue:

> " I'm sure this Jesus will not do
> Either for Englishman or Jew."

Scarcely, as far as one sees: we may surely allow him that. And yet, having somehow steered right through this chaotic evangel, we may as surely admit that none but a great man with a great gift of belief could have conceived or wrought it out even as roughly as it is here set down. There is more absolute worship implied in it than in most works of art that pass muster as religious; a more perfect power of noble adoration, an intenser faculty of faith and capacity of love, keen as flame and soft as light; a more uncontrollable desire for right and lust after justice, a more inexhaustible grace of pity for all evil and sorrow that is not of itself pitiless, a more deliberate sweetness of mercy towards all that are cast out and trodden under. This "vision of Christ," though it be to all seeming the "greatest enemy" of other men's visions, can hardly be regarded as the least significant or beautiful that the religious world has yet been brought into contact with. It is at least not effeminate, not unmerciful, not ignoble, and not incomprehensible: other "visions" have before now been any or all of these. Thus much it is at least; the "vision" of a perfectly brave, tender,

subtle and faithful spirit; in which there was no
fear and no guile, nothing false and nothing base.
Of the technical theology or "spiritualism" each
man who cares to try will judge as it may please
him; it goes at least high and deep enough to draw
down or pluck up matter for absolution or condemna-
tion. It is no part of our affair further to vindicate,
to excuse, or to account for the singular gospel here
preached.*

* In a briefer and less important fragment of verse Blake as
earnestly inculcates this faith of his: that all mere virtues and vices
were known before Christ; of right and wrong Plato and Cicero,
men uninspired, were competent to speak as well as he; but until
his advent "the moral virtues in their pride" held rule over the
world, and among them as they rode clothed with war and sacrifice,
driving souls to hell before them, shone "upon the rivers and the
streams" the face of the Accuser, holy God of this Pharisaic world.
Then arose Christ and said to man "Thy sins are all forgiven thee;"
and the "moral virtues," in terror lest their reign of war and
accusation should now draw to an end, cried out "Crucify him,"
and formed with their own hands the cross and the nails and the
spear: and the Accuser spoke to them saying:

> " Am I not Lucifer the great
> And ye my daughters, in great state,
> The fruit of my mysterious tree
> Of Good and Evil and Misery?"

It, the preacher adds, moral virtue was Christianity, Christ's pre-
tensions were madness, "and Caiaphas and Pilate men praise-
worthy;" and the lion's den a fitter emblem of heaven than the
sheepfold. "The moral Christian is the cause of the unbeliever;"
and Antichrist is incarnate in those who close heaven against
sinners

> " With iron bars in virtuous state
> And Rhadamanthus at the gate."

But men have so long allowed the heathen virtues, whose element
is war and whose essence retaliation, to "take Jesus' and Jehovah's

Space may be made here (before we pass on to larger things if not greater) for another stray note or two on separate poems. *The Crystal Cabinet*, one of the completest short poems by Blake which are not to be called songs, is an example of the somewhat jarring and confused mixture of apparent "allegory" with actual "vision" which is the great source of trouble and error to rapid readers of his verse or students of his designs. The "cabinet" is either passionate or poetic vision—a spiritual gift, which may soon and easily become a spiritual bondage; wherein a man is locked up, with keys of gold indeed, yet is he a prisoner all the same: his prison built by his love or his art, with a view open beyond of exquisite limited loveliness, soft quiet and light of dew or moon, and a whole fresh world to rest in or look into, but intangible and simply reflective; all present pleasure or power trebled in it, until you try at too much and attempt to turn spiritual to physical reality—"to seize the inmost form" with "hands of flame" laid upon things of the spirit which will endure no such ardent handling—to translate eternal existence into temporal, essential into accidental, substantial into attributive; when at once the whole framework, which was meant otherwise to last out your present life, breaks up and

name" that the Accuser, Antichrist and Lucifer though he be, is now worshipped by those holy names over all the world: and the era called Christian is the era of his reign. For the rest, this new relic has no special merit, although it may be allowed some share of interest as a supplement or illustration to the larger poem or sermon.

leaves you stranded or cast out, feeble and sightless
"like a weeping babe ; " so that whereas at first you
were full of light natural pleasure, "dancing merrily"
in "the wild" of animal or childish life, you are now
a child again, but unhappy instead of happy—less
than a child, thrown back on the crying first stage
of babyhood—having had the larger vision, and lost
your hold of it by too great pressure of impatience
or desire—unfit for the old pleasure and deprived of
the new ; and the maiden-mother of your spiritual
life, your art or your love, is become wan and tearful
as you, "pale reclined" in the barren blowing air
which cannot again be filled with the fire and the
luminous life of vision. In *Mary* we come again
upon the main points of inner contact between
Blake's mind and Shelley's. This frank acceptance
of pleasure, this avowal without blushing or doubt-
ing "that sweet love and beauty are worthy our
care," was as beautiful a thing to Shelley as to Blake :
he has preached the excellence of it in " Rosalind and
Helen " and often elsewhere : touching also, as Blake
does here, on the persecution of it by all "who
amant miserè : "

> " Some said she was proud, some called her a whore,
>   And some when she passed by shut to the door ; "

for in their sight the tender and outspoken purity of
instinct and innocence becomes confounded with base
desire or vanity. This rather than genius or mere
beauty seems to be the thing whose persecution by
the world is here symbolized.

Many others of these brief poems are not less
excellent ; the slightest among them have the grace
of form and heat of life which are indivisible in all
higher works of poetry. One, *The Mental Traveller*,
is full of sweet and vigorous verses turned loose
upon a somewhat arid and thorny pasture. By a
miracle of patient ingenuity this poem has been com-
pelled to utter some connected message ; but it may
perhaps be doubted whether the message be not too
articulate and coherent for Blake. Thus limited and
clarified, the broad chafing current of mysticism
seems almost too pure and too strait to issue from
such a source : a well-head of living speech that
bursts up with sudden froth and steam through
more outlets than one at once. To have contrived
such an elaborate allegory, so welded link by sequent
link together, seems an exercise of logical patience
to which Blake would hardly have submitted his
passionate genius, his overstrained and wayward
will. Separate stanzas may be retraced wellnigh
through every word in other books. The latter
part seems again to record, as in two preceding
poems, the perversion of love ; which having annihi-
lated all else, falls at last to feed upon itself, to seek
out strange things and barren ways, to invent new
loves and invert the old, to fill the emptied heart and
flush the subsiding veins with perverse passion.
Alone in the desert it has made, beguiled to second
youth by the incessant diet of joy, fear comes upon
love ; fear, and seeming hate, and weariness and
cunning ; fruits of the second graft of love, not

native to the simple stock : till reduced at last to the likeness of the two extremes of life, age and infancy, love can be no further abused or consumed. These stages of love, once seen or heard of, allure lovers to eat of the strange fruits and herd with the strange flocks of transforming or transformed desire ; the visible world, destroyed at the first advent of love and absorbed into the soul by a single passion, is again felt nearer ; the trees bring forth their pleasure, and the planets lavish their light. For the second love, in its wayward and strange delights, is a thing half material ; not alien at least from material forms, as was the first simple and spiritual ardour of equal love. Passionate and perverse emotion touches all things with some fervent colour of its own, mixes into all water and all wine some savour of the dubious honey gathered from its foreign flowers. Pure first love will not coexist with out-ward things, burns up with white fire all tangible form, and so, an unfed lamp, must at last burn itself down to the stage of life and sensation which breeds those latter loves. The babe that is "born a boy," often painfully begot and joyfully brought forth, I take to signify human genius or intellect, which none can touch and not be consumed except the "woman old," faith or fear : all weaker things, pain and pleasure, hatred and love, fly with shrieking averted faces from before it. The grey and cruel nurse, custom or religion, crucifies and torments the child, feeding herself upon his agony to false fresh youth ; an allegory not even literally inapt. Grown older,

and seeing her made fair with his blood and strong
by his suffering, he weds her, and constrains her to
do him service, and turns her to use ; custom, the
daily life of men, once married to the fresh intellect,
bears fruit to him of profit and pleasure, and becomes
through him nobler than she was ; but through such
union he grows old the sooner, soon can but wander
round and look over his finished work and gathered
treasure, the tragic passions and splendid achieve-
ments of his spirit, kept fresh in verse or colour ;
which he deals to all men alike, giving to the poorest
of this divine meat and drink, the body and the blood
of genius, caught in golden vessels of art and rhyme,
that sight and hearing may be fed.   This, the
supreme and most excellent delight possible to man,
is the fruit of his pain ; of his suffering at the hands
of life, of his union with her as with a bride.   The
"female* babe" sprung from the fire that burns
always on his hearth, is the issue or result of genius,
which, being too strong for the father, flows into
new channels and follows after fresh ways ; the thing
which he has brought forth knows him no more, but

* The words " female " and " reflex " are synonymous in all
Blake's writings.   What is feminine in its material symbol is deri-
vative in its spiritual significance ; "there is no such thing in
eternity as a female will ; " for in eternity substances lose their
shadows, and essence puts off accident.   The " frowning babe " of
the last stanzas is of course the same or such another as the one
whose birth is first spoken of ; not the latter female growth born in
the earthly house of art, but genius itself, whose likeness is terrible
and unlovely at first sight to the run of men, filling them with
affright and scandal, with wonder and the repellent sense that a new
and strange thing is brought into the world.

must choose its own mate or living form of expression, and expel the former nature—casting off (as theologians say) the old man.   The outcast intellect can then be vivified only by a new love, or by a new aim of which love is the type; a bride unlike the first, who was old at root and in substance, young only in seeming and fair only through cruel theft of his own life and strength; unlike also the art which has now in its ultimate expression turned against him; love which can change the face of former things and scatter in sunder the gatherings of former friends; love which masters the senses and transfigures the creatures of the earthly life, leaving no light or sustenance but what comes of itself.   Then follow the stages of love, and the phases of action and passion bred from either stage; of these we have already taken account.   If this view of the poem be wholly or partially correct, then we may roughly sum up the problem by saying that its real obscurity arises in the main from a verbal confusion between the passion of art and the passion of love. These are always spoken of by Blake in terms which prove that in his nature the two feelings had actually grown into each other; had become interfused past all chance of mutual extrication.   Art was to him as a lust of the body; appetite as an emotion of the soul.   This saying, true as to some extent it must be of all great men, was never so exclusively and finally true of any other man as of this one.   It is no bad sample of Blake's hurried manner of speech, that having sustained halfway through his poem an

allegory of intellect in its relations to art and to
common life, he should suddenly stumble over a type
of his own setting up, and be led off into a new
allegory of love which might better have made a
separate poem.   As it is, the two symbols are
welded together not without strength and cunning
of hand.

Some further and final notice may here be taken
of the manifold designs scattered about the MS.
pages which we have found so prodigal of verse.
Among the most curious of these we rank a series of
drawings not quite so roughly pencilled as the rest,
each inscribed with a brief text or metrical motto.
Many of these have been wrought up into the
" Gates of Paradise ; " many more remain to speak
and shift for themselves as they may.* Published
as it stands here, the series would exceed in length
the whole of that little book : and there is evidently
some thread of intended connexion between all, worn
thin and all but broken. They are numbered in a
different order from that in which they stand, which
is indeed plainly a matter of chance. Several have
great grace and beauty ; one in especial, where
Daphne passes into the laurel ; her feet are roots
already and grasp the ground with strong writhing
fibres ; her lifted arms and wrestling body struggle

---

* It seems not impossible that this series may have been intended,
in its complete form, to bear the title of " Ideas of Good and Evil,"
which we find loosely attached to the general MS. When the
designer broke it up into different sets, this name would naturally
have been abandoned.

into branch and stem, with strange labour of the
supple limbs, with agony of convulsed and loosen-
ing hair. One of the larger designs seems to be
a rough full-length study for Adam and Eve, with
these lines opposite by way of suggested epigraph :

> " What is it men in women do require ?
> The lineaments of gratified desire.
> What is it women do in men require ?
> The lineaments of gratified desire."

These are barely to be recognised in the crude
sketch : the faces are merely serious and rather
grim : though designed to reproduce the sweet
silence of beauty, filling features made fair with soft
natural pleasure and a clear calm of soul and body.
There is however a certain grace and nobility of
form in the straight limbs and flowing hair, not
unworthy the typical man and woman. Another
design which deserves remark is a fine sketch after
the manner of the illustrations to Blake's prophe-
cies, in which a figure caught in the fierce slanting
current of a whirlwind is drifted sideways like a
drowning swimmer under sea, below the orbit of
three mingling suns or planets seen above thick
drifts of tempestuous air. Other and better notices
than ours, of various studies hidden away in the
chaos of this MS., the reader will find on reference
to that admirable Catalogue which will remain
always the great witness for Blake's genius before
the eyes of all who read his life.

We have done now with the lyrical side of this

poet's work,* and pass on to things of less direct attraction. Those who have found any in the record of his life and character, the study of his qualities and abilities, may safely follow him further. The perfect sweetness and sufficiency of his best lyrics and his best designs, we may not find ; of these we take now farewell, with thanks and final praise such as we have to give ; but we shall not fail to find the traces of a great art and an exalted spirit, to feel about us the clear air of a great man's presence.

* Of Blake's prose other samples are extant besides the notes on art published in the second volume of the " Life and Selections." These strays are for the most part, as far as I have seen, mere waifs of weed and barren drift. One fragment, not without some grace and thoughtfulness curiously used up and thrown away, is an allegory of " the Gods which came from Fear," of Shame born of the " poisonous seed " of pride, and such things ; written much in the manner of those early Ossianic studies which dilate and deform the volume of " Poetical Sketches : " perhaps composed (though properly never composed at all) about the same time. Another, a sort of satire on critics and " philosophers," seems to emulate the style of Sterne in his intervals of lax and dull writing ; in execution it is some depths below the baby stories of little Malkin, whose ghost might well have blushed rejection of the authorship. The fragment on *Laocoon* is a mere cento of stray notes on art which reaffirm in a chaotic and spluttering manner Blake's theories that the only real prayer is study of art, the only real praise, its practice ; that excellence of art, not moral virtue, is the aim and the essence of Christianity ; and much more of the same sort. These notes, crammed into every blank space and corner of the engraved page, burst out as it were and boil over, disconnected but irrepressible, in a feverish watery style. All really good or even passable prose of Blake's seems to be given in the volume of " Selections."

III

THE PROPHETIC BOOKS

BEFORE entering upon any system of remark or comment on the "Prophetic Books," we may set down in as few and distinct words as possible the reasons which make this a thing seriously worth doing; nay, even requisite to be done, if we would know rather the actual facts of the man's nature than the circumstances and accidents of his life. Now, first of all, we are to recollect that Blake himself regarded these works as his greatest, and as containing the sum of his achieved ambitions and fulfilled desires: as in effect inspired matter, of absolute imaginative truth and eternal import. We shall not again pause to rebut the familiar cry of response, to the effect that he was mad and not accountable for the uttermost madness of error.. It must be enough to reply here that he was by no means mad, in any sense that would authorize us.in rejecting his own judgment of his own aims and powers on a plea which would be held insufficient in another man's case. Let all readers and all critics get rid of that notion for good —clear their minds of it utterly and with all haste; let them know and remember, having once been told it, that in these strangest of all written books there is purpose as well as power, meaning as well as mystery. Doubtless, nothing quite like them was ever pitched out headlong into the world as they were. The confusion, the clamour, the jar of words that half suffice and thoughts that half exist —all these and other more absolutely offensive qualities—audacity, monotony, bombast, obscure play of licence and tortuous growth of fancy—cannot quench or even wholly conceal the living purport and the imperishable beauty which are here latent.

And secondly we are to recollect this ; that these books are not each a set of designs with a text made by order to match, but are each a poem composed for its own sake and with its own aim, having illustrations arranged by way of frame or appended by way of ornament. On all grounds, therefore, and for all serious purpose, such notices as some of those given in this biography are actually worse than worthless. Better have done nothing than have done this and no more. All the criticism included as to the illustrative parts merely, is final and faultless, nothing missed and nothing wrong ; this could not have been otherwise, the work having fallen under hands and eyes of practical taste and trained to actual knowledge, and the assertions being therefore issued by authority. So much otherwise has it fared with the books themselves, that (we are compelled in this case to say it) the clothes are all right and the body is all wrong. Passing from some phrase of high and accurate eulogy to the raw ragged extracts here torn away and held up with the unhealed scars of mutilation fresh and red upon them, what is any human student to think of the poet or his praisers? what, of the assertion of his vindicated sanity with such appalling counterproof thrust under one's eyes? In a word, it must be said of these notices of Blake's " Prophetic Books " * (except perhaps that insufficient but pains-taking and well-meant chapter on the " Marriage of Heaven and Hell ") that what has been done should not have been done, and what should have been done has not been done.

Not that the thing was easy to do. If any one would realize to himself for ever a material notion of chaos, let him take a blind header into the midst of the whirling foam and rolling weed of this sea of words. Indeed the sound and savour of these prophecies constantly recall some such idea or some such memory. This poetry has the huge various mono-tonies, the fervent and fluent colours, the vast limits, the fresh sonorous strength, the certain confusion and

* It should not be overlooked that this part of his work was left unfinished, all but untouched, by the author of the " Life." Without as long a study and as deep a sympathy as his, it would seem to any follower, however able and zealous, the most toilsome as well as the most sterile part of the task in hand. The fault therefore lies with chance or fate alone. Less than I have said above could not here be said; and more need not be. I was bound at starting to register my protest against the contempt and condemnation which these books have incurred, thinking them as I do not unworthy the trouble of commentary; but no word was designed to depreciate the careful and admirable labour which has completed a monument cut short with the life of the sculptor, joined now in death to the dead whom he honoured.

tumultuous law, the sense of windy and weltering space, the intense refraction of shadow or light, the crowded life and inanimate intricacy, the patience and the passion of the sea. By no manner of argument or analysis will one be made able to look back or forward with pure confidence and comprehension. Only there are laws, strange as it must sound, by which the work is done and against which it never sins. The biographer once attempts to settle the matter by asserting that Blake was given to contradict himself, by mere impulse if not by brute instinct, to such an extent that consistency is in no sense to be sought for or believed in throughout these works of his : and quotes, by way of ratifying this quite false notion, a noble sentence from the *Proverbs of Hell*, aimed by Blake with all his force against that obstinate adherence to one external opinion which closes and hardens the spirit against all further message from the new-grown feelings or inspiration from the altering circumstances of a man. Never was there an error more grave or more complete than this. The expression shifts perpetually, the types blunder into new forms, the meaning tumbles into new types ; the purpose remains, and the faith keeps its hold.

There are certain errors and eccentricities of manner and matter alike common to nearly all these books, and distinctly referable to the character and training of the man. Not educated in any regular or rational way, and by nature of an eagerly susceptible and intensely adhesive mind, in which the lyrical faculty had gained and kept a preponderance over

all others visible in every scrap of his work, he had
saturated his thoughts and kindled his senses with a
passionate study of the forms of the Bible as trans-
lated into English, till his fancy caught a feverish
contagion and his ear derived a delirious excitement
from the mere sound and shape of the written words
and verses.   Hence the quaint and fervent imitation
of style, the reproduction of peculiarities which to
most men are meaningless when divested of their old
sense or invested with a new.   Hence the bewilder-
ing catalogues, genealogies, and divisions which (es-
pecially in such later books as the *Jerusalem*) seem
at first invented only to strike any miserable reader
with furious or lachrymose lunacy.   Hence, though
heaven knows by no fault of the originals, the insane
cosmogony, blatant mythology, and sonorous aber-
ration of thoughts and theories.   Hence also much of
the special force and supreme occasional loveliness or
grandeur in expression.   Conceive a man incompar-
ably gifted as to the spiritual side of art, prone beyond
all measure to the lyrical form of work, incredibly
contemptuous of all things and people dissimilar to
himself, of an intensely sensitive imagination and
intolerant habit of faith, with a passionate power of
peculiar belief, taking with all his might of mental
nerve and strain of excitable spirit to a perusal and
reperusal of such books as Job and Ezekiel.   Observe
too that his tone of mind was as far from being
critical as from being orthodox.   Thus his ecstasy
of study was neither on the one side tempered and
watered down by faith in established forms and

P

external creeds, nor on the other side modified and
directed by analytic judgment and the lust of facts.
To Blake either form of mind was alike hateful. Like
the Moses of Rabbinical tradition, he was "drunken
with the kisses of the lips of God." Rational deism
and clerical religion were to him two equally abhor-
rent incarnations of the same evil spirit, appearing
now as negation and now as restriction. He wanted
supremacy of freedom with intensity of faith. Hence
he was properly neither Christian nor infidel : he was
emphatically a heretic. Such men, according to the
temper of the times, are burnt as demoniacs or pitied
as lunatics. He believed in redemption by Christ, and
in the incarnation of Satan as Jehovah. He believed
that by self-sacrifice the soul should attain freedom
and victorious deliverance from bodily bondage and
sexual servitude ; and also that the extremest fulness
of indulgence in such desire and such delight as the
senses can aim at or attain was absolutely good,
eternally just, and universally requisite. These
opinions, and stranger than these, he put forth in
the cloudiest style, the wilfullest humour, and the
stormiest excitement. No wonder the world let his
books drift without caring to inquire what gold or
jewels might be washed up as waifs from the dregs
of. churned foam and subsiding surf. He was the
very man for fire and faggot ; a mediæval inquisitor
would have had no more doubt about him than a
materialist or "theophilanthropist" of his own day
or of ours.

A wish is expressed in the " Life " that we could

accompany the old man who appears entering an
open door, star in hand, at the beginning of the
Jerusalem, and thread by his light those infinite dark
passages and labyrinthine catacombs of invention or
thought. In default of that desirable possibility,
let us make such way as we can for ourselves into
this submarine world, along its slippery and unpaven
ways, under its roof of hollow sound and tumbling
storm.

> " We shall see, while above us
>   The waves roar and whirl,
>   A ceiling of amber,
>   A pavement of pearl."

At the entrance of the labyrinth we are met by
huge mythologic figures, created of fire and cloud.
Titans of monstrous form and yet more monstrous
name obstruct the ways ; sickness or sleep never
formed such savage abstractions, such fierce vanities
of vision as these : office and speech they seem at
first to have none : but to strike or clutch at the
void of air with feeble fingers, to babble with vast
lax lips a dialect barren of all but noise, loud and
loose as the wind. Slowly they grow into some-
thing of shape, assume some foggy feature and
indefinite colour : word by word the fluctuating
noise condenses into music, the floating music
divides into audible notes and scales. The sound
which at first was as the mere collision of cloud with
cloud is now the recognizable voice of god or
dæmon. Chaos is cloven into separate elements ;
air divides from water, and earth releases fire.

P 2

Upon each of these the prophet, as it were, lays
hand, compelling the thing into shape and speech,
constraining the abstract to do service as a man
might. These and such as these make up the
personal staff or executive body of his prophecies.
But it would be waste of time to conjecture how or
why he came to inflict upon them such incredible
names. These hapless energies and agencies are
not simply cast into the house of allegoric bondage,
and set to make bricks without straw, to con-
struct symbols without reason ; but find themselves
baptized with muddy water and fitful fire, by names
inconceivable, into a church full of storm and
vapour ; regenerated with a vengeance, but dis-
embodied and disfigured in their resurrection. Space
fell into sleep, and awoke as Enitharmon : Time
suffered eclipse, and came forth as Los. The Christ
or Prometheus of this faith is Orc or Fuzon ; Urizen
takes the place of "Jehovah, Jove, or Lord."
Hardly in such chaotic sounds can one discern the
slightest element of reason gone mad, the narrowest
channel of derivation run dry. In this last word,
one of incessant recurrence, there seems to flicker a
thin reminiscence of such names as Uranus, Uriel,
and perhaps Urien ; for the deity has a diabolic
savour in him, and Blake was not incapable of
mixing the Hellenic, the Miltonic, and the Celtic
mythologies into one drugged and adulterated com-
pound. He had read much and blindly ; he had
no leaning to verbal accuracy, and never acquired
any faculty of comparison. Any sound that in the

dimmest way suggested to him a notion of hell or heaven, of passion or power, was significant enough to adopt and register. Commentary was impossible to him : if his work could not be apprehended or enjoyed by an instinct of inspiration like his own, it was lost labour to dissect or expound ; and here, if ever, translation would have been treason. He took the visions as they came ; he let the words lie as they fell. These barbarous and blundering names are not always without a certain kind of melody and an uncertain sort of meaning. Such as they are, they must be endured ; or the whole affair must be tossed aside and thrown up. Over these clamorous kingdoms of speech and dream some few ruling forces of supreme discord preside : and chiefly the lord of the world of man ; Urizen, God of cloud and star, "Father of jealousy," clothed with a splendour of shadow, strong and sad and cruel ; his planet faintly glimmers and slowly revolves, a horror in heaven ; the night is a part of his thought, rain and wind are in the passage of his feet ; sorrow is in all his works ; he is the maker of mortal things, of the elements and sexes ; in him are incarnate that jealousy which the Hebrews acknowledged and that envy which the Greeks recognized in the divine nature ; in his worship faith remains one with fear. Star and cloud, the types of mystery and distance, of cold alienation and heavenly jealousy, belong of right to the God who grudges and forbids : even as the spirit of revolt is made manifest in fiery incarnation—pure prolific fire, "the cold loins of Urizen

dividing." These two symbols of "cruel fear" or
"starry jealousy" in the divine tyrant, of ardent
love or creative lust in the rebellious saviour of man,
pervade the mystical writings of Blake. Orc, the
man-child, with hair and flesh like fire, son of Space
and Time, a terror and a wonder from the hour of
his birth, containing within himself the likeness of
all passions and appetites of men, is cast out from
before the face of heaven; and falling upon earth,
a stronger Vulcan or Satan, fills with his fire the
narrowed foreheads and the darkened eyes of all
that dwell thereon; imprisoned often and fed from
vessels of iron with barren food and bitter drink,* a
wanderer or a captive upon earth, he shall rise again
when his fire has spread through all lands to inflame
and to infect with a strong contagion the spirit and
the sense of man, and shall prevail against the law
and the commandments of his enemy. This endless

* Something like this may be found in a passage of Werner
translated by Mr. Carlyle, but mixed with much of meaner matter,
and debased by a feebleness and a certain spiritual petulance proper
to a man so much inferior. The German mystic, though ingenious
and laborious, is also tepid, pretentious, insecure; half terrified at
his own timid audacities, half choked by the fumes of his own
alembic. He labours within a limit, not fixed indeed, but never
expansive; narrowing always at one point as it widens at another:
his work is weak in the head and the spine; he ventures with half
a heart and strikes with half a hand; throughout his myth of Phos-
phorus he goes halting and hinting; not ungracefully, nay with a
real sense of beauty, but never like a man braced up for the work
requisite; he labours under a dull devotion and a cloudy capacity.
Above all, he can neither speak nor do well, being no artist or
prophet; and so makes but a poor preacher or essayist. The light
he shows is thick and weak; Blake's light, be it meteor or star,
rises with the heat and radiance of fire or the morning.

myth of oppression and redemption, of revelation and revolt, runs through many forms and spills itself by strange straits and byways among the sands and shallows of prophetic speech.   But in these books there is not the substantial coherence of form and reasonable unity of principle which bring within scope of apprehension even the wildest myths grown out of unconscious idealism and impulsive tradition. A single man's work, however exclusively he may look to inspiration for motive and material, must always want the breadth and variety of meaning, the supple beauty of symbol, the infectious intensity of satisfied belief, which grow out of creeds and fables native to the spirit of a nation, yet peculiar to no man or sect, common yet sacred, not invented or constructed, but found growing and kept fresh with faith.   But for all the dimness and violence of expression which pervert and darken the mythology of these attempts at gospel, they have qualities great enough to be worth finding out.   Only let none conceive that each separate figure in the swarming and noisy life of this populous dæmonic creation has individual meaning and vitality.   Blake was often taken off his feet by the strong currents of fancy, and indulged, like a child during its first humour of invention, in wild byplay and erratic excesses of simple sound ; often lost his way in a maze of wind-music, and transcribed as it were with eyes closed and open ears the notes caught by chance as they drifted across the dream of his subdued senses. Alternating between lyrical invention and gigantic

allegory, it is hard to catch and hold him down to
any form or plan.   At one time we have mere music,
chains of ringing names, scattered jewels of sound
without a thread, tortuous network of harmonies
without a clue; and again we have passages, not
always unworthy of an Æschylean chorus, full of
fate and fear; words that are strained wellnigh in
sunder by strong significance and earnest passion;
words that deal greatly with great things, that strike
deep and hold fast; each inclusive of some fierce
apocalypse or suggestive of some obscure evangel.
Now the matter in hand is touched with something
of an epic style; the narrative and characters lose
half their hidden sense, and the reciter passes from
the prophetic tripod to the seat of a common singer;
mere names, perhaps not even musical to other ears
than his, allure and divert him; he plays with
stately cadences, and lets the wind of swift or slow
declamation steer him whither it will.   Now again
he falls with renewed might of will to his purpose;
and his grand lyrical gift becomes an instrument
not sonorous merely but vocal and articulate.   To
readers who can but once take their stand for a
minute on the writer's footing, look for a little with
his eyes and listen with his ears, even the more inco-
herent cadences will become not undelightful; some-
thing of his pleasure, with something of his percep-
tion, will pass into them; and understanding once
the main gist of the whole fitful and high-strung
tune, they will tolerate, where they cannot enjoy, the
strange diversities and discords which intervene.

Among many notable eccentricities we have touched upon but two as yet; the huge windy mythology of elemental dæmons, and the capricious passion for catalogues of random names, which make obscure and hideous so much of these books. Akin to these is the habit of seeing or assuming in things inanimate or in the several limbs and divisions of one thing, separate forms of active and symbolic life. This, like many other of Blake's habits, grows and swells enormously by progressive indulgence. At first, as in *Thel*, clouds and flowers, clods and creeping things, are given speech and sense; the degree of symbolism is already excessive, owing to the strength of expression and directness of dramatic vision peculiar to Blake; but in later books everything is given a soul to feel and a tongue to speak; the very members of the body become spirits, each a type of some spiritual state. Again, in the prophecies of *Europe* and *America*, there is more fable and less allegory, more overflow of lyrical invention, more of the divine babble which sometimes takes the place of earthly speech or sense, more vague emotion with less of reducible and amenable quality than in almost any of these poems. In others, a habit of mapping out and marking down the lines of his chaotic and Titanic scenery has added to Blake's other singularities of manner this above all, that side by side with the jumbled worlds of Tharmas and Urthona, the whirling skies and plunging planets of Ololon and Beulah, the breathless student of prophecy encounters places and names absurdly familiar;

London streets and suburbs make up part of the
mystic antediluvian world ; Fulham and Lambeth,
Kentish Town and Poland Street, cross the courses
and break the metres of the stars. This apparent
madness of final absurdity has also its root in the
deepest and soundest part of Blake's mind and faith.
In the meanest place as in the meanest man he
beheld the hidden spirit and significance of which the
flesh or the building is but a type. If continents have
a soul, shall suburbs or lanes have less ? where life
is, shall not the spirit of life be there also ?   Europe
and America are vital and significant ; we mean by
all names somewhat more than we know of ; for
where there is anything visible or conceivable, there
is also some invisible and inconceivable thing.   This
is but the rough grotesque result of the tenet that
matter apart from spirit is non-existent. Launched
once upon that theory, Blake never thought it worth
while to shorten sail or tack about for fear of any
rock or shoal.   It is inadequate and even inaccurate
to say that he allotted to each place as to each world
a presiding dæmon or deity.   He averred implicitly
or directly, that each had a soul or spirit, the
quintessence of its natural life, capable of change
but not of death ; and that of this soul the visible
externals, though a native and actual part, were
only a part, inseparable as yet but incomplete.   Thus
whenever, to his misfortune and ours, he stumbles
upon the proper names of terrene men and things,
he uses these names as signifying not the sensual
form or body but the spirit which he supposed to

animate these, to speak in them and work through them. In *America* the names of liberators, in *Jerusalem* the names of provinces, have no separate local or mundane sense whatever; throughout the prophecies "Albion" is the mythical and typical fatherland of human life, much what the East might seem to other men : and by way of making this type actual and prominent enough, Blake seizes upon all possible divisions of the modern visible England in town or country, and turns them in his loose symbolic way into minor powers and serving spirits. That he was wholly unconscious of the intolerably laughable effect we need not believe. He had all the delight in laying snares and giving offence, which is proper to his kind. He had all the confidence in his own power and right to do such things and to get over the doing of them which accompanies in such men the subtle humour of scandalizing. And unfortunately he had not by training, perhaps not by nature, the conscience which would have reminded him that whether or not an artist may allowably play with all other things in heaven and earth, one thing he must certainly not play with ; the material forms of art : that levity and violence are here prohibited under grave penalties. Allowing however for this, we may notice that in the wildest passages of these books Blake merely carries into strange places or throws into strange shapes such final theories as in the dialect of calmer and smaller men have been accounted not unreasonable.

Further preface or help, however loudly the

subject might seem to call for it, we have not in
this place to give; and indeed more words would
possibly not bring with them more light. What
was explicable we have endeavoured to explain; to
suggest where a hint was profitable; to prepare
where preparation was feasible: but many voices
might be heard crying in this wilderness before the
paths were made straight. The pursuivant would
grow hoarse and the outrider saddle-sick long before
the great man's advent; and for these offices we
have no further taste or ability. Those who will
may now, with what furtherance they have here,
follow us through some brief revision of each book
in its order.*

* A word in passing may here be spared to the singular MS. of
Tiriel. This little poem or mythical episode is evidently a growth
of the crude Ossianic period; in style it is somewhat weak and
inadequate to any grave or subtle expression of thought: a few
noticeable lines intervene, but the general execution is heavy, faint,
and rough even for a sketch. Here however (if I am not incorrect
in referring it to a date earlier than the earliest of the prophetic
books) we may see the dull dawn of a day full of fiery presage, of
the light and vapour of tempestuous revelation. The name of
Tiriel king of the West, father of a rebellious race of children who
perish by his curse, hardly reappears once as "Thiriel" the cloud-
born son of Urizen; Har and Heva, the gentler father and mother
of the great eastern family, who in the *Song of Los* are seen flying
before the windy flames of a broad-blown sunset, chased over Asia
with fire and sword by the divine tyrant and his tributary kings,
are here seen forsaken of their sons in extreme and childish age,
but tended by "Mutha" their mother; "they are holy and for-
giving, filled with loving mercy, forgetting the offences of their
most rebellious children." Into the story or subject-matter we
need not go far; but it is worth notice that the series of twelve
designs classified in the Catalogue, section B, No. 156, pp. 253-4
of vol. 2, must evidently (as is there half suggested) be a set of

The Book of Thel, first in date and simplest in tone of the prophecies, requires less comment than illustrations to this *Tiriel*. In one of these any reader will recognize the serpentine hair which at her father's imprecation rose and hissed around the brows of "Hela" (*Tiriel*, ch. 6); but these designs have as evidently fallen out of order; thus the one lettered (*k*) appears to illustrate the very first lines of the poem; and others seem equally misarranged. In this faint allegory of the blind discrowned king with his two brothers, the mad invulnerable giant of the woods and the fettered dotard dwelling in caves, some fresh incomplete symbol is discernible of tyranny and error, of strength made insane or perverse and weakness made cruel or imbecile by oppression of the spirit or the flesh; the "eloquent" outcast oppressor might then be the uninspired intellect, against whose errors and tyrannies its own children revolt, and perish by the curse of their perishing father and mother, blind reason and powerless faith: but from such shallow and sandy soil the conjectural Muse of commentary can reap little worth her pains to garner, and at every sweep of her sickle must risk being blinded by the sand blown into her eyes. Some stray verses might be gathered up, perhaps worth a place in the gleaner's loose sheaf; such as these:

"And aged Tiriel stood and said: Where does the thunder sleep?
  Where doth he hide his terrible head? and his swift and fiery daughters,
  Where do they shroud their fiery wings and the terrors of their hair?"

Anything better worth citation than such crude sonorous snatches of lyric style I have not found here, except in chap. vii., where the dying Tiriel lays his final curse on Har—"weak mistaken father of a lawless race," whose "laws and Tiriel's wisdom end together in a curse." Here, in words afterwards variously repeated and enlarged, he appeals against the laws of mere animal life, the narrowed senses and material bondage of men upon earth; against unnatural training and abstinence through which "milk is cut off from the weeping mouth with difficulty and pain," when first "the little lids are lifted and the little nostrils opened;" against "hypocrisy, the idiot's wisdom and the wise man's folly," by which men are "compelled to pray repugnant and to handle the

the others. This poem is as the one sister, feeblest
if also fairest, among that Titanic brotherhood of
books. It has the clearness and sweetness of spring-
water ; they have in their lips the speech, in their
limbs the pulses of the sea. In this book, as in the
illustrations to Blair, the poet attempts to comfort
life through death; to assuage by spiritual hope
the fleshly fear of man. The "shining woman,"
youngest and mortal daughter of the angels of
God, leaving her sisters to tend the flocks and close
the folds of the stars, fills herself with the images
of perishable things ; she feeds upon the sorrow
that comes of beauty, the heathen weariness of
heart, that is sick of life because death will come,
seeing how " our little life is rounded with a sleep."
Let all these things go, for they are mortal ; but if
I die with the flowers, let me also die as they die.
This is the end of all things, to sleep ; but let me
fall asleep softly, not without the lulling sound of
God's voice audible in my ears. The flower makes
answer ; does God not care for the least of these?
they shall not die, they shall all be changed. She

immortal spirit" till like Tiriel they become as subtle serpents in
a paradise which they consume fruit by fruit and flower by flower
till at its fall they themselves are left desolate. Thus too he
inveighs against faith in matter and "respect of persons" under
their perishable and finite forms: "Can wisdom be put in a silver
rod or love in a golden bowl? is the son of a king warmed without
wool? or does he cry with a voice of thunder? does he look upon
the sun and laugh, or stretch his little hands into the depths of the
sea?" Much of this has been half erased, probably with a view
to remoulding the whole: for here alone does anything in tone or
thought recall the nobler mysticism of Blake's later writings.

answers again; the flower is serviceable to God's
creatures, giving food to the pasturing lambs and
flavour to the honey of the gleaning bees: but her
beauty is barren as a lighted cloud's; wherefore
should she live? She is bidden to seek counsel
then of the cloud; and of him she asks the secret of
his glad ephemeral life; for she, not less ephemeral,
has no such joy of her life. Here again she is
shown that life and permanence are twain; the
cloud has drunk at the springs of the sun, whence
all hours are renewed; and shall not die though he
pass away; for his falling drops find out the living
flowers, and are wedded to the dew in these; and
they are made one before the sun, and kept alive
to feed other flowers: and all these are as women
and men, having souls and senses, capable of love
and prayer. But she answers, that of her fair body
no cloud or bird gets food, but the worm only;
why should anything survive of her who has been
helpful to nothing? The worm therefore is called
to witness; and appears in an infant's likeness,
inarticulate, naked, weeping; but upon it too the
divine earth has mercy, and the clay finds a voice
to speak for it; this likewise is not the sad un-
profitable thing it seems; for the very earth, baser
and liker death than the least thing bred of it, is
the bride of God, a fruitful mother of all his children.
"We live not for ourselves;" else indeed were
earth and the worm of earth things mournful and
fruitless. The secret of creation is sacrifice; the
very act of growth is a sacrament: and through

this eternal generation in which one life is given
for another and shed into new veins of existence,
each thing is redeemed from perpetual death by
perpetual change. This secret once made evident
to Thel, her fear is in a measure removed; for the
very deathbed of earth in which she must lie is now
revealed as a mother's bosom, warm and giving
warmth, living and prodigal of life. That God
would care for the least thing he made she knew
always; but now knows also that in the least thing
there is something of God's life infused, which makes
it substantially imperishable. So far one may say
the poem is as fluent and translucent as the merest
sermon on faith, hope, and charity could well be:
and not less inoffensive. The earth, who has over-
heard and gathered up all the flitting sighs of this
unwedded Eve, now unveils to her the mysteries of
the body, bred in the grave whither all sorrows
tend and whence all tears arise. The forces of
material nature give way before her; passing to
her own grave, she hears thence a voice lamenting
over the nature of all the senses, their sweet perilous
gifts and strange limits, and all their offices which
fill and discolour the days of mortal life. To this,
the question lying at the root of life and under
the shadow of death, nothing makes answer; as
though no word spoken upon earth or under
could explain the marvel of the flesh, the infinite
beauty and delight of it, the infinite subtlety and
danger; its prodigalities and powers, its wide
capacity and utter weakness. Set face to face with

this bodily mystery, and affrighted at the sudden
nakedness of natural life, the soul recoils ; and Thel
regains the common air and quiet light of earth.
Such, cut short and melted down, is the purport of
this poem : a prophecy as literally as any other of
Blake's, being professedly an inspired exposition
of material things ; for none of course pretend to
be prophecies in the inaccurate and vulgar sense of
prediction.   It is full of small sweet details, bright
and soft as summer grass, regular to monotony in
its cadence until the last division, where the tone
suddenly strengthens and deepens.   There and not
for the last time the strong imagination of Blake
wrestles with the great questions of physical life,
constraining the mute rebellious flesh as in a fervent
and strenuous grasp of spirit, if perchance it will
yield up the heart of its mystery.   Throughout the
book his extreme and feminine tenderness of faith
speaks more softly and shows a simpler face than
elsewhere.   One might almost say that *Thel* had
overmuch of this gracious and delicate beauty ; that
the intense faith and compassion which thus animate
all matter give a touch of almost dubious and
effeminate sweetness to the thought and style.   Not
however justly ; for there is a firm body of significance
in the poem, and the soft light leaves in which the
fruit lies wrapped are solid as well as sweet.

It is well worth while to compare any average
copy of *Thel* with the smaller volume of designs
now in the British Museum, which reproduces
among others the main illustrations of this book.

The clear, sweet, pallid colour of the fainter version
will then serve to throw into full effect the splen-
dour of the more finished work.   Especially in the
separate copy of the frontispiece, the sovereignty
of colour and glorious grace of workmanship double
and treble its original beauty ; give new light and
new charm to the fervent heaven, to the bowing
figure of the girl, to the broad cloven blossoms
whose flickering and sundering petals release the
bright leaping forms of loving spirits, raindrop and
dewdrop wedded before the sun ; and again, where
Thel sees the worm in likeness of a new-born child,
the colours of tree and leaf and sky are of a more
excellent and lordly beauty than in any copy known
to me of the book itself ; though in all good copies
these designs appear full of great and gracious
qualities.   Of the book of designs here referred to
more must not now be said ; not even of the twelfth
plate where the mother-goddess and her fiery first-
born child exult with flying wingless limbs through
splendid spaces of the infinite morning, coloured
here like opening flowers and there like climbing
fire, where all the light and all the wind of heaven
seem to unite in fierce gladness as of a supreme em-
brace and exultation ; for to these better praise than
ours has been already given at p. 374 of the "Life,"
in words of choice and incomparable sufficiency,
not less bright and sweet, significant and subtle, than
the most tender or perfect of the designs described.

In 1790 Blake produced the greatest of all his
books ; a work indeed which we rank as about the

greatest produced by the eighteenth century in the line of high poetry and spiritual speculation. "The Marriage of Heaven and Hell" gives us the high-water mark of his intellect. None of his lyrical writings show the same sustained strength and radiance of mind; none of his other works in verse or prose give more than a hint here and a trace there of the same harmonious and humorous power, of the same choice of eloquent words, the same noble command and liberal music of thought; small things he could often do perfectly, and great things often imperfectly; here for once he has written a book as perfect as his most faultless song, as great as his most imperfect rhapsody. His fire of spirit fills it from end to end; but never deforms the body, never singes the surface of the work, as too often in the still noble books of his later life. Across the flicker of flame, under the roll and roar of water, which seem to flash and to resound throughout the poem, a stately music, shrill now as laughter and now again sonorous as a psalm, is audible through shifting notes and fitful metres of sound. The book swarms with heresies and eccentricities; every sentence bristles with some paradox, every page seethes with blind foam and surf of stormy doctrine; the humour is of that fierce grave sort, whose cool insanity of manner is more horrible and more obscure to the Philistine than any sharp edge of burlesque or glitter of irony; it is huge, swift, inexplicable; hardly laughable through its enormity of laughter, hardly significant through its

condensation of meaning; but as true and thought-
ful as the greatest humourist's. The variety and
audacity of thoughts and words are incomparable:
not less so their fervour and beauty. "No bird
soars too high if he soars with his own wings."
This proverb might serve as motto to the book: it
is one of many *Proverbs of Hell*, as forcible and as
finished.

It was part of Blake's humour to challenge
misconception, conscious as he was of power to
grapple with it : to blow dust in their eyes who
were already sandblind, to strew thorns under their
feet who were already lame. Those whom the
book in its present shape would perplex and repel
he knew it would not in any form have attracted;
and how such readers may fare is no concern of
such writers; nor in effect need it be. Aware that
he must at best offend a little, he did not fear to
offend much. To measure the exact space of safety,
to lay down the precise limits of offence, was an
office neither to his taste nor within his power.
Those who try to clip or melt themselves down to
the standard of current feeling, to sauce and spice
their natural fruits of mind with such condiments
as may take the palate of common opinion, deserve
to disgust themselves and others alike. It is hope-
less to reckon how far the timid, the perverse, or
the malignant irrelevance of human remarks will
go; to set bounds to the incompetence or devise
landmarks for the imbecility of men. Blake's way
was not the worst; to indulge his impulse to the

full and write what fell to his hand, making sure
at least of his own genius and natural instinct. In
this his greatest book he has at once given him-
self freer play and set himself to harder labour than
elsewhere : the two secrets of great work. Passion
and humour are mixed in his writing like mist and
light ; whom the light may scorch or the mist con-
fuse it is not his part to consider.

In the prologue Blake puts forth, not without
grandeur if also with an admixture of rant and
wind, a chief tenet of his moral creed. Once the
ways of good and evil were clear, not yet confused
by laws and religions ; then humility and benevo-
lence, the endurance of peril and the fruitful labour
of love, were the just man's proper apanage ; behind
his feet the desert blossomed ; by his toil and danger,
by his sweat and blood, the desolate places were
made rich and the dead bones clothed with flesh
as the flesh of Adam. Now the hypocrite has
come to reap the fruits, to divide and gather and
eat ; to drive forth the just man and to dwell
in the paths which he found perilous and barren,
but left safe and fertile. Churches have cast out
apostles ; creeds have rooted out faith. Henceforth
anger and loneliness, the divine indignation of
spiritual exile, the salt bread of scorn and the bitter
wine of wrath, are the portion of the just man ; he
walks with lions in the waste places, not worth
making fertile that others may reap and feed.
" Rintrah," the spirit presiding over this period, is
a spirit of fire and storm ; darkness and famine,

wrath and want, divide the kingdoms of the world. "Prisons are built with stones of Law; brothels with bricks of Religion." "As the caterpillar chooses the fairest leaves to lay her eggs on, so the priest lays his curse on the fairest joys." In a third proverb the view given of prayer is no less heretical; "As the plough follows words, so God rewards prayers." This was but the outcome or corollary of his main doctrine; as what we have called his "evangel of bodily liberty" was but the fruit of his belief in the identity of body with soul. The fear which restrains and the faith which refuses were things as ignoble as the hypocrisy which assumes or the humility which resigns. Veils and chains must be lifted and broken. "Folly is the cloak of knavery; shame is pride's cloak." Again; "He who desires but acts not breeds pestilence." "Sooner murder an infant in its cradle than nurse unacted desires." The doctrine of freedom could hardly run further or faster. Translated into rough practice, and planted in a less pure soil than that of the writer's mind, this philosophy might bring forth a strange harvest. Together with such width of moral pantheism as will hardly admit a "tender curb," leave "a little curtain of flesh on the bed of our desire," there is a vehemence of faith in divine wrath, in the excellence of righteous anger and revenge, to be outdone by no prophet or Puritan. "A dead body revenges not injuries." Sincerity and plain dealing at least are virtues not to be thrown over; Blake indeed could not conceive an impulse to mendacity, a tortuous habit of mind, a soul born crooked. This one quality of falsehood remains damnable in his sight, to be consumed with all that comes of it. In man or beast or any other part of God he found no native taint or birthmark of this. Upon all else the divine breath and the divine hand are sensible and visible.

> " The pride of the peacock is the glory of God ;
> The lust of the goat is the bounty of God ;
> The wrath of the lion is the wisdom of God ;
> The nakedness of woman is the work of God."

All form and all instinct is sacred ; but no invention or device of man's. All crafts and creeds of theirs are " the serpent's meat : " and that a man should be born cruel and false is barely imaginable. " If the lion was advised by the fox he would be cunning." Such counsel was always wasted on the high clear spirit and stainless intellect of Blake.

We have given some of the most subtle and venturous *Proverbs of Hell*—samples of their depth of doctrine and plainness of speech. But even here Blake rarely indulges in such excess and exposure. There are jewels in this treasure-house neither set so roughly nor so sharply cut as these ; they may be seen in the "Life," taken out and reset, so as to offend no customer. And these sayings must themselves be read by the light of Blake's life and weighed against others of his words not less weighty than they. Apology shall now and always remain as far from us as it was in life from

Blake himself ; to excuse and to explain are different
offices. To plead for his acquittal on the base and
foolish ground that he meant no harm, knew not
what he did, had no design or desire to afflict or
offend, is no office for his counsel ; who must strive
at least to speak not less frankly and clearly than
did Blake when he could speak in his own cause.
Neither have we to approve or condemn ; but only
to endeavour that we may see the right and deliver
the truth as to this man and his life. "That I
cannot live," he says, in the Butts correspondence,
"without doing my duty to lay up treasures in
heaven, is certain and determined, and to this I
have long made up my mind. And why this should
be made an objection to me, while drunkenness,
lewdness, gluttony, and even idleness itself does
not hurt other men, let Satan himself explain. The
thing I have most at heart—more than life, or all
that seems to make life comfortable without (it)—is
the interest of true religion and science." His one
fear is to "omit any duty to my station as a soldier
of Christ ;" a fear that "gives him the greatest
torments ;" for "if our footsteps slide in clay, how
can we do otherwise than fear and tremble?" And
such books as these were part of his spiritual task-
work. From whencesoever the inspiration of them
came, inspiration it was and no invention. He is
content with that knowledge ; and if it please the
hearer to call it diabolic, diabolic it shall be. If he
has a devil, he will make the most and the best of
him. If these things come from hell, let us look to

it and hold them fast, that we may see what it is
that divides hell from heaven.

" As a new heaven is begun, and it is now thirty-three years
since its advent: the Eternal Hell revives.   And lo ! Swedenborg
is the Angel sitting at the tomb : his writings are the linen clothes
folded up. Now is the dominion of Edom, and the return of Adam
into Paradise ; see Isaiah xxxiv. and xxxv. chap.

" Without Contraries is no progression.   Attraction and Repul-
sion, Reason and Energy, Love and Hate, are necessary to Human
existence.

" From these Contraries spring what the religious call Good
and Evil.   Good is the passive that obeys Reason.

" Evil is the active springing from Energy.

" *Good is Heaven.   Evil is Hell.*

" THE VOICE OF THE DEVIL.

" All Bibles or sacred codes have been the causes of the follow-
ing Errors.

" 1. That man has two real existing principles—viz., a Body
and a Soul.

" 2. That Energy, called Evil, is alone from the Body ; and
that Reason, called Good, is alone from the Soul.

" 3. That God will torment Man in Eternity for following his
Energies.

" But the following contraries to these are True.

" 1. Man has no Body distinct from his Soul, for that called
Body is a portion of Soul discerned by the five Senses, the chief
inlets of Soul in this age.

" 2. Energy is the only life, and is from the Body ; and Reason
is the bound or outward circumference of Energy.

" 3. Energy is Eternal Delight.

" Those who restrain desire do so because theirs is weak enough
to be restrained ; and the restrainer, or reason, usurps its place and
governs the unwilling.

" And being restrained it by degrees becomes passive, till it is
only the shadow of desire.

" The history of this is written in ' Paradise Lost,' and the
Governor, or Reason, is called Messiah.

" And the original Archangel, or possessor of the command of he heavenly host, is called the Devil or Satan, and his children are called Sin and Death.

" But in the Book of Job Milton's Messiah is called Satan.

" For this history has been adopted by both parties.

" It indeed appeared to Reason as if Desire was cast out; but the Devil's account is, that the Messiah fell, and formed a heaven of what he stole from the Abyss.

" This is shewn in the Gospel, where he prays to the Father to send the comforter or Desire, that Reason may have Ideas to build on, the Jehovah of the Bible being no other than he who dwells in flaming fire. Know that after Christ's death, he became Jehovah.

" But in Milton the Father is Destiny, the Son a Ratio of the five Senses, and the Holy Ghost, Vacuum.

" NOTE.—The reason Milton wrote in fetters when he wrote ot Angels and God, and at liberty when of Devils and Hell, is because he was a true Poet, and of the Devil's party without knowing it."

Something of these high matters we have seen before, and should now be able to allow for the subtle intricate fashion in which Blake labours to invert the weapons of his antagonists upon themselves. Neither can the banns of marriage be published between heaven and hell with the voice of a parish clerk. This prophet came to do what Swedenborg his precursor had left undone, being but the watchman by the empty sepulchre, and his writings as the grave-clothes cast off by the risen Christ. Blake's estimate of Swedenborg, right or wrong, was, as we shall see, distinct and consistent; to this effect; that his inspiration was limited and timid, superficial and derivative; that he was content with leaves and husks, and had not the courage to examine the root and the kernel of things; that he clove to the heaven and shrank from the hell of other men; whereas, to men in whom "a new heaven is begun," the one must not be terrible nor the other desirable. To them the "flaming fire" wherein dwells a God whom men call devil, must seem a purer element of life than the starry and cloudy space wherein dwells a devil whom they call God. ¶ It must be remembered that Blake uses the current terms of religion, now as types of his own peculiar faith, now in the sense of ordinary preachers: impugning therefore at one time what at another he will seem to vindicate. Vague and violent as this overture may appear, it must be followed with care, that the writer's intensity of spiritual faith may be hereafter kept in sight. The senses, "the chief inlets of soul in this age" of brute doubt and brute belief, are worthy only as parts of the soul. This, it cannot be too much repeated and insisted on, this and no prurience of porcine appetite for rotten apples, no vulgarity of porcine adoration for unctuous wash, is what lies at the root of Blake's sensual doctrine. Let no reader now or ever forget, that while others will admit nothing beyond the body, the mystic will admit nothing outside the soul. That the two extremes, if reduced to hard practice, might run round and meet, not without lamentably curious consequences, those may assert who will; it is none of our business to decide. Even granting that the result will be about equivalent if one man does for his soul's sake all that another would do for his body's sake, we might plead that the difference of thought and eye between these two would remain great and

important. Indulgence bracketed to faith and vivi-
fied by that vigorous contact with things divine is
not (we might say) the same, whether seen from the
actual side of life or from the speculative, as indul-
gence cut loose and left to decompose. But these
pleas we will leave the mystic to advance, if it
please him, on his own behalf.

"A MEMORABLE FANCY.

"As I was walking among the fires of hell, delighted with the
enjoyments of Genius, which to Angels look like torment and
insanity, I collected some of their Proverbs: thinking that as the
sayings used in a nation mark its character, so the Proverbs of Hell
show the nature of the Infernal wisdom better than any description
of buildings or garments. When I came home, on the abyss of the
five senses, where a flat-sided steep frowns over the present world,
I saw a mighty Devil folded in black clouds, hovering on the sides
of the rock ; with corroding fires he wrote the following sentence,
now perceived by the minds of men, and read by them on earth :

" ' How do you know but ev'ry Bird that cuts the airy way
Is an immense world of delight, clos'd by your senses five ? ' "

Here follow the *Proverbs of Hell*, which give
us the quintessence and the most fine gold of
Blake's alembic. Each, whether earnest or satirical,
slight or great in manner, is full of that passionate
wisdom and bright rapid strength proper to the step
and speech of gods. The simplest give us a measure
of his energy, as this : " Think in the morning, act
in the noon, eat in the evening, sleep in the night."
The highest have a light and resonance about them,
as though in effect from above or beneath ; a spirit
which lifts thought upon the high levels of verse.

From the ensuing divisions of the book we shall give full extracts ; for these detached sections have a grace and coherence which we shall not always find in Blake ; and the crude excerpts given in the " Life " are inadequate to help the reader much towards a clear comprehension of the main scheme.

" The ancient Poets animated all sensible objects with Gods or Geniuses, calling them by the names and adorning them with the properties of woods, rivers, mountains, lakes, cities, nations, and whatever their enlarged and numerous senses could perceive.

" And, particularly, they studied the genius of each city and country, placing it under its mental deity.

" Till a system was formed, which some took advantage of and enslaved the vulgar by attempting to realise or abstract the mental deities from their objects : thus began Priesthood,

" Choosing forms of worship from poetic tales ;

" And at length they pronounced that the Gods had ordered such things.

" Thus men forgot that All deities reside in the human breast."

From this we pass to higher tones of exposition. The next passage is one of the clearest and keenest in the book, full of faith and sacred humour, none the less sincere for its dramatic form. The subtle simplicity of expression is excellently subservient to the intricate force of thought.

" A Memorable Fancy.

" The Prophets Isaiah and Ezekiel dined with me, and I asked them how they dared so roundly to assert that God spoke to them : and whether they did not think at the time that they would be misunderstood, and so be the cause of imposition.

" Isaiah answered, ' I saw no God, nor heard any, in a finite or organical perception ; but my senses discovered the infinite in everything, and as I was then persuaded, I remain confirmed, that the voice of honest indignation is the voice of God. I cared not for consequences, but wrote.'

"Then I asked, 'Does a firm persuasion that a thing is so, make it so?'

"He replied, 'All poets believe that it does, and in ages of imagination this firm persuasion removed mountains. But many are not capable of a firm persuasion of anything.'

"Then Ezekiel said, 'The philosophy of the East taught the first principles of human perception. Some nations held one principle for the origin and some another. We of Israel taught that the Poetic Genius (as you now call it) was the first principle, and all the others merely derivative, which was the cause of our despising the Priests and Philosophers of other countries, and prophesying that all Gods would at last be proved to originate in ours, and to be the tributaries of the Poetic Genius. It was this that our great poet King David desired so fervently and invokes so pathetically, saying by this he conquers enemies and governs kingdoms; and we so loved our God, that we cursed in his name all the deities of surrounding nations, and asserted that they had rebelled; from these opinions the vulgar came to think that all nations would at last be subject to the Jews.

"'This,' said he, 'like all firm persuasions, is come to pass, for all nations believe the Jews' code and worship the Jews' God, and what greater subjection can be?'

"I heard this with some wonder, and must confess my own conviction. After dinner, I asked Isaiah to favour the world with his lost works. He said none of equal value was lost.

"Ezekiel said the same of his.

"I also asked Isaiah what made him go naked and barefoot three years? He answered, the same that made our friend Diogenes the Grecian.

"I then asked Ezekiel, why he eat dung, and lay so long on his right and left side? he answered, the desire of raising other men into a perception of the infinite. This the North American tribes practise; and is he honest who resists his genius or conscience, only for the sake of present ease or gratification?"

The doctrine of perception through not with the senses, beyond not in the organs, as also of the absolute existence of things thus apprehended, is

again directly enforced in our next excerpt ; in praise
of which we will say nothing, but leave the words to
burn their way in as they may.

" The ancient tradition that the world will be consumed in fire
at the end of six thousand years is true, as I have heard from Hell.

" For the cherub with his flaming sword is hereby commanded
to leave his guard at the tree of life ; and when he does, the whole .
creation will be consumed, and appear infinite and holy, whereas it
now appears finite and corrupt.

" This will come to pass by an improvement of sensual enjoy-
ment.

." But first the notion that man has a body distinct from his soul
is to be expunged ; this I shall do, by printing in the infernal
method, by corrosives, which in Hell are salutary and medicinal,
melting apparent surfaces away and displaying the infinite which
was hid.

" If the doors of perception were cleansed, everything would
appear to man as it is, infinite.

" For man has closed himself up, till he sees all things through
narrow chinks of his cavern."

After which corrosive touch of revelation there
follows a vision of knowledge ; first, the human
nature is cleansed and widened into shape, then
decorated, then enlarged and built about with stately
buildings for guest-chambers and treasure-houses ;
then the purged metal of knowledge, melted into
form with divine violence, is made fluid and vital,
that it may percolate and permeate the whole man
through every pore of his spirit ; then the metal is
cast forth and put to use. All forms and forces of
the world, viper and lion, half-human things and
nameless natures, serve to help in this work ; all
manner of aspiration and inspiration, wrath and
faith, love and labour, do good service here.

" The Giants who formed this world into its sensual existence, and now seem to live in it in chains, are in truth the causes of its life and the sources of all activity; but the chains are, the cunning of weak and tame minds, which have power to resist energy; according to the proverb, the weak in courage is strong in cunning.

" Thus one portion of being is the Prolific, the other, the Devouring; to the devourer it seems as if the producer was in his chains; but it is not so; he only takes portions of existence and fancies that the whole.

" But the Prolific would cease to be Prolific, unless the Devourer as a sea received the excess of his delights.

" Some will say, Is not God alone the Prolific?

" I answer, God only Acts and Is in existing beings or Men.

" These two classes of men are always upon earth, and they should be enemies; whoever tries to reconcile them, seeks to destroy existence.

" Religion is an endeavour to reconcile the two.

" NOTE.—Jesus Christ did not wish to unite but to separate them, as in the Parable of sheep and goats! and he says I came not to send Peace but a Sword.

" Messiah or Satan or Tempter was formerly thought to be one of the Antediluvians who are our Energies."

These are hard sayings; who can hear them? At first sight also, as we were forewarned, this passage seems at direct variance with that other in the overture, where our prophet appears at first sight, and only appears, to speak of the fallen " Messiah " as the same with the Christ of his belief. Verbally coherent we cannot hope to make the two passages; but it must be remarked and remembered that the very root or kernel of this creed is not the assumed humanity of God, but the achieved divinity of Man; not incarnation from without, but development from within; not a miraculous passage into flesh, but a natural growth into godhead. Christ, as the type or sample of manhood, thus becomes after death the true Jehovah; not, as he seems to the vulgar, the extraneous and empirical God of creeds and churches, human in no necessary or absolute sense, the false and fallen phantom of his enemy, Zeus in the mask of Prometheus. We are careful to note and as far as may be to correct any apparent slips or shortcomings in expression, only because if left without a touch of commentary they may seem to make worse confusion than they do actually make. Subtle, trenchant and profound as is this philosophy, there is no radical flaw in the book, no positive incongruity, no inherent contradiction. A single consistent principle keeps alive the large relaxed limbs, makes significant the dim great features of this strange faith. It is but at the opening that the words are even partially inadequate and obscure. Revision alone could have righted and straightened them; and revision the author would not give. Impatient of their insufficiency, and incapable of any labour that implies rest, he shook them together and flung them out in an irritated hurried manner, regardless who might gather them up or let them lie.

In the next and longest division of the book, direct allegory and imaginative vision are indivisibly mixed into each other. The stable and mill, the twisted root and inverted fungus, are transparent symbols enough: the splendid and stormy apocalypse of the abyss is a chapter of pure vision or poetic invention. Why "Swedenborg's volumes" are the weights used to sink the travellers from the "glorious clime" to the passive and iron void between the fixed stars and the coldest of the remote planets, will be conceivable in due time.

"An Angel came to me and said, 'O pitiable foolish young man! O horrible! O dreadful state! Consider the hot burning dungeon thou art preparing for thyself to all eternity, to which thou art going in such career.'

"I said, 'Perhaps you will be willing to show me my eternal lot and we will contemplate upon it and see whether your lot or mine is most desirable.'

"So he took me through a stable and through a church and down into the church vault at the end of which was a mill; through the mill we went, and came to a cave; down the winding cavern we groped our tedious way, till a void, boundless as a nether sky, appeared beneath us, and we held by the roots of trees and hung over this immensity; but I said, 'If you please, we will commit ourselves to this void, and see whether Providence is here also; if you will not, I will.'

"But he answered, 'Do not presume, O young man, but as we here remain, behold thy lot, which will soon appear when the darkness passes away.'

"So I remained with him, sitting in the twisted root of an oak; he was suspended in a fungus, which hung with the head downward into the deep.

"By degrees we beheld the infinite Abyss, fiery as the smoke of a burning city; beneath us at an immense distance was the sun, black but shining; round it were fiery tracks on which revolved vast spiders, crawling after their prey; which flew or rather swam in the infinite deep, in the most terrific shapes of animals sprung from corruption; and the air was full of them, and seemed composed of them; these are Devils, and are called Powers of the air. I now asked my companion which was my eternal lot? he said, between the black and white spiders.

"But now, from between the black and white spiders a cloud and fire burst and rolled through the deep blackening all beneath, so that the nether deep grew black as a sea and rolled with a terrible noise: beneath us was nothing now to be seen but a black tempest, till looking east between the clouds and the waves, we saw a cataract of blood mixed with fire, and not many stones' throw from us appeared and sunk again the scaly fold of a monstrous serpent; at last, to the east, distant about three degrees, appeared a fiery crest above the waves; slowly it reared, like a ridge of golden rocks, till we discovered two globes of crimson fire, from which the sea fled away in clouds of smoke: and now we saw it was the head of Leviathan; his forehead was divided into streaks of green and purple, like those on a tiger's forehead: soon we saw his mouth and red gills hang just above the raging foam, tinging the black deep with beams of blood, advancing toward us with all the fury of a spiritual existence.

" My friend the Angel climbed up from his station into the mill; I remained alone, and then this appearance was no more; but I found myself sitting on a pleasant bank beside a river by moonlight, hearing a harper who sung to the harp, and his theme was, The man who never alters his opinion is like standing water, and breeds reptiles of the mind.

" But I arose, and sought for the mill, and there I found my Angel, who, surprised, asked me how I escaped?

" I answered, ' All that we saw was owing to your metaphysics: for when you ran away, I found myself on a bank by moonlight hearing a harper. But now we have seen my eternal lot, shall I show you yours?' He laughed at my proposal: but I by force suddenly caught him in my arms, and flew westerly through the night, till we were elevated above the earth's shadow: then I flung myself with him directly into the body of the sun; here I clothed myself in white, and taking in my hand Swedenborg's volumes, sunk from the glorious clime, and passed all the planets till we came to Saturn: here I staid to rest, and then leaped into the void, between Saturn and the fixed stars.

" ' Here,' said I, ' is your lot, in this space, if space it may be called.' Soon we saw the stable and the church, and I took him to the altar and opened the Bible, and lo! it was a deep pit, into which I descended, driving the Angel before me; soon we saw seven houses of brick; one we entered; in it were a number of monkeys, baboons, and all of that species chained by the middle, grinning and snatching at one another, but withheld by the shortness of their chains; however, I saw that they sometimes grew numerous, and then the weak were caught by the strong and, with a grinning aspect, first coupled with and then devoured, by plucking off first

R 2

one limb and then another, till the body was left a helpless trunk ; this, after grinning and kissing it with seeming kindness, they devoured too ; and here and there I saw one savourily picking the flesh off of his own tail. As the stench terribly annoyed us both, we went into the mill, and I in my hand brought the skeleton of a body, which in the mill was Aristotle's ' Analytics.'

" So the Angel said ; ' Thy phantasy has imposed upon me, and thou oughtest to be ashamed.'

" I answered ; ' We impose on one another, and it is but lost time to converse with you, whose works are only Analytics.' "

The " seven houses of brick " we may take to be a reminiscence of the seven churches of St. John ; as indeed the traces of former evangelists and prophets are never long wanting when we track the steps of this one. Lest however we be found unawares on the side of these hapless angels and baboons, we will abstain with all due care from any not indispensable analysis. It is evident that between pure "phantasy" and mere "analytics" the great gulf must remain fixed, and either party appear to the other deceptive and deceived. That impulsive energy and energetic faith are the only means, whether used as tools of peace or as weapons of war, to pave or to fight our way toward the realities of things, was plainly the creed of Blake ; as also that these realities, once well in sight, will reverse appearance and overthrow tradition : hell will appear as heaven, and heaven as hell. The abyss once entered with due trust and courage appears a place of green pastures and gracious springs : the paradise of resignation once beheld with undisturbed eyes appears a place of emptiness or bondage, delusion or cruelty. On the humorous

beauty and vigour of these symbols we need not
expatiate ; in these qualities Rabelais and Dante
together could hardly have excelled Blake at his
best. What his meaning is should by this time be
as clear as the meaning of a mystic need be ; it is
but partially expressible by words, as (to borrow
Blake's own symbol) the inseparable soul is yet but
incompletely expressible through the body. Whether
it be right or wrong, foolish or wise, we will neither
inquire nor assert : the autocercophagous monkeys
of the mill may be left to settle that for themselves
with " Urizen."

We come now to a chapter of comments, inter-
calated between two sufficiently memorable "fancies."

"I have always found that Angels have the vanity to speak
of themselves as the only wise ; this they do with a confident
insolence sprouting from systematic reasoning.

" Thus Swedenborg boasts that what he writes is new, though
it is only the Contents or Index of already published books.

" A man carried a monkey about for a show, and because he
was a little wiser than the monkey, grew vain, and conceived
himself as much wiser than seven men. It is so with Swedenborg :
he shows the folly of churches and exposes hypocrites, till he
imagines that all are religious and himself the single one on earth
that ever broke a net.

" Now hear a plain fact : Swedenborg has not written one new
truth.

" Now hear another : He has written all the old falsehoods.

" And now hear the reason : He conversed with Angels who
are all religious and conversed not with Devils who all hate religion ;
for he was incapable, through his conceited notions.

" Thus Swedenborg's writings are a recapitulation of all super-
ficial opinions, and an analysis of the more sublime, but no further.

" Hear now another plain fact : Any man of mechanical talents
may, from the writings of Paracelsus or Jacob Behmen, produce
ten thousand volumes of equal value with Swedenborg's ; and from

those of Dante or Shakespeare, an infinite number. But when
he has done this, let him not say that he knows better than his
master, for he only holds a candle in sunshine."

This also we will leave for those to decide who
please, and attend to the next and final vision.
That the fire of inspiration should absorb and
convert to its own nature all denser and meaner
elements of mind, was the prophet's sole idea of
redemption: the dead cloud of belief consumed
becomes the vital flame of faith.

"A MEMORABLE FANCY.

"Once I saw a Devil in a flame of fire, who arose before an
Angel that sat on a cloud, and the Devil uttered these words.

"The worship of God is: Honouring his gifts in other men,
each according to his genius, and loving the greatest men best;
those who envy or calumniate great men hate God, for there is no
other God.

"The Angel hearing this became almost blue, but mastering
himself, he grew yellow, and at last white, pink, and smiling;
and then replied, Thou Idolator, is not God one? and is not he
visible in Jesus Christ? and has not Jesus Christ given his sanction
to the law of ten commandments? and are not all other men fools,
sinners, and nothings?

"The Devil answered; Bray a fool in a mortar with wheat,
yet shall not his folly be beaten out of him: if Jesus Christ is the
greatest man, you ought to love him in the greatest degree; now
hear how he has given his sanction to the law of the ten command-
ments: did he not mock at the sabbath, and so mock the sabbath's
God? murder those who were murdered, because of him? turn
away the law from the woman taken in adultery? steal the labour
of others to support him? bear false witness when he omitted
making a defence before Pilate? covet when he prayed for his
disciples, and when he bid them shake off the dust of their feet
against such as refused to lodge them? I tell you, no virtue can
exist without breaking these ten commandments. Jesus was all
virtue, and acted from impulse, not from rules.

"When he had so spoken, I beheld the Angel who stretched out his arms embracing the flame of fire, and he was consumed, and arose as Elijah.

"NOTE. This Angel, who is now become a Devil, is my particular friend : we often read the Bible together in its infernal or diabolical sense, which the world shall have if they behave well.

"I have also the Bible of Hell, which the world shall have, whether they will or no."

Under this title at least the world was never favoured with it ; but we may presumably taste some savour of that Bible in these pages. After this the book is wound up in a lyric rapture, not without some flutter and tumour of style, but full of clear high music and flame-like aspiration. Epilogue and prologue are both nearer in manner to the dubious hybrid language of the succeeding books of prophecy than to the choice and noble prose in which the rest of this book is written. The overture must be read by the light of its meaning ; of the mysterious universal mother and her son, the latest birth of the world, we have already taken account. The date of 1790 must here be kept in mind, that all may remember what appearances of change were abroad, what manner of light and tempest was visible upon earth, when the hopes of such men as Blake made their stormy way into speech or song.

"A SONG OF LIBERTY.

1. The Eternal Female groan'd ! it was heard over all the Earth.

2. Albion's coast is sick silent ; the American meadows faint !

3. Shadows of Prophecy shiver along by the lakes and the rivers, and mutter across the ocean. France, rend down thy dungeon ;

4. Golden Spain, burst the barriers of old Rome ;

5. Cast thy keys, O Rome, into the deep down falling, even to eternity down falling ;

6. And weep.

7. In her trembling hands she took the new-born terror howling :

8. On those infinite mountains of light now barred out by the Atlantic sea, the new-born fire stood before the starry King !

9. Flag'd with grey-browed snows and thunderous visages the jealous wings waved over the deep.

10. The speary hand burned aloft, unbuckled was the shield, forth went the hand of jealousy among the flaming hair, and hurled the new-born wonder thro' the starry night.

11. The fire, the fire is falling !

12. Look up ! look up ! O citizen of London, enlarge thy countenance : O Jew, leave counting gold ! return to thy oil and wine ; O African ! black African ! (go, winged thought, widen his forehead.)

13. The fiery limbs, the flaming hair, shot like the sinking sun into the western sea.

14. Waked from his eternal sleep, the hoary element roaring fled away.

15. Down rushed, beating his wings in vain, the jealous King ; his grey-browed councillors, thunderous warriors, curled veterans, among helms and shields, and chariots, horses, elephants ; banners, castles, slings and rocks ;

16. Falling, rushing, ruining ! buried in the ruins, on Urthona's dens ;

17. All night beneath the ruins, then their sullen flames faded emerge round the gloomy King.

18. With thunder and fire, leading his starry hosts thro' the waste wilderness, he promulgates his ten commands, glancing his beamy eyelids over the deep in dark dismay ;

19. Where the son of fire in his eastern cloud, while the morning plumes her golden breast,

20. Spurning the clouds written with curses, stamps the stony law to dust, loosing the eternal horses from the dens of night, crying, Empire is no more ! and now the lion and the wolf shall cease.

CHORUS.

Let the Priests of the Raven of dawn no longer in deadly black
with hoarse note curse the sons of joy ; Nor his accepted brethren,
whom, tyrant, he calls free, lay the bound or build the roof ; Nor
pale religious letchery call that virginity that wishes but acts not ;
For everything that lives is Holy."

And so, as with fire and thunder—"thunder of
thought, and flames of fierce desire"—is this *Marriage
of Heaven and Hell* at length happily consummated ;
the prophet, as a fervent paranymph, standing by to
invoke upon the wedded pair his most unclerical
benediction. Those who are not bidden to the
bridegroom's supper may as well keep away, lest
worse befall them, not having a wedding garment.
For us there remains little to say, now that the
torches are out, the nuts scattered, the songs silent,
and the saffron faded from the veil. We will wish
them a quiet life, and an heir who may combine the
merits and capacities of either parent. It were
pleasant enough, but too superfluous, to dwell upon
the beauty of this nuptial hymn ; to bid men remark
what eloquence, what subtlety, what ardour of
wisdom, what splendour of thought, is here ; how
far it outruns, not in daring alone but in sufficiency,
all sayings of minor mystics who were not also
poets ; how much of lofty love and of noble faith
underlies and animates these rapid and fervent
words ; what greatness of spirit and of speech there
was in the man who, living as Blake lived, could
write as Blake has written. Those who cannot see
what is implied may remain unable to tolerate what

is expressed; and those who can read aright need
no index of ours.*

* Before we dismiss the matter from view, it may be per-
missible to cast up in a rough and rapid way the sum of Blake's
teaching in these books, if only because this was also the doctrine
or moral of his entire life and life's work. I will therefore, as
leave has been given, append a note extracted from a manuscript
now before me, which attempts to embody and enforce, if only by
dint of pure and simple exposition, the pantheistic evangel here set
forth in so strange a fashion. Thus at least I read the passage; if
misinterpreted, my correspondent has to thank his own laxity of
expression. "These poems or essays at prophecy" (he says)
"seem to me to represent in an obscure and forcible manner the
real naked question to which all theologies and all philosophies
must in the end be pared down. Strained and filtered clear of
extraneous matter, pruned of foreign fruit and artificial foliage, this
radical question lies between Theism and Pantheism. When the
battles of the creeds have been all fought out, this battle will remain
to fight. I do not see much likelihood on either hand of success or
defeat. Faith and reason, evidence and report, are alike inadequate
to decide the day. This prophet or that prophet, this God or that
God, is not here under debate. Histories, religions, all things
born of rumour or circumstance, accident or change, are out of
court; are, for the moment, of necessity set aside. Gentile or Jew,
Christian or Pagan, Eastern or Western, can but be equal to us—
for the moment. No single figure, no single book, stands out for
special judgment or special belief. On the right hand, let us say
(employing the old figure of speech), is the Theist—the 'man of
God,' if you may take his own word for it; the believer in a
separate or divisible deity, capable or conceivably capable of
existence apart from ours who conceive of it; a conscious and
absolute Creator. On the left hand is the Pantheist; to whom
such a creed is mainly incredible and wholly insufficient. His
creed is or should be much like that of your prophet here;" (I
must observe in passing that my correspondent seems so unable to
conceive of a comment apart from the text, an exponent who is not
an evangelist,—so inclined to confuse the various functions of critic
and of disciple, and assume that you must mean to preach or teach
whatever doctrine you may have to explain—in a word, so obtuse
or perverse on this point that he might be taken for a professional

The decorations of this great work, though less
large and complete than those of the subsequent

man-of-letters or sworn juryman of the press; but I will hope
better things of him, though anonymous;) "and that creed, as I
take it, is simply enough expressible in Blake's own words, or
deducible from them; that 'all deities reside in the human breast;'
that except humanity there is no divine thing or person. Clearly
therefore, in the eyes of a Theist, he lies open to the charge of
atheism or antitheism. The real difference is perhaps this; God
appears to a Theist as the root, to a Pantheist as the flower of
things. It does not follow logically or actually that to this latter
all things are alike. For us (he might say), for us, within the
boundaries of time and space, evil and good do really exist, and live
no empirical life—for a certain time, and within a certain range.
'There is no God unless man can become God.' That is no saying
for an Atheist. 'There is no man unless the child can become a
man;' is that equivalent to a denial of manhood? But if a man is
to be born into the world, the mother must abstain from the drugs
that produce abortion, the child from strong meats and drinks, the
man from poisons. So it is in the spiritual world; tyranny and
treachery, indolence and dulness, cannot but impede and impair the
immutable law of nature and necessary growth. These and their
like must be and must pass away; the eternal body of things must
change. As the fanatic abstains through fear of God or of hell, the
free-thinker abstains from what he sees or thinks to be evil (*i.e.*,
adverse or alien to his nature at its best) through respect for what
he is and reverence for what he may be. Pantheism therefore is no
immoral creed, and cannot be, if only because it is based upon faith
in nature and rooted in respect for it. By faith in sight it attains
to sight through faith. It follows that pure Theism is more
immediately the contrary of this belief, more unacceptable and
more delusive in the eyes of its followers, than any scheme of
doctrine or code of revelation. These, as we see by your Blake"
(again), "the Pantheist may seize and recast in the mould of his
own faith. But Theism, but the naked distinct figure of God,
whether or not he assume the nature of man, so long as this is mere
assumption and not the essence of his being—the clothes and not
the body, the body and not the soul—this is to him incredible, the
source of all evil and error. Grant such a God his chance of exist-
ence, what reason has the Theist to suppose or what right to

prophecies, are full of noble and subtle beauty. Over every page faint fibres and flickering threads of colour weave a net of intricate design. Skies cloven with flame and thunder, half-blasted trees round which huddled forms of women or men cower and cling, strange beasts and splendid flowers, alternate with the engraved text; and throughout all the sunbeams of heaven and fires of hell shed fiercer or softer light. In minute splendour and general effect the pages of Blake's next work fall short of these; though in the *Visions of the Daughters of Albion* the separate designs are fuller and more composed. This poem, written in a sort of regular though quasi-lyrical blank verse, is more direct and lucid in purpose than most of these books ; but the style is already laxer, veers more swiftly from point to point, stands weaker on its feet, and speaks with more of a hurried and hysterical tone. With "formidable moral questions," as the biographer has observed, it does assuredly deal ; and in a way somewhat formidable. This, we are told, "the exemplary man had good right to do." Exem-

assume his wisdom or his goodness? why this and not that? whence his acceptance and whence his rejection of anything that is ? 'Shall the clay demand of the potter, why hast thou made me thus ?' Shall it not? and why? Of whom else should a man ask? and if sure of his God, what better should he do? Theism is not expansive, but exclusive : and the creeds begotten or misbegotten on this lean body of belief are 'Satanic' in the eyes of a Pantheist, as his faith is in the eyes of their followers." There is much more, but it were superfluous to mix a narcotic over strong : and in pursuit of his flying "faith" my friend's ideal "Pantheist" is apt to become heretical.

plary or not, he in common with all men had
undoubtedly such a right ; and was not slow to use
it.   Nowhere else has the prophet so fully and
vehemently set forth his doctrine of indulgence ; too
Albigensian or antinomian this time to be given out
again in more decorous form.   Of pure mythology
there is happily little ; of pure allegory even less.
"The eye sees more than the heart knows ;" these
words are given on the title-page by way of motto
or key-note.   Above this inscription a single design
fills the page ; in it the title is written with characters
of pale fire upon cloud and rainbow ; the figure of
the typical woman, held fast to earth but by one foot,
seems to soar and yearn upwards with straining
limbs that flutter like shaken flame : appealing in
vain to the mournful and merciless Creator, whose
sad fierce face looks out beyond and over her,
swathed and cradled in bloodlike fire and drifted
rain.   In the prologue we get a design expressive of
plain and pure pleasure ; a woman gathers a child
from the heart of a blossom as it breaks, and the sky
is full of the golden stains and widening roses of a
sundawn.   But elsewhere, from the frontispiece to
the end, nothing meets us but emblems of restraint
and error ; figures rent by the beaks of eagles though
lying but on mere cloud, chained to no solid rock by
the fetters only of their own faiths or fancies ; leafless
trunks that rot where they fell ; cold ripples of
barren sea that break among caves of bondage.
The perfect woman, Oothoon, is one with the spirit
of the great western world ; born for rebellion and

freedom, but half a slave yet, and half a harlot.
"Bromion," the violent Titan, subject himself to
ignorance and sorrow, has defiled her;* "Theo-
tormon," her lover, emblem of man held in bondage
to creed or law, will not become one with her
because of her shame; and she, who gathered in
time of innocence the natural flower of delight, calls
now for his eagles to rend her polluted flesh with
cruel talons of remorse and ravenous beaks of shame :
enjoys his infliction, accepts her agony, and reflects
his severe smile in the mirrors of her purged spirit.†

---

* That is, woman has become subject to oppression of customs;
suffers violence at the hands of marriage laws and other such con-
demnable things. "Emancipation" and the cognate creeds of
which later days have heard so much never had a more violent and
vehement preacher. Not love, not the plucking of the flower, but
error, fear, submission to custom and law, is that which "defiles"
a woman in the sight of our prophet.

† Even thus told, the myth is plain enough; a word or two
of briefer translation may serve also to light up future allusions.
"I plucked Leutha's flower," says Oothoon in the prelude of this
poem, "and I was not ashamed;" the flower that brings forth
a child, which nature permits and desires her to gather : Leutha
is the spirit emblematic of physical pleasure, of sensual impulse
and indulgence, from whom comes the "loose Bible" of Mahomet
(*Song of Los*). But crossing the seas eastward to find her lover,
the strong enslaved spirit of Europe, she, type of womanhood and
freedom, is caught and chained as he by the force of conventional
error and tyrannous habit, which makes her seem impure in his
eyes; so they sit bound back to back, afraid to love; the eagles
that tear her flesh are emblems of her lover's scorn; vainly, a
virgin at heart, she appeals to all the fair and fearless face of
nature against her rival, the prurient modesty of custom, a virgin
in face, a harlot at heart; against unnatural laws of restraint upon
youths and maidens, whose inevitable outcome is in the licentious
alternative not less unnatural; he will not answer but with vain
and vague lamentation, will not turn himself and love her for all

But he
> " sits wearing the threshold hard
> With secret tears ; beneath him sound like waves on a desert shore
> The voice of slaves beneath the sun, and children bought with
>   money."

From her long melodious lamentation we give
one continuous excerpt here. Sweet and lucid as
Thel, it is more subtle and more strong ; the
allusions to American servitude and English aspira-
tion, which elsewhere distract and distort the sense
and scheme of the poem, are here well cleared away.

> " I cry Arise, O Theotormon ; for the village dog
>   Barks at the breaking day ; the nightingale has done lamenting ;
>   The lark does rustle in the green corn, and the eagle returns
>   From nightly prey and lifts his golden beak to the pure east ;
>   Shaking the dust from his immortal pinions, to awake
>   The sun that sleeps too long.   Arise my Theotormon, I am pure
>   Because the night is gone that closed me in its deadly black.
>   They told me that the night and day were all that I could see ;
>   They told me that I had five senses to enclose me up,
>   And they enclosed my infinite beam into a narrow circle,
>   And sank my heart into the abyss, a red round globe hotburning
>   Till all from life I was obliterated and erased.
>
>   Instead of morn arises a bright shadow like an eye
>   In the eastern cloud ; instead of night a sickly charnel-house.
>
>   But Theotormon hears me not : to him the night and morn
>   Are both alike ; a night of sighs, a morning of fresh tears.
>   And none but Bromion can hear my lamentations.
>
>   With what sense is it that the chicken shuns the ravenous hawk ?
>   With what sense does the tame pigeon measure out the expanse ?

---

her crying : the mystery of things and thoughts, the tyranny of
times and laws, is heavy upon them to the end.   All forms of life
but these are free to be fair and happy : only from east to west the
prison-houses are full of the wailing of women.

With what sense does the bee form cells? have not the mouse
    and frog
Eyes and ears and sense of touch? yet are their habitations
And their pursuits as different as their forms and as their joy.
Ask the wild ass why he refuses burdens, and the meek camel
Why he loves man: is it because of eye, ear, mouth or skin,
Or breathing nostrils? no: for these the wolf and tiger have.
Ask the blind worm the secrets of the grave and why her spires
Love to curl around the bones of death: and ask the ravenous
    snake
Where she gets poison; and the winged eagle why he loves the
    sun;
And then tell me the thoughts of man, that have been hid of old.

Silent I hover all the night, and all day could be silent,
If Theotormon once would turn his loved eyes upon me;
How can I be defiled when I reflect thy image pure?
Sweetest the fruit that the worm feeds on, and the soul prey'd
    on by woe;
The new-washed lamb tinged with the village smoke, and the
    bright swan
By the red earth of our immortal river; I bathe my wings
And I am white and pure to hover round Theotormon's breast.

Then Theotormon broke his silence, and he answered;
Tell me what is the night or day to one overflowed with woe?
Tell me what is a thought? and of what substance is it made?
Tell me what is joy? and in what gardens do joys grow?
And in what rivers swim the sorrows? and upon what mountains
Wave shadows of discontent? and in what houses dwell the
    wretched
Drunken with woe forgotten, and shut up from cold despair?

Tell me where dwell the thoughts forgotten till thou call them
    forth?
Tell me where dwell the joys of old? and where the ancient
    loves?
And when will they renew again and the night of oblivion be
    past?
That I might traverse times and spaces far remote and bring
'omfort into a present sorrow and a night of pain!

Where goest thou, O thought? to what remote land is thy flight?
If thou returnest to the present moment of affliction
Wilt thou bring comforts on thy wings and dews and honey and
    balm
Or poison from the desert wilds, from the eyes of the envier? "

After this Bromion, with less musical lamentation, asks whether for all things there be not one law established? " Thou knowest that the ancient trees seen by thine eyes have fruit; but knowest thou that trees and fruits flourish upon the earth to gratify senses unknown, in worlds over another kind of seas? " Are there other wars, other sorrows, and other joys than those of external life? But the one law surely does exist "for the lion and the ox," for weak and strong, wise and foolish, gentle and fierce ; and for all who rebel against it there are prepared from everlasting the fires and the chains of hell. So speaks the violent slave of heaven ; and after a day and a night Oothoon lifts up her voice in sad rebellious answer and appeal.

" O Urizen, Creator of men ! mistaken Demon of heaven !
    Thy joys are tears : thy labour vain, to form man to thine image ;
    How can one joy absorb another? are not different joys
    Holy, eternal, infinite? and each joy is a Love.

    Does not the great mouth laugh at a gift? and the narrow eyelids
        mock
    At the labour that is above payment? and wilt thou take the ape
    For thy counsellor, or the dog for a schoolmaster to thy children?
        *   *   *   *   *   *
    Does the whale worship at thy footsteps as the hungry dog?
    Or does he scent the mountain prey, because his nostrils wide
    Draw in the ocean? does his eye discern the flying cloud
    As the raven's eye? or does he measure the expanse like the
        vulture ?

S

Does the still spider view the cliffs where eagles hide their
   young ?
Or does the fly rejoice because the harvest is brought in ?
Does not the eagle scorn the earth and despise the treasures
   beneath ?
But the mole knoweth what is there, and the worm shall tell
   it thee."

Perhaps there is no loftier note of music and of
thought struck anywhere throughout these prophe-
cies. For the rest, we must tread carefully over the
treacherous hot ashes strewn about the latter end of
this book : which indeed speaks plainly enough for
once, and with high equal eloquence ; but to no
generally acceptable effect. The one matter of
marriage laws is still beaten upon, still hammered at
with all the might of an insurgent prophet : to whom
it is intolerable that for the sake of mere words and
mere confusions of thought "she who burns with
youth and knows no fixed lot " should be "bound by
spells of law to one she loathes," should "drag the
chain of life in weary lust," and "bear the wintry
rage of a harsh terror driven to madness, bound to
hold a rod over her shrinking shoulders all the day,
and all the night to turn the wheel of false desire ;"
intolerable that she should be driven by "longings
that wake her womb" to bring forth not men but
some monstrous "abhorred birth of cherubs," im-
perfect, artificial, abortive ; counterfeits of holiness
and mockeries of purity ; things of barren or perverse
nature, creatures inhuman or diseased, that live as a
pestilence lives and pass away as a meteor passes ;
"till the child dwell with one he hates, and do the

deed he loathes, and the impure scourge force his
seed into its unripe birth ere yet his eyelids can
behold the arrows of the day : " the day whose blind-
ing beams had surely somewhat affected the prophet's
own eyesight, and left his eyelids lined with strange
colours of fugitive red and green that fades into
black.   However, all these things shall be made
plain by death ; for " over the porch is written Take
thy bliss, O man ! and sweet shall be thy taste, and
sweet thy infant joys renew."   On the one hand is
innocence, on the other modesty ; infancy is " fearless,
lustful, happy ; " who taught it modesty, " subtle
modesty, child of night and sleep " ?   Once taught
to dissemble, to call pure things impure, to " catch
virgin joy, and brand it with the name of whore and
sell it in the night ; " once corrupted and misled,
" religious dreams and holy vespers light thy smoky
fires : once were thy fires lighted by the eyes of
honest morn."   Not pleasure but hypocrisy is the
unclean thing ; Oothoon is no harlot, but " a virgin
filled with virgin fancies, open to joy and to delight
wherever it appears ; if in the morning sun I find it,
there my eyes are fixed in happy copulation : " and
so forth—further than we need follow.

" Is it because acts are not lovely that thou seekest solitude
   Where the horrible darkness is impressed with reflections of
      desire ?—

Father of Jealousy, be thou accursed from the earth !
Why hast thou taught my Theotormon this accursed thing ?
Till beauty fades from off my shoulders, darkened and cast out,
A solitary shadow wailing on the margin of non-entity ; "

as in a later prophecy Ahania, cast out by the jealous God, being the type or embodiment of this sacred natural love "free as the mountain wind."

"Can that be love which drinks another as a sponge drinks water?
That clouds with jealousy his nights, with weepings all the days?

* * * * * *

Such is self-love, that envies all; a creeping skeleton
With lamp-like eyes watching around the frozen marriage-bed."

But instead of the dark-grey "web of age" spun around man by self-love, love spreads nets to catch for him all wandering and foreign pleasures, pale as mild silver or ruddy as flaming gold; beholds them without grudging drink deep of various delight, "red as the rosy morning, lustful as the first-born beam." No single law for all things alike; the sun will not shine in the miser's secret chamber, nor the brightest cloud drop fruitful rain on his stone threshold; for one thing night is good and for another thing day: nothing is good and nothing evil to all at once.

"'The sea-fowl takes the wintry blast for a covering to her limbs,
And the wild snake the pestilence, to adorn him with gems and
gold;
And trees and birds and beasts and men behold their eternal joy.
Arise, you little glancing wings, and sing your infant joy!
Arise and drink your bliss! For everything that lives is holy.'

Thus every morning wails Oothoon, but Theotormon sits
Upon the margined ocean, conversing with shadows dire.

The daughters of Albion hear her woes, and echo back her sighs."

It may be feared that Oothoon has yet to wait long before Theotormon will leave off "conversing with shadows dire ; " nor is it surprising that this poem won such small favour ; for had it not seemed inexplicable it must have seemed unbearable. Blake, as evidently as Shelley, did in all innocence believe that ameliorated humanity would be soon qualified to start afresh on these new terms after the saving advent of French and American revolutions. " All good things are in the West ; " thence in the teeth of " Urizen " shall human deliverance come at length. In the same year Blake's prophecy of *America* came forth to proclaim this message over again. Upon this book we need not dwell so long ; it has more of thunder and less of lightning than the former prophecies ; more of sonorous cloud and less of explicit fire. The prelude, though windy enough, is among Blake's nobler myths : the divine spirit of rebellious redemption, imprisoned as yet by the gods of night and chaos, is fed and sustained in secret by the " nameless " spirit of the great western continent ; nameless and shadowy, a daughter of chaos, till the day of their fierce and fruitful union.

"Silent as despairing love and strong as jealousy,
  The hairy shoulders rend the links, free are the wrists of fire."

At his embrace " she cast aside her clouds and smiled her first-born smile, as when a black cloud shows its lightnings to the silent deep."

"Soon as she saw the terrible boy then burst the virgin's cry ;
  I love thee ; I have found thee, and I will not let thee go.
  Thou art the image of God who dwells in darkness of Africa,
  And thou art fallen to give me life in regions of dark death."

Then begins the agony of revolution, her frost and
his fire mingling in pain ; and the poem opens as
with a sound and a light of storm.   It is throughout
in the main a mere expansion and dilution of the
Song of Liberty which we have already heard ;
and in the interludes of the great fight between
Urizen and Orc the human names of American or
English leaders fall upon the ear with a sudden
incongruous clash : not perhaps unfelt by the
author's ear also, but unheeded in his desire to make
vital and vivid the message he came to deliver.   The
action is wholly swamped by the allegory ; hardly is
it related how the serpent-formed "hater of dignities,
lover of wild rebellion and transgressor of God's
Law," arose in red clouds, "a wonder, a human
fire ;" "heat but not light went from him ;" "his
terrible limbs were fire ;" his voice shook the ancient
Druid temple of tyranny and faith, proclaiming free-
dom and "the fiery joy that Urizen perverted to ten
commands ;" the "punishing demons " of the God of
jealousy

"Crouch howling before their caverns deep like skins dried in the
      wind ;
  They cannot smite the wheat nor quench the fatness of the earth ;
  They cannot smite with sorrows nor subdue the plough and spade ;
  For terrible men stand on the shores, and in their robes I see
  Children take refuge from the lightnings.   *   *   *
  Ah vision from afar ! ah rebel form that rent the ancient heavens !
        *   *   *   *   Red flames the crest rebellious
  And eyes of death ; the harlot womb oft opened in vain
  Heaves in eternal circles, now the times are returned upon thee."

"Thus wept the angel voice" of the guardian-
angel of Albion ; but the thirteen angels of the

American provinces rent off their robes and threw
down their sceptres and cast in their lot with the
rebel; gathered together where on the hills

"called Atlantean hills,
Because from their bright summits you may pass to the golden
  world,
An ancient palace, archetype of mighty emperies,
Rears its immortal pinnacles, built in the forest of God
By Ariston the king of beauty for his stolen bride."

A myth of which we are to hear no more, significant
probably of the rebellion of natural beauty against
the intolerable tyranny of God, from which she has
to seek shelter in the darkest part of his creation
with the angelic or dæmonic bridegroom (one of the
descended "sons of God") who has wedded her by
stealth and built her a secret shelter from the strife
of divine things; where at least nature may breathe
freely and take pleasure; whither also in their time
congregate all other rebellious forces and spirits at
war with the Creator and his laws. But the speech
of "Boston's angel" we will at least transcribe: not
without a wish that he had never since then spoken
more incoherently and less musically.

"Must the generous tremble and leave his joy to the idle, to the
  pestilence,
That mock him? who commanded this? what God? what Angel?
To keep the generous from experience, till the ungenerous
Are unrestrained performers of the energies of nature,
Till pity is become a trade and generosity a science
That men get rich by; and the sandy desert is given to the
  strong?
What God is he writes laws of peace and clothes him in a
  tempest?

What pitying Angel lusts for tears and fans himself with sighs ?
What crawling villain preaches abstinence and wraps himself
In fat of lambs ? no more I follow, no more obedience pay."

This is perhaps the finest and clearest passage in the book ; and beyond this point there is not much extractable from the clamorous lyrical chaos.   Here again besides the mere outward violence of battle, the visible plague and fire of war, we have sight of a subtler and wider revolution.

" For the female spirits of the dead pining in bonds of religion
Run from their fetters reddening and in long-drawn arches sitting.
They feel the nerves of youth renew, and desires of ancient times."

Light and warmth and colour and life are shed from the flames of revolution not alone on city and valley and hill, but likewise

"Over their pale limbs, as a vine when the tender grape appears ;
*   *   *   *   *   *
The heavens melted from north to south ; and Urizen who sat
Above all heavens in thunders wrapt, emerged his leprous head
From out his holy shrine ; his tears in deluge piteous
Falling into the deep sublime."

Notwithstanding for twelve years it was fated that "angels and weak men should govern o'er the strong, and then their end should come when France received the demon's light : " and the ancient European guardians " slow advance to shut the five gates of their law-built heaven, filled with blasting fancies and with mildews of despair, with fierce disease and lust ; " but these gates were consumed in the final fire of revolution that went forth upon the world. So ends the poem ; and of the decoration we have

barely space to say enough. On one page are the
visions of the renewed world, on another the emblems
of oppression and war : children sleeping nestled in
the fleece of a sleeping ram with heavy horns and
quiet mouth pressing the soft ground, while over-
head shapely branches droop and gracious birds are
perched ; or what seems the new-born body of Orc
cast under the sea, enmeshed in a web of water
whose waves are waves of corn when you come
to look ; maidens and infants that bridle a strong
dragon, and behind them a flight of birds through
the clouds of a starry moonlit night, where a wild
swan with vast wings and stretching neck is be-
stridden by a spirit looking eagerly back as he
clutches the rein ; eagles that devour the dead on a
stormy sea-beach, while underneath fierce pikes and
sharks make towards a wrecked corpse that has
sunk without drifting, and sea-snakes wind about
it in soft loathsome coils ; women and children
embrace in bitter violence of loving passion among
ripples of fruitful flame, out of which rise roots and
grasses of the field and laden branches of the vine.
Of all these we cannot hope to speak duly ; nor can
we hope to give more than a glimpse of the work
they illustrate.

Throughout the Prophecy of *Europe* the fervent
and intricate splendours of text and decoration are
whirled as it were and woven into spreading webs
or twining wheels of luminous confusion. The
Museum copy, not equal in nobility of colour to
some others, is crowded with MS. notes and mottos

of some interest and significance. To the frontis-
piece a passage of Milton is appended; to the first
page is prefixed a transcript of some verses by
Mrs. Radcliffe concerning a murdered pilgrim,
sufficiently execrable and explanatory; and so
throughout. These notes will help us at least to
measure the amount of connexion between the text
and the designs; an amount easily measurable,
being in effect about the smallest possible. Fierce
fluctuating wind and the shaken light of meteors
flutter or glitter upon the stormy ways of vision;
serving rather for raiment than for symbol. The
outcast gods of star and comet are driven through
tempestuous air: "forms without body" leap or
lurk under cloud or water; War, a man coated
with scales of defiled and blackening bronze, hand-
ling a heavy sword-hilt, averts his face from
appealing angels; Famine slays and eats her
children; fire curls about the caldron in which their
limbs are to be sodden for food; starved plague-
stricken shapes of women and men fall shrieking
or silent as the bell-ringer, a white-haired man with
slouched hat drawn down and long straight cassock,
passes them bell in hand; a daughter clings to her
father in the dumb pain of fear, while he with arms
thrust out in repulsion seems to plead against the
gathering deluges that "sweep o'er the yellow
year;" mildews are seen incarnate as foul flushed
women with strenuous limbs contorted, blighting
ears of corn with the violent breath of their inflated
mouths; "Papal Superstition," with the triple crown

on a head broader across cheek and jowl than across
the forehead, with bat's wings and blood-like gar-
ments dripping and rent, leers across the open book
on his knees; behind his reptile face a decoration as
of a cleft mitre, wrought in the shape of Gothic
windows that straiten as it ascends, shows grey
upon the dead black air; this is "Urizen seen on
the Atlantic; and his brazen book that kings and
priests had copied on earth, expanded from north to
south;" all the creeping things of the prison-house,
bloated leaf and dropping spider, crawl or curl above
a writhing figure overgrown with horrible scurf of
corruption as with network; the gaoler leaves his
prisoner fast bound by the ankles, with limbs stained
and discoloured; (the motto to this is from "The
Two Noble Kinsmen," Act ii. Sc. 1, "The vine
shall grow, but we shall never see it," &c.); snakes
and caterpillars, birds and gnats, each after their
own kind take their pleasure and their prey among
the leaves and grasses they defile and devour;
flames chase the naked or swooning fugitives from a
blazing ruin. The prelude is set in the frame of two
large designs; one of the assassin waiting for the
pilgrim as he turns round a sharp corner of rock;
one of hurricane and storm in which "Horror,
Amazement and Despair" appear abroad upon the
winds. A sketch of these violent and hideously
impossible figures is pasted into the note-book on a
stray slip of paper. The MS. mottos are mostly
from Milton and Dryden; Shakespeare and Fletcher,
Rowe and Mason, are also dragged into service.

The prophecy itself is full of melody and mist; of music not wholly unrecognisable and vapour not wholly impermeable. In a lull of intermittent war, the gods of time and space awake with all their children; Time bids them "seize all the spirits of life and bind their warbling joys to our loud strings, bind all the nourishing sweets of earth to give us bliss." Orc, the fiery spirit of revolution, first-born of Space, his father summons to arise; "and we will crown thy head with garlands of the ruddy vine; for now thou art bound; and I may see thee in the hour of bliss, my eldest born." Allegory, here as always, is interfused with myth in a manner at once violent and intricate; but in this book the mere mythologic fancy of Blake labours for the most part without curb or guide. Enitharmon, the universal or typical woman, desires that "woman may have dominion" for a space over all the souls upon earth; she descends and becomes visible in the red light of Orc; and she charges other spirits born of her and Los to "tell the human race that woman's love is sin," for thus the woman will have power to refuse or accede, to starve or satiate the perverted loves and lives of man; "that an eternal life awaits the worms of sixty winters, in an allegorical abode where existence hath never come; forbid all joy, and from her childhood shall the little female spread nets in every secret path." To this end the goddess of Space calls forth her chosen children, the "horned priest" of animal nature, the "silver-bowed queen" of desolate places, the "prince of the sun" with his innumerable race " thick as the summer stars ; each one, ramping, his golden mane shakes, and thine eyes rejoice because of strength, O Rintrah, furious King." Moon and sun, spirit and flesh, all lovely jealous forces and mysteries of the natural world are gathered together under her law, that throughout the eighteen Christian centuries she may have her will of the world. For so long nature has sat silent, her harps out of tune ; the goddess herself has slept out all those years, a dream among dreams, the ghostly regent of a ghostly generation. The angels of Albion, satellites once of the ancient Titan, are smitten now with their own plagues, crushed in their own council-house, and rise again but to follow after Rintrah, the fiery minister of his mother's triumph. Him the chief " Angel " follows to " his ancient temple serpent-formed," ringed round with Druid oaks, massive with pillar and porch built of precious stones ; " such eternal in the heavens, of colours twelve, few known on earth, give light in the opaque."

" Placed in the order of the stars, when the five senses whelmed
In deluge o'er the earth-born man : then bound the flexile eyes
Into two stationary orbs concentrating all things :
The ever-varying spiral ascents to the heaven of heavens
Were bended downward, and the nostril's golden gates shut,
Turned outward, barred and petrified against the infinite.
Thought changed the infinite to a serpent ; that which pitieth
To a devouring flame ; and man fled from its face and hid
In forests * of night ; then all the eternal forests were divided
Into earths rolling in circles of space, that like an ocean rushed

* Night, or the darkness of worlds yet undivided and chaotic, is always typified by Blake as a "forest" dark with involved and implicated leaf or branch. Compare *The Tiger*.

And overwhelmed all except this finite wall of flesh.
Then was the serpent temple formed, image of (the) infinite
Shut up in finite revolutions,* and man became an Angel ;
Heaven a mighty circle turning ; God a tyrant crowned."

Thus again recurs the doctrine that the one inlet
left us for spiritual perception—that namely of the
senses—is but one and the least of many inlets and
channels of communication now destroyed or per-
verted by the creative demon ; a tenet which once
well grasped and digested by the disciple will further
his understanding of Blake more than anything else
can : will indeed, pushed to the full extreme of its
logical results, elucidate and justify much that seems
merely condemnable and chaotic. To resume our
somewhat halting and bewildered fable : the southern
porch of this temple, "planted thick with trees of
blackest leaf, and in a vale obscure, enclosed the
stone of night ; oblique it stood, o'erhung with purple
flowers and berries red ;" image of the human intel-
lect "once open to the heavens" as the south to the
sun ; now, as the head of fallen man, "overgrown
with hair and covered with a stony roof ;" sunk deep
"beneath the attractive north," where evil spirits are
strongest, where the whirlpool of speculation sucks
in the soul and entombs it. Standing on this, as on
a watch-tower, the "Angel" beholds Religion en-
throned over Europe, and the pale revolution of
cloud and fire through the night of space and time ;

* Along this page a serpent of imperious build rears the strong
and sinuous length of his dusky glittering body, and spits forth keen
undulating fire.

beholds "Albion," the home once of ancient freedom
and faith, trodden underfoot by laws and churches,
that the God of Religion may have wherewithal to
"feed his soul with pity." At last begins the era of
rebellion and change ; the fires of Orc lay hold upon
law* and gospel ; yet for a little while the ministers
of his mother have power to fight against him, and
she, allied now and making common cause with the
God alien to her children, "laughs in her sleep,"
seeing through the veil and vapour of dreams the
subjection of male to female, the false attribute of
unnatural power given to women by faith and fear.
Not as yet can the Promethean fire utterly dissolve
the clouds of Urizen, though the flesh of the minister-
ing angel of religion is already consumed or con-
suming ; nor as yet can the trumpet of revolution
summon the dead to judgment. That first blast of
summons must be blown by material science, which
destroys the letter of the law and the text of the
covenant. When the "mighty spirit" of Newton
had seized the trumpet and blown it,

> "Yellow as leaves of Autumn the myriads of Angelic hosts
> Fell thro' the wintry skies seeking their graves,
> Rattling their hollow bones in howling and lamentation ;"

as to this day they do, and did in Blake's time,
throughout whole barrowfuls of controversial "apolo-
gies" and "evidences." Then the mother-goddess

---

* It is possible that Blake intended here some grotesque em-
blematic reference to the riots witnessed by himself, in which Lord
Mansfield's house and MSS. were destroyed by fire. At all events,
here alone is there any visible allusion to a matter of recent history.

awoke from her eighteen centuries of sleep, the
"Christian era" being now wellnigh consummated,
and all those years "fled as if they had not been;" she
called her children around her, by many monstrous
names and phrases of chaotic invocation; comfort
and happiness here, there sweet pestilence and soft
delusion; the "seven churches of Leutha" seek the
love of "Antamon," symbolic of Christian faith
reconciled to "pagan" indulgence and divorced from
Jewish prohibition; even as we find in the prophet
himself equal faith in sensual innocence and spiritual
truth. Of "the soft Oothoon" the great goddess
asks now "Why wilt thou give up woman's secrecy,
my melancholy child? Between two moments bliss
is ripe." Last she calls upon Orc; "Smile, son of
my afflictions; arise and give our mountains joy of
thy red light."

> "She ceased; for all were forth at sport beneath the solemn moon,
>   Waking the stars of Urizen with their immortal songs,
>   That nature felt thro' all her pores the enormous revelry.
>   Till morning oped her eastern gate;
>   Then every one fled to his station; and Enitharmon wept."

But with the dawn of that morning Orc descended
in fire, "and in the vineyards of red France appeared
the light of his fury." The revolution begins; all
space groans; and lion and tiger are gathered
together after their prey: the god of time arises as
one out of a trance,

> "And with a cry that shook all nature to the utmost pole
>   Called all his sons to the strife of blood."

Our study of the *Europe* might bring more profit if we could have genuine notes appended to the text as well as to the designs. Such worth or beauty as the poem has burns dim and looms distant by comparison ; but there is in it more of either than we have here time or means to indicate. At least the prelude so strangely selected for citation and thrown loose upon the pages of the biography in so crude and inexplicable a manner, may now be seen to have some tangible or presumable sense. The spirit of Europe rises revealed in the advent of revolution, sick of time and travail ; pleading with the mother-goddess, Cybele of this mythology ; wrapping about her veils of water and garments of cloud, in vain ; "the red sun and moon and all the overflowing stars rain down prolific pains." Out of her overlaboured womb arise forms and forces of change, fugitive fires of wrath, sonorous shapes of fear ; and they take substance in space, but bring to their mother no help or profit, no comfort or light ; to the virgin daughter of America freedom has come and fruitful violence of love, but not to the European mother. She has no hope in all the infinity of space and time ; "who shall bind the infinite with an eternal band, to compass it with swaddling bands?" By comparison of the two preludes the relations of the two kindred poems may be better understood : the one is plaintive as the voice of a world in pain, and decaying kingdom by kingdom ; the other fierce and hopeful as the cry of a nation in travail, whose agony is not that of death, but rather that of birth.

T

The First Book of Urizen is perhaps more shapeless and chaotic at a first glimpse than any other of these prose poems. Clouds of blood, shadows of horror, worlds without form and void, rise and mingle and wane in indefinite ways, with no special purpose or appreciable result. The myth here is of an active but unprolific God, warring with shapes of the wilderness, and at variance with the eternals : beaten upon by Time, who figures always in all his various shapes and actions as the saviour and friend of man. "Earth was not, nor globes of attraction ; the will of the Immortal expanded or contracted at will his all-flexible senses. Death was not ; but eternal life sprang." (1. Urizen, ii. 1.) Urizen, the God of restraint, creator of prohibition, whose laws are for-bearance and abstinence, is for ages divided from Eternity and at war with Time ; "long periods in burning fires labouring, till hoary, and age-broken, and aged, in despair and the shadows of death." (1. Urizen, iii. 6.) In time the formless God takes form, creating and assuming feature by feature ; bones, heart, eyes, ears, nostrils, throat with tongue, hands with feet ; an age of agony being allotted to each of the seven created features ; still toiling in fire and beset by snares, which the Time-Spirit kindles and weaves to avert and destroy in its birth the desolate influence of the Deity who forbids and restrains These transformations of Urizen make up some of Blake's grandest and strangest prophetic studies. First the spinal skeleton, with branchwork of rib and savage nudity of joint and clavicle, shaped

mammoth-wise, in grovelling involution of limb.   In
one copy at least these bones are touched with dim
green and gold colour ; such a faint fierce tint as one
might look for on the cast scales or flakes of dragons
left astrand in the ebb of a deluge.   Next a huge
fettered figure with blind shut eyes overflowing into
tears, with convulsed mouth and sodden stream of
beard : then bones painfully gathering flesh, twisted
forms round which flames break out fourfold, tortured
elemental shapes that plunge and writhe and moan.
Until Time, divided against himself, brings forth
Space, the universal eternal female element, called
Pity among the gods, who recoil in fear from the
dawn of human creation and division.   Of these two
divinities, called in the mythology Los and Enith-
armon, is born the man-child Orc.   "The dead
heard the voice of the child and began to awake
from sleep ; all things heard the voice of the child
and began to awake to life." (vii. 5.)   Here again
we may spare a word or two for that splendid figure
(p. 20) of the new-born child falling aslant through
cloven fire that curls and trembles into spiral
blossoms of colour and petals of feverish light.   And
the children of Urizen were Thiriel, born from cloud ;
Utha, from water ; Grodna, from earth ; Fuzon
"first-begotten, last-born," from fire—"and his
daughters from green herbs and cattle, from monsters
and worms of the pit.   He cursed both sons and
daughters ; for he saw that no flesh nor spirit could
keep his iron laws one moment." (viii. 3, 4.)   Then
from his sorrows for these his children begotten on

the material body of nature, the web of religion begins to unwind and expand, "throwing out from his sorrowing soul, the dungeon-like heaven dividing" (viii. 6)—and the knotted meshes of the web to involve all races and cities. "The Senses inward rushed shrinking beneath the dark net of infection : till the shrunken eyes, clouded over, discerned not the woven hypocrisy ; but the streaky slime in their heavens, brought together by narrowing perceptions, appeared transparent air ; for their eyes grew small like the eyes of a man. Six days they shrank up from existence, and the seventh day they rested, and they blessed the seventh day, in sick hope ; and forgot their eternal life." (1. Urizen, ix. 1, 2, 3.) Hence grows the animal tyranny of gravitation, and hence also the spiritual tyranny of law ; "they lived a period of years, then left a noisome body to the jaws of devouring darkness ; and their children wept, and built tombs in the desolate places ; and formed laws of prudence and called them the eternal laws of God." (ix. 4, 5.) Seeing these his brethren degraded into life and debased into flesh, the son of the fire, Fuzon, called together "the remaining children of Urizen ; and they left the pendulous earth : they called it Egypt, and left it. And the salt ocean rolled englobed." (ix. 8, 9.) The freer and stronger spirits left the world of men to the dominion of earth and water ; air and fire were withdrawn from them, and there were left only the heaviness of imprisoning clay and the bitterness of violent sea.

This is a hurried and blotted sketch of the main

myth, which is worth following up by those who would enter on any serious study of Blake's work ; all that is here indicated in dim hints being afterwards assumed as the admitted groundwork of later and larger myths. In this present book (and in it only) the illustrative work may be said almost to overweigh and stifle the idea illustrated. Strange semi-human figures, clad in sombre or in fiery flesh, racing through fire or sinking through water, allure and confuse the fancy of the student. Every page vibrates with light and colour ; on none of his books has the artist lavished more noble profusion of decorative work. It is worth observing that while some copies are carefully numbered throughout "First Book," in others the word "First" is erased from every leaf: as in effect the Second Book never was put forth under that title. Next year however the *Book of Ahania* came out—if one may say as much of a quarto of six leaves which has hardly yet emerged into sight of two or three readers. This we may take—or those may who please—to be the *Second Book of Urizen.* It is among the choicer spoils of Blake, not as yet cast into the public treasury ; for the Museum has no copy, though possessing (in its blind confused way) duplicates of *America*, *Albion*, and *Los.* Some day, one must hope, there will at least be a complete accessible collection of Blake's written works arranged in rational order for reference. Till the dawn of that day people must make what shift they can in chaos.

In *Ahania*, though a fine and sonorous piece of

wind-music, we have not found many separate notes worth striking. Formless as these poems may seem, it is often the floating final impression of ˌpower which makes them memorable and valuable, rather than any stray gleam of purple or glitter of pearl on the skirt. Thus the myth runs—to the best of its power; but the tether of it is but short.

Fuzon, born of the fiery part of the God of nature, in revolt against his father, divides him in twain as with a beam of fire; the desire of Urizen is separated from him; this divided soul, "his invisible lust," he sees now as she is apart from himself, and calls Sin; seizes her on his mountains of jealousy; kisses and weeps over her, then casts her forth and hides her in cloud, in dumb distance of mysterious space; "jealous though she was invisible." Divided from him, she turns to mere shadow "unseen, unbodied, unknown, the mother of Pestilence." But the beam cast by Fuzon was light upon earth—light to "Egypt," the house of bondage and place of captivity for the outcast human children of Urizen. Thus far the book floats between mere allegory and creative myth; not difficult however to trace to the root of its purport. From this point it grows, if not wilder in words, still mistier in build of limb and shape of feature. Fuzon, smitten by the bow of Urizen, seems to typify dimly the Christian or Promethean sacrifice; the revolted God or son of God, who giving to men some help or hope to enlighten them, is slain for an atonement to the wrath of his father: though except for the mythical

sonship Prometheus would be much the nearer
parallel. The bow, formed in secrecy of the nerves
of a slain dragon "scaled and poisonous-horned,"
begotten of the contemplations of Urizen and
destroyed by him in combat, must be another type,
half conceived and hardly at all wrought out, of
the secret and jealous law of introspective faith
divided against itself and the god of its worship, but
strong enough to smite the over-confident champion
of men even in his time of triumph, when he
"thought Urizen slain by his wrath: I am God,
said he, eldest of things." (ii. 8.) Suddenly the
judgment of the jealous wrath of God falls upon him ;
the rock hurled as an arrow "enters his bosom ; his
beautiful visage, his tresses that gave light to the
mornings of heaven, were smitten with darkness.—
But the rock fell upon the earth, Mount Sinai, in
Arabia :" being indeed a type of the moral law of
Moses, sent to destroy and suppress the native
rebellious energies and active sins of men. Here
one may catch fast hold of one thing—the identity of
Blake's "Urizen," at least for this time, with the
Deity of the earlier Hebrews ; the God of the Law
and Decalogue rather than of Job or the Prophets.
"On the accursed tree of mystery" that shoots up
under his heel from "tears and sparks of vegeta-
tion" fallen on the barren rock of separation, where
"shrunk away from Eternals," alienated from the
ancient freedom of the first Gods or Titans, averse
to their large and liberal laws of life, the jealous
God sat secret—on the topmost stem of this tree

Urizen "nailed the corpse of his first-begotten." Thenceforward there fell upon the half-formed races of men sorrow only and pestilence, barren pain of unprofitable fruit and timeless burden of desire and disease. One need not sift the myth too closely; it would be like winnowing water and weighing cloud with scale or sieve. The two illustrations, it may here be said, are very slight—mere hints of a design, and merely touched with colour. In the frontispiece Ahania, divided from Urizen, floats upon a stream of wind between hill and cloud, with haggard limbs and straightened spectral hair; on the last leaf a dim Titan, wounded and bruised, lies among rocks flaked with leprous lichen and shaggy with bloodlike growths of weed and moss. One final glimpse we may take of Ahania after her division—the love of God, as it were, parted from God, impotent therefore and a shadow, if not rather a plague and blight; mercy severed from justice, and thus made a worse thing than useless. Such may be the hinted meaning, or at least some part of it; but the work, it must be said, holds by implication dim and great suggestions of something more than our analytic ingenuities can well unravel by this slow process of suggestion. Properly too Ahania seems rather to represent the divine generative desire or love, translated on earth into sexual expression; the female side of the creative power—mother of all things made.

> "The lamenting voice of Ahania weeping upon the void and
> d the Tree of Fuzon. Distant in solitary night her voice was

heard, but no form had she; but her tears from clouds eternal fell round the Tree. And the voice cried ' Ah Urizen! Love! Flower of morning! I weep on the verge of non-entity: how wide the abyss between Ahania and thee! I lie on the verge of the deep, I see thy dark clouds ascend; I see thy black forests and floods, a horrible waste to my eyes. Weeping I walk over the rocks, over dens, and through valleys of death. Why dost thou despise Ahania, to cast me from thy bright presence into the world of loneness? I cannot touch his hand; nor weep on his knees; nor hear his voice and bow; nor see his eyes and joy; nor hear his footsteps, and my heart leap at the lovely sound; I cannot kiss the place where his bright feet have trod: but I wander on the rocks with hard necessity. Where is my golden palace? where my ivory bed? where the joy of my morning hour? where the sons of eternity singing to awake bright Urizen my king to arise to the mountain sport, to the bliss of eternal valleys, to awake my king in the morn, to embrace Ahania's joy on the breath of his open bosom; from my soft cloud of dew to fall in showers of life on his harvest? When he gave my happy soul to the sons of eternal joy; when he took the daughters of life into my chambers of love; when I found babes of bliss on my beds and bosoms of milk in my chambers, filled with eternal seed. O! eternal births sung round Ahania in interchange sweet of their joys; swelled with ripeness and fat with fatness, bursting n clouds my odours, my ripe figs and rich pomegranates, in infant joy at thy feet, O Urizen, sported and sang: then thou with thy lap full of seed, with thy hand full of generous fire, walkedst forth from the clouds of morning, on the virgins of springing joy, on the human soul, to cast the seed of eternal science. The sweat poured down thy temples, to Ahania returned in evening; the moisture awoke to birth my mother's joys sleeping in bliss. But now alone over rocks, mountains—cast out from thy lovely bosom—cruel jealousy! selfish fear! self-destroying! how can delight renew in these chains of darkness, where bones of beasts are strewn on the bleak and snowy mountains, where bones from the birth are buried before they see the light?' "—*Ahania*, ch. v., v. 1—14.

With the prolonged melody of this lament the *Book of Ahania* winds itself up; one of the most musical among this crowd of singing shadows. In

the same year the last and briefest of this first
prophetic series was engraved. The *Song of Los*,
broken into two divisions headed *Africa* and *Asia*,
has more affinity to *Urizen* and *Ahania* than to
Europe and *America*. The old themes of delusion
and perversion are once again rehandled ; not with-
out vigorous harmonies of choral expression. The
illustrations are of special splendour, as though
designed to atone for the lean and denuded form in
which *Ahania* had been sent forth. In the frontis-
piece a grey old giant, clothed from the waist only
with heavy raiment of livid and lurid white, bows
down upon a Druid altar before the likeness of a
darkened sun low-hung in heaven, filled with sombre
and fiery forms of things, and shooting out upon
each quarter a broad reflected ray like the reflection
struck by sunlight from a broad bare sword-blade,
but touched also, as with strange infection, with
flakes of deadly colour that vibrate upon the starless
solid ground of an intolerable night. Less of
menace with more of sadness is in the landscape and
sky on the title-page : a Titan, with one weighty
hand lying on a gigantic skull, rests at the edge
of a green sloping moor, himself seeming a grey
fragment of moorland rock ; brown fire of waste
grass or rusted flower stains crag and bent all round
him ; the sky is all night and fire, bitter red and
black. On the first page a serpent, splendid with
blood-red specks and scales of greenish blue, darts
the cloven flame of its tongue against a brilliant
swarm of flies ; and again throughout the divided

lines a network of fair tortuous things, of flickering leaf and sinuous tendril and strenuous root, flashes and curls from margin to margin.

This song is the song of Time, sung to the four harps of the world, each continent a harp struck by Time as by a harper. In brief dim words it celebrates the end of the world of the patriarchs where faith and freedom were one, the advent of the iron laws and ages, when God the Accuser gave his laws to the nations by the hands of the children of Time : when to the extreme east was given mere abstract philosophy for faith instead of clear pure belief, and man became slave to the elements, the slave and not the lord of the nature of things ; but not yet was philosophy a mere matter of the five senses. Thus they fared in the east ; meantime the spirits of the patriarchal world shrank beneath waters or fled in fires, Adam from Eden, Noah from Ararat ; and "Moses beheld upon Mount Sinai forms of dark delusion." Over each religion, Indian and Jewish and Grecian, some special demon or god of the mythology is bidden preside ; Christianity, the expression of human sorrow, human indulgence and forgiveness, was given as gospel to "a man of sorrows" by the two afflicted spirits who typify man and woman, in whom the bitter errors and the sore needs of either several sex upon earth are reproduced in vast vague reflection ; to them therefore the gentler gospel belongs as of right. Next comes Mahometanism, to give some freedom and fair play to the controlled and abused senses ; but northwards other spirits set on foot a code of war to satiate their violent delight. So on all sides is the world overgrown with kingdoms and churches, codes and creeds; inspiration is crushed and erased; the sons of Time and Space reign alone; Har and Heva, the spirits of loftier and purer kind who were not as the rest of the Titan brood that "lived in war and lust," are fled and fallen, become as mere creeping things; and the world is ripe to bring forth for its cruel and mournful God the final fruit of reason debased and faith distorted.

> " Thus the terrible race of Los and Enitharmon gave
> Laws and Religions to the sons of Har, binding them more
> And more to Earth, closing and restraining ;
> Till a Philosophy of Five Senses was complete ;
> Urizen wept, and gave it into the hands of Newton and Locke."

These " terrible sons" of Time and Space are the presiding demons of each creed or code; the sons of men are in their hands now, for the father and mother of men are fallen gods, oblivious and transformed : and these minor demons are all subservient to the Creator, whose soul, sorrowful but not merciful, animates the whole pained world. So, with cloud of menace and fire of wrath shed out about the deceased gods and the new philosophies, the first part ends. In the second part the clouds have broken and the fire has come forth; revolution has begun in Europe; the ancient lords of Asia are startled from their dens and cry in bitterness of soul for help of the old oppressions; for councillors and taxes, for plagues and for priests, " to turn man

from his path ; to restrain the child from the womb ;
to cut off the bread from the city, that the remnant
may learn to obey : that the pride of the heart may
fail ; that the lust of the eye may be quenched ; that
the delicate ear in its infancy may be dulled, and the
nostrils closed up ; to teach mortal worms the path
that leads from the gates of the grave." At their
cry Urizen arose, the lord of Asia from of old, ever
since he cast down the patriarchal law and set up the
Mosaic code ; "his shuddering waving wings went
enormous above the red flames," to contend with the
rekindled revolution, "the thick-flaming thought-
creating fires of Orc ; "

> " His books of brass, iron, and gold
> Melted over the land as he flew,
> Heavy-waving, howling, weeping.
> And he stood over Judea,
> And stayed in his ancient places,
> And stretched his clouds over Jerusalem.
> For Adam, a mouldering skeleton,
> Lay bleached on the garden of Eden ;
> And Noah, as white as snow,
> On the mountains of Ararat."

Thus, with thunder from eastward and fire from
westward, the God of jealousy and the Spirit of
freedom met together ; earth shrank at the meeting
of them.

> " Forth from the dead dust rattling bones to bones
> Came ; shaking, convulsed, the shivering clay breathes ;
> And all flesh naked stands ; Fathers and Friends ;
> Mothers and Infants ; Kings and Warriors ;
> The Grave shrieks with delight, and shakes
> Her hollow womb, and clasps the solid stem ;

Her bosom swells with wild desire ;
And milk and blood and glandous wine
In rivers rush and shout and dance
On mountain, dale and plain.
        The Song of Los is ended.
            Urizen wept."

So much for the text ; which has throughout a con-
tagious power of excitement in the musical passion
of its speech. For these books, above all, it is
impossible to read continuously and not imbibe a
certain half-nervous enjoyment from their long
cadences and tempestuous undulations of melody.
Such passion went to the writing of them that some
savour of that strong emotion infects us also in
reading pages which seem still hot from the violent
touch of the poet. The design of Har and Heva
flying from their lustful and warlike brethren across
green waste land before a late and thunder-coloured
sky, he grasping her with convulsive fear, she
looking back as she runs with lifted arm and
flame-like hair and fiery flow of raiment ; and
that succeeding where they reappear fallen to
mere king and queen of the vegetable world, them-
selves half things of vegetable life ; are both
noble if somewhat vehement and reckless. In this
latter, the deep green-blue heaven full of stars like
flowers is set with sweet and deep effect against the
darkening green of the vast lily-leaves supporting
the fiery pallor of those shapely chalices which
enclose as the heart of either blossom the queen
lying at her length, and the king sitting with bright
plucked-out pistil in hand by way of sceptre or

sword ; and below them the dim walls of the world alone are wholly black : his robes of soft shot purple and red, her long chrysalid shell or husk of tarnished gold, are but signs of their bondage and fall from deity ; they are fallen to be mere flowers. More might be said of the remaining designs ; the fierce glory of sweeping branches and driven leaves in a strong wind, the fervent sky and glimmering hill, the crouching figures above and under, the divine insane luxuriance of cloudy and flowery colour which makes twice luminous the last page of the poem ; the strange final design where a spirit with huge childlike limbs and lifted hair seems to smite with glittering mallet the outer rim of a huger blood-red sun ; but for this book we have no more space ; and much laborious travel lies ahead of us yet.

With the *Song of Los* the first or London series of prophecies came to a close not unfit or unmelodious. As their first word had been Revelation, their last was Revolution. We have now to deal with the two later and larger books written at Felpham, but not put forth till 1804. To one of these at least we must allow some tolerably full notice. The *Milton* shall here take precedence. This poem, though sufficiently vexatious to the human sense at first sight, is worth some care and some admiration. Its preface must here be read in full.

"The stolen and perverted writings of Homer and Ovid, of Plato and Cicero, which all men ought to contemn, are set up by artifice against the sublime of the Bible ; but when the New Age is at leisure to pronounce, all will be set right, and those grand works of the more ancient and consciously and professedly inspired men, will hold their proper rank ; and the daughters of memory shall become the daughters of inspiration. Shakespeare and Milton were both curbed by the general malady and infection from the silly Greek and Latin slaves of the sword. Rouse up, O young men of the New Age ! set your foreheads against the ignorant hirelings ! For we have hirelings in the camp, the court, and the university ; who would, if they could, for ever depress mental and prolong corporeal war. Painters ! on you I call ! Sculptors ! Architects ! suffer not the fashionable fools to depress your powers by the prices they pretend to give for contemptible works or the expensive advertising boasts that they make of such works : believe Christ and his Apostles, that there is a class of men whose whole delight is in destroying. We do not want either Greek or Roman models if we are but just and true to our own imaginations, those worlds of eternity in which we shall live for ever, in Jesus our Lord.

> And did those feet in ancient time
> Walk over England's mountains green ?
> And was the holy Lamb of God
> On England's pleasant pastures seen ?
>
> And did the Countenance Divine
> Shine forth upon our clouded hills ?
> And was Jerusalem builded here,
> Among these dark Satanic mills ?
>
> Bring me my bow of burning gold ;
> Bring me my arrows of desire ;
> Bring me my spear : O clouds, unfold ;
> Bring me my chariot of fire.
>
> I will not cease from mental fight,
> Nor shall my sword sleep in my hand,
> Till we have built Jerusalem
> In England's green and pleasant land.

'Would to God that all the Lord's people were prophets.'— Numbers xi. 29."

After this strange and grand prelude, which, though taken in the letter it may read like foolish-

ness, is in the spirit of it certainty and truth for all
time, we pass again under the shadow and into the
land that shifts and slips under our feet. Something
however out of the chaos of fire and wind and stormy
colour may be caught at by fits and stored up for
such as can like it. Thus the poem opens, with not
less fervour and splendour of sound than usual.

" Daughters of Beulah ! Muses who inspire the Poet's Song !
  Record the journey of immortal Milton thro' your realms
  Of terror and mild moony lustre, in soft sexual delusions
  Of varied beauty, to delight the wanderer and repose
  His burning thirst and freezing hunger ! Come into my hand,
  By your mild power descending down the Nerves of my right arm
  From out the Portals of my Brain, where by your ministry
  The Eternal Great Humanity Divine planted his Paradise
  And in it caused the Spectres of the Dead to take sweet forms
  In likeness of himself."

(Observe here the answer by anticipation to the old
foolish charge of madness and belief in mere material
visions ; a charge indeed refuted and confuted at
every turn we take. Thus, and no otherwise, did
Blake believe in his dead visitors and models : as
spectres formed into new and significant shape by
God, after his own likeness ; *not* called up as by some
witch of Endor and reclothed with the rags and
rottenness of their dead old bodies ; creatures exist-
ing within the brain and imagination of the workman,
not as they were once externally and by accident, but
as they will be for ever by the essence and substance
of their nature. For the "vegetated shadow." or
"human vegetable" no mystic ever had deeper or
subtler contempt than Blake ; nor was ever a man

U

less likely to care about raising or laying it after death.)

> " Tell also of the False Tongue ! vegetated
> Beneath your land of shadows ; of its sacrifices, and
> Its offerings : even till Jesus, the image of the Invisible God,
> Became its prey ; a curse, an offering, and an atonement
> For Death Eternal, in the heavens of Albion, and before the gates
> Of Jerusalem his Emanation, in the heavens beneath Beulah."

Let the Súfis of the West make what construction they can of that doctrine. We will help them, before passing on, with another view of the Atonement, taken from *The Everlasting Gospel.*

> " But when Jesus was crucified,
> Then was perfected his galling pride.
> In three days he devoured his prey,
> *And still he devours the body of clay ;*
> For dust and clay is the serpent's meat,
> Which never was meant for man to eat."

That is, the spirit must be eternally at work consuming and destroying the likeness of things material and the religions made out of them. This over-fervent prophet of freedom for the senses as well as the soul would have them free, one may say, only for the soul's sake : talking as we see he did of redemption from the body and salvation by the spirit at war with it, in words which literally taken would hardly have misbecome a monk of Nitria.

Returning to the *Milton,* we are caught again in the mythologic whirlpools and cross-currents of symbol and doctrine ; our ears rung deaf and dazed by the hammers of Los (Time) and our eyes bewildered by the wheels and woofs of Enitharmon (Space):

"her looms vibrate with soft affections, weaving the Web of Life out from the ashes of the Dead." This is a fragment of the main myth, whose details Los and Enitharmon themselves for the present forbid our following out.

" The Three Classes of men regulated by Los's hammer, and woven
By Enitharmon's Looms, and spun beneath the Spindle of
Tirzah :
The first : The Elect from before the foundation of the World ;
The second : The Redeemed. The third : The Reprobate and
formed
To destruction from the mother's womb."

Into the myth of the harrow and horses of Palamabron, more Asiatic in tone than any other of Blake's, and full of the vast proportion and formless fervour of Hindoo legends, we will not haul any reluctant reader. Let him only take enough by way of extract to understand how thoroughly one vein of fiery faith runs through all the " Prophetic Books," and one passionate form of doctrine is enforced and beaten in upon the disciple again and again ; not hitherto with much material effect.

" And in the midst of the Great Assembly Palamabron prayed ;
O God, protect me from my friends that they have not power
over me ;
Thou hast given me power to protect myself from my bitterest
enemies."

Then the wrath of Rintrah, the most fiery of the spirits who are children of Time, having entered by lot into Satan, who was of the Elect from the first, "seeming a brother, being a tyrant, even thinking himself a brother while he is murdering the just,"

"with incomparable mildness," believing "that he
had not oppressed"—a symbolic point much insisted
on—

" He created Seven deadly Sins, drawing out his infernal scroll
    Of moral laws and cruel punishments upon the clouds of Jehovah,
    To pervert the divine voice in its entrance to the earth
    With thunders of war and trumpet's sound, with armies of
        disease ;
    Punishments and deaths mustered and numbered ; saying, I am
        God alone,
    There is no other ; let all obey my principles of moral in-
        dividuality
    I have brought them from the uppermost innermost recesses
    Of my Eternal Mind ; transgressors I will rend off for ever ;
    As now I rend this accursed Family from my covering."

This is the Satan of Blake, sufficiently unlike the
Miltonic. Of himself he cannot conceive evil and
bring forth destruction ; the absolute Spirit of Evil
is alien from this mythology ; he must enter into the
body of a law or system and put on the qualities of
spirits strange to himself (Rintrah) ; he is divided,
inconsistent, a mystery and error to himself ; he
represents Monotheism with its stringent law and
sacerdotal creed, Jewish or Christian, as opposed to
Pantheism whereby man and God are one, and by
culture and perfection of humanity man makes himself
God. The point of difference here between Blake
and many other western Pantheists is that in his
creed self-abnegation (in the mystic sense, not the
ascetic—the Oriental, not the Catholic) is the highest
and only perfect form of self-culture : and as Satan
(under "names divine"—see the Epilogue to the
Gates of Paradise) is the incarnate type of Mono-

theism, so is Jesus the incarnate type of Pantheism. To return to our myth; the stronger spirit rears walls of rocks and forms rivers of fire round them;

" And Satan, *not having the Science of Wrath but only of Pity*,*
   Rent them asunder ; and Wrath was left to Wrath, and Pity to Pity."

This is Blake's ultimate conception of active evil; not wilful wrong-doing by force of arm or of spirit; but mild error, tender falsehood innocent of a purpose, embodied in an external law of moral action and restrictive faith, and clothed with a covering of cruelty which adheres to and grows into it (Decalogue and Law). A subtle and rather noble conception, developing easily and rapidly into what was once called the Manichean doctrine as to the Old Testament.

" If the guilty should be condemned, he must be an Eternal Death,
   And one must die for another throughout all Eternity ;
   Satan is fallen from his station and can never be redeemed,
   But must be new-created continually moment by moment,
   And therefore the class of Satan shall be called the Elect, and those
   Of Rintrah the Reprobate, and those of Palamabron the Redeemed ;
   For he is redeemed from Satan's law, the wrath falling on Rintrah.

---

   * That is, being unable to reconcile qualities, to pass beyond the legal and logical grounds of good and evil into the secret places where they are not. The whole argument hinges on this difference between Pantheism, which can, and Theism, which cannot, and is therefore no surer or saner than a mere religion based on Church or Bible, nor less incompetent to include, to expound, to redeem the world.

And therefore Palamabron cared not to call a solemn Assembly
Till Satan had assumed Rintrah's wrath in the day of mourning,
In a feminine delusion * of false pride self-deceived."

The words of the text recur not unfrequently in
the "Prophetic Books." A single final act of redemp-
tion by sacrifice and oblation of one for another is not
admitted as sufficient, or even possible. The favourite
dogma is this, of the eternity of sacrifice ; endless
redemption to be bought at no less a price than
endless self-devotion. To this plea of " an Eternal "
before the assembly succeeds the myth of Leutha
" offering herself a ransom for Satan : " † a myth,

* Compare, for the doctrine as to delusion and jealousy being
feminine principles (destructive by their weakness, not by their
strength), this strange expostulation with God, recalling the tone of
earlier prophets :

" Why art thou silent and invisible,
　　Father of Jealousy ?
Why dost thou hide thyself in clouds
　　From every searching eye ?

Why darkness and obscurity
　　In all thy words and laws,
That none dare eat the fruit but from
　　The wily serpent's jaws?
Or is it because Jealousy ‡
　　Gives feminine applause ? "

† Leutha, the spirit or guardian goddess of natural pleasure and
physical beauty, is sacrificed as a ransom to redeem the spirit or
guardian god of prohibitive law or judicial faith ; to him she is
sacrificed that through her he may be saved. Thus, in the *Visions
of the Daughters of Albion*, the maiden who " plucks Leutha's
flower," who trusts and indulges Nature, has her " virgin mantle
torn in twain by the terrible thunders " of religious and moral law :

‡ his word, half rubbed off in the MS., may be "secrecy ;" and the point
emain the same.

not an allegory ; for of allegory pure and simple
there is scarcely a trace in Blake.

> "I formed the Serpent
> Of precious stones and gold turned poison on the sultry waste.
> To do unkind things with kindness ; with power armed, to say
> The most irritating things in the midst of tears and love ;
> These are the stings of the Serpent."

This whole myth of Leutha is splendid for colour,
and not too subtle to be thought out : the imagina-
tive action of the poem plays like fire and palpitates
like blood upon every line, as the lips of caressing
flame and the tongues of cleaving light in which the
text is set fold and flash about the margins.

> " The Elect shall meet the Redeemed, on Albion's rocks they shall
>   meet,
> Astonished at the Transgressor, in him beholding the Saviour.
> And the Elect shall say to the Redeemed ; We behold it is of
>   Divine
> Mercy alone, of free gift and Election, that we live ;
> Our Virtues and cruel Goodnesses have deserved Eternal
>   Death."

Forgiveness of sin and indulgence, the disciple per-
ceives, is not enough for this mythology ; it must
include forgiveness of virtue and abstinence, the
hypocritic holiness made perfect in the body of death
for six thousand years under the repressive and
restrictive law called after the name of the God of

woman was sacrificed and man " fast bound in misery " during the
eighteen centuries—through which the mother goddess lay asleep,
to weep over her children at her waking ; as in the Prophecy of
Europe Time the father and Space the mother of men are afflicted
and spellbound until the sleep of faith be slept out. There again
the emblematic name of Leutha recurs in passing.

the Jews, who "was leprous." Thus prophesies
Blake, in a fury of supra-Christian dogmatism.

Here ends the "Song of the Bard" in the First
Book. "Many condemned the high-toned song,
saying, Pity and Love are too venerable for the im-
putation of guilt. Others said, If it is true!" Let
us say the same, and pass on: listening only to the
Bard's answer:

> "I am inspired! I know it is Truth! for I sing
> According to the Inspiration of the Poetic Genius
> Who is the Eternal all-protecting divine Humanity
> To whom be Glory and Power and Dominion evermore. Amen."

Then follows the incarnation and descent into earth
and hell of Milton, who represents here the redemp-
tion by inspiration, working in pain and difficulty
before the expiration of the six thousand Satanic
years. His words are worth quoting:

> "When will the Resurrection come, to deliver the sleeping body
> From corruptibility? O when, Lord Jesus, wilt thou come?
> Tarry no longer; for my soul lies at the gates of death:
> I will arise and look forth for the morning of the grave:
> I will go down to the sepulchre and see if morning breaks.
> I will go down to self-annihilation and eternal death
> Lest the Last Judgment come and find me unannihilate
> And I be seized and given into the hands of my own selfhood."

This grand dogma, that personal love and selfish-
ness make up the sin which defies redemption, is in
a manner involved in that former one of the necessary
"eternity of sacrifice," for

> "I in my selfhood am that Satan; I am that Evil One;
> He is my Spectre."

Now by the light of these extracts let any student examine the great figure at p. 13, where "he beheld his own Shadow—and entered into it." Clothed in the colours of pain, crowned with the rays of suffering, it stands between world and world in a great anguish of transformation and change : Passion included by Incarnation. Erect on a globe of opaque shadow, backed by a sphere of aching light that opens flower-wise into beams of shifting colour and bitter radiance as of fire, it appeals with a doubtful tortured face and straining limbs to the flat black wall and roof of heaven. All over the head is a darkness not of transitory cloud or night that will some time melt into day ; recalling that great verse : "Neither could the bright flames of the stars endure to lighten that horrible night."

"As when a man dreams he reflects not that his body sleeps,
Else he would wake; so seemed he entering his Shadow; but
With him the Spirits of the Seven Angels of the Presence
Entering, they gave him still perceptions of his Sleeping Body
Which now arose and walked with them in Eden, as an Eighth
Image, Divine tho' darkened, and tho' walking as one walks
In Sleep; and the Seven comforted and supported him."

The whole passage is full of a deep and dim beauty which grows clearer and takes form of feature to those only who bring with them eyes to see and patience to desire it. Take next this piece of cosmo-graphy, worth comparing with Dante's vision of the worlds :

"The nature of infinity is this; That everything has its
Own vortex: and when once a traveller thro' Eternity
Has passed that vortex, he perceives it roll backward behind

His path into a globe itself enfolding, like a sun
Or like a moon or like a universe of starry majesty,
While he keeps onward in his wondrous journey thro' the earth,
Or like a human form, a friend with whom he lived benevolent :
As the eye of man views both the east and west encompassing
Its vortex, and the north and south, with all their starry host ;
Also the rising and setting moon he views surrounding
His cornfields and his valleys of five hundred acres square ;
Thus is the earth one infinite plane, and not as apparent
To the weak traveller confined beneath the moony shade ;
Thus is the heaven a vortex passed already, and the earth
A vortex not yet passed by the traveller thro' Eternity."

One curious piece of symbolism may be extracted
from the myth, as the one reference to anything
actual :

" Then Milton knew that the Three Heavens of Beulah were
    beheld
By him on earth in his bright pilgrimage of sixty years
In those three Females whom his Wives, and those three whom
    his Daughters
Had represented and contained, that they might be resumed
By giving up of Selfhood."

But of Milton's flight, of the cruelties of Ulro, of his
journey above the Mundane Shell, which " is a vast
concave earth, an immense hardened shadow of all
things upon our vegetated earth, enlarged into
dimension and deformed into indefinite space," we
will take no more account here ; nor of the strife
with Urizen, " one giving life, the other giving
death, to his adversary ;" hardly even of the tempta-
tion by the sons and daughters of Rahab and Tirzah,
when

" The twofold Form Hermaphroditic, and the Double-sexed,
    The Female-male and the Male-female, self-dividing stood
    Before him in their beauty and in cruelties of holiness."

(Compare the beautiful song *To Tirzah*, in the "Songs of Experience.") This Tirzah, daughter of Rahab the holy, is "Natural Religion" (Theism as opposed to Pantheism), which would fain have the spiritual Jerusalem offered in sacrifice to it.

> "Let her be offered up to holiness: Tirzah numbers her:
>   She numbers with her fingers every fibre ere it grow:
>   Where is the Lamb of God? where is the promise of his coming?
>   Her shadowy sisters form the bones, even the bones of Horeb
>   Around the marrow; and the orbed scull around the brain;
>   She ties the knot of nervous fibres into a white brain;
>   She ties the knot of bloody veins into a red-hot heart;
>   She ties the knot of milky seed into two lovely heavens,
>   Two yet but one; each in the other sweet reflected; these
>   Are our Three Heavens beneath the shades of Beulah, land of
>   rest."

Here and henceforward the clamour and glitter of the poem become more and more confused; nevertheless every page is set about with jewels; as here, in a more comprehensible form than usual:

> "God sent his two servants Whitfield and Wesley; were they
>   prophets?
>   Or were they idiots and madmen? 'Show us Miracles'?
>   Can you have greater Miracles than these? Men who devote
>   Their life's whole comfort to entire scorn, injury, and death?"

Take also these scraps of explanation mercifully vouchsafed us:

> "Bowlahoola is named Law by Mortals: Tharmas founded it
>   Because of Satan: *   *   *   *
>   But Golgonooza is named Art and Manufacture by mortal men.
>   In Bowlahoola Los's Anvils stand and his Furnaces rage.
>   Bowlahoola thro' all its porches feels, tho' too fast founded
>   Its pillars and porticoes to tremble at the force
>   Of mortal or immortal arm;   *   *   *

> The Bellows are the Animal Lungs; the Hammers the Animal
>   Heart;
> The Furnaces the Stomach for digestion; "

(Here we must condense instead of transcribing. While thousands labour at this work of the Senses in the halls of Time, thousands "play on instruments stringed or fluted" to lull the labourers and drown the painful sound of the toiling members, and bring forgetfulness of this slavery to the flesh: a myth of animal life not without beauty, and to Blake one of great attraction.)

> "Los is by mortals named Time, Enitharmon is named Space;
> But they depict him bald and aged who is in eternal youth
> All-powerful, and his locks flourish like the brows of morning;
> He is the Spirit of Prophecy, the ever-apparent Elias.
> Time is the mercy of Eternity; without Time's swiftness
> Which is the swiftest of all things, all were eternal torment."

At least this last magnificent passage should in common charity and sense have been cited in the biography, if only to explain the often-quoted words Los and Enitharmon. Neither blindness to such splendour of symbol, nor deafness to such music of thought, can excuse the omission of what is so wholly necessary for the comprehension of extracts already given, and given (as far as one can see) with no available purpose whatever.

The remainder of the first book of the *Milton* is a vision of Nature and prophecy of the gathering of the harvest of Time and treading of the winepress of War; in which harvest and vintage work all living things have their share for good or evil.

"How red the sons and daughters of Luvah ! here they tread the
    grapes,
Laughing and shouting, drunk with odours ; many fall o'erwearied,
Drowned in the wine is many a youth and maiden ; those around
Lay them on skins of Tigers and of the spotted Leopard and the
    wild Ass
Till they revive, or bury them in cool grots, making lamentation.
This Winepress is called War on Earth ; it is the printing-press
Of Los, there he lays his words in order above the mortal brain
As cogs are formed in a wheel to turn the cogs of the adverse
    wheel."

All kind of insects, of roots and seeds and creeping
things—"all the armies of disease visible or in-
visible "—are there ;

" The slow slug ; the grasshopper that sings and laughs and drinks
    (Winter comes, he folds his slender bones without a murmur) ; "

wasp and hornet, toad and newt, spider and snake,

" They throw off their gorgeous raiment ; they rejoice with loud
    jubilee
Around the winepresses of Luvah, naked and drunk with wine.
There is the nettle that stings with soft down ; and there
The indignant thistle whose bitterness is bred in his milk ;
Who feeds on contempt of his neighbour ; there all the idle weeds
That creep around the obscure places show their various limbs
Naked in all their beauty, dancing round the winepresses.
But in the winepresses the human grapes sing not nor dance,
They howl and writhe in shoals of torment, in fierce flame
    consuming ; "

tortured for the cruel joy and deadly sport of Luvah's
sons and daughters ;

" They dance around the dying and they drink the howl and groan ;
    They catch the shrieks in cups of gold, they hand them one to
        another ;

> These are the sports of love, and these the sweet delights of
> 　　amorous play ;
> Tears of the grape, the death-sweat of the cluster ; the last sigh
> Of the mild youth who listens to the luring songs of Luvah."

Take also this from the speech of Time to his
reapers.

> " You must bind the sheaves not by nations or families,
> 　You shall bind them in three classes ; according to their classes
> 　So shall you bind them, separating what has been mixed
> 　Since men began to be woven into nations.　　*　　　*
> 　　　*　　　　　*　　　　　*　　　　The Elect is one class ; you
> Shall bind them separate ; they cannot believe in eternal life
> Except by miracle and a new birth.　The other two classes,
> 　The Reprobate * who never cease to believe, and the Redeemed
> Who live in doubts and fears, perpetually tormented by the Elect,
> These you shall bind in a twin bundle for the consummation."

The constellations that rise in immortal order,
that keep their course upon mountain and valley,
with sound of harp and song, "with cups and
measures filled with foaming wine ; " that fill the
streams with light of many visions and leave in
luminous traces upon the extreme sea the peace of
their passage ; these too are sons of Los, and labour
in the vintage. The gorgeous flies on meadow or
brook, that weave in mazes of music and motion the
delight of artful dances, and sound instruments of
song as they touch and cross and recede ; the trees
shaken by the wind into sound of heavy thunder till
they become preachers and prophets to men ; these

---

* That is of course the reprobate according to theology, such
as the heretical prophet himself : the class of men upon which is
laid the burden of the sins of the elect, as Satan's upon Rintrah in
the myth.

are the sons of Los, these the visions of eternity ; and we see but as it were the hem of their garments.

A noble passage follows, in which are resumed the labours of the sons of time in fashioning men and the stations of men. They make for doubts and fears cabinets of ivory and gold ; when two spectres "like lamps quivering" between life and death stand ready for the blind malignity of combat, they are taken and moulded instead into shapes fit for love, clothed with soft raiment by softer hands, drawn after lines of sweet and perfect form. Some " in the optic nerve " give to the poor infinite wealth of insight, power to know and enjoy the invisible heaven, and to the rich scorn and ignorance and thick darkness. Others build minutes and hours and days ;

" And every moment has a couch of gold for soft repose
(A moment equals a pulsation of the artery)
And every minute has an azure tent with silken veils,
And every hour has a bright golden gate carved with skill,
And every day and night has walls of brass and gates of adamant ·
Shining like precious stones and ornamented with appropriate signs,
And every month a silver-paved terrace builded high,
And every year invulnerable barriers with high towers,
And every age is moated deep, with bridges of silver and gold,
And every Seven Ages are encircled with a flaming fire."

There is much ·more of the same mythic sort concerning the duration of time, the offices of the nerves (e.g., in the optic nerve sleep was transformed to death by Satan· the father of sin and death, even as we have seen sensual death re-transformed by Mercy into sleep), and such-like huge matters ; full,

one need not now repeat, of subtle splendour and
fanciful intensity. But enough now of this over-
careful dredging in such weedy waters; where
nevertheless, at risk of breaking our net, we may
at every dip fish up some pearl.

At the opening of the second book the pearls lie
close and pure. From this (without explanation or
reference) has been taken the lovely and mutilated
extract at p. 197 of the "Life." Thus it stands in
Blake's text :

" Thou hearest the nightingale begin the song of spring ;
  The lark, sitting upon his earthy bed, just as the morn
  Appears, listens silent ; then, springing from the waving corn-
    field, loud
  He leads the choir of day : trill—trill—trill—trill—
  Mounting upon the wings of light into the great expanse,
  Re-echoing against the lovely blue and shining heavenly shell
  His little throat labours with inspiration ; every feather
  On throat, and breast, and wing, vibrate with the effluence divine.
  All nature listens to him silent ; and the awful Sun
  Stands still upon the mountains, looking on this little bird
  With eyes of soft humility, and wonder, love, and awe.
  Then loud, from their green covert, all the birds began their
    song,—
  The thrush, the linnet and the goldfinch, robin and the wren,
  Awake the Sun from his sweet reverie upon the mountains ;
  The nightingale again essays his song, and through the day
  And through the night warbles luxuriant ; every bird of song
  Attending his loud harmony with admiration and love.

(This is a vision of the lamentation of Beulah over Ololon.)

Thou perceivest the flowers put forth their precious odours,
And none can tell how from so small a centre come such sweets,
Forgetting that within that centre eternity expands
Its ever-during doors that Og and Anak fiercely guard.*

---

* This line appears to have been too much for the writer in the
" Life," who here breaks his quotation short off by the head, anni-

First ere the morning breaks joy opens in the flowery bosoms,
Joy even to tears, which the sun rising dries; first the wild
thyme

---

hilating with a quite ingenious violence at once grammar, sense,
and sound. It is but a small nut to have broken his critical tooth
upon; the evident meaning being simply this: that within the
centre of everything living by animal or vegetative life there is by
way of kernel something imperishable; the fleshly or material life of
form contains the infinite spiritual life, lurking under leaf or latent
under limb: man and flower and beast have each the separate secret
of a soul or divisible indestructible spirit (compare even the "Songs
of Innocence"); but while the earthly and fleshly form remains
there stand as wardens of the ways the two material giants, Strength
and Force, binding the soul in the body with chains of flesh and
sex, the spirit in the petals with bonds of vegetable form, fashioned
fastenings of chalice and anther, sprinklings of dusty gold on leaf
or pistil; always, without hammer or rivet of Vulcanic forging,
able to hold fast Prometheus in blind bondage to the flesh and
form of things; so that except by inspiration there can be no chance
of seeing what does exist and work in man or beast or flower; only
by vision or by death shall one be brought safe past the watch
guarded by the sentinels of material form and bodily life, the crude
tributary "Afrites" (as in the Æschylean myth) of the governing
power which fashions and fetters life in men and things. And thus
this, the singing of birds and dancing of flowers, the springing of
colour and kindling of music at each day's dawn, is a symbol—
"a vision of the lamentation of Beulah over Ololon"—of the
dwellers in that milder and moonlight-coloured world of reflex
mortal spirits over the imperishable influences of a higher spiritual
world, which descending upon earth must be clothed with material
mystery and become subject to sensuous form and likeness in the
body of the shadow of death. This glorious passage, almost to be
matched for wealth of sound, for growth and gradation of floral
and musical splendour, for mastery of imperial colour, even against
the great interlude or symphony of flowers in "Maud," was not cast
at random into the poem, but has also a "soul" or meaning in it—
though the ways of seeing and understanding are somewhat too
closely guarded by "Og and Anak." Reading it as an excerpt
indeed one need hardly wish to see beyond the form or material
figure. That "innumerable dance" of tree and flower and herb

X

And meadow-sweet downy and soft waving among the reeds,
Light springing on the air, lead the sweet dance; they wake
The honeysuckle sleeping on the oak, the flaunting beauty
Revels along upon the wind; the white-thorn, lovely May,
Opens her many lovely eyes; listening, the rose still sleeps,
None dare to wake her: soon she bursts her crimson-curtained
    bed
And comes forth in the majesty of beauty; every flower,
The pink, the jessamine, the wallflower, the carnation,
The jonquil, the mild lily, opes her heavens; every tree
And flower and herb soon fill the air with an innumerable dance,
Yet all in order sweet and lovely; men are sick with love.

Such is a vision of the lamentation of Beulah over Ololon."

This Beulah is "a place where contrarieties are equally true;" "it is a pleasant lovely shadow where no dispute can come because of those who sleep:" made to shelter, before they "pass away in winter," the temporary emanations "which trembled exceedingly neither could they live, because the life of man was too exceeding unbounded." Of the incarnation and descent of Ololon, of the wars and prophecies of Milton, and of all the other Felpham visions here put on record, we shall say no more in this place; but all these things are written in the Second Book. The illustrative work is also noble and worth study in all ways. One page for example is covered by a design among the grandest of Blake's. Two figures lie half embraced, as in a deadly sleep without dawn of dream or shadow of rest, along a bare slant ledge of rock washed against by wintry water. Over these two stoops an eagle balanced on the heavy-laden

is not unfit for comparison with the old ἀνήριθμον γέλασμα of the waves of the sea.

air, with stretching throat and sharpened wings, opening beak, and eyes full of a fierce perplexity of pity. All round the greenish and black slope of moist sea-cliff the weary tidal ripple plashes and laps, thrusting up as it were faint tongues and listless fingers tipped with foam. On an earlier page, part of the text of which we have given, crowd and glitter all shapes and images of insect or reptile life, sprinkling between line and margin keen points of jewel-coloured light and soft flashes as of starry or scaly brilliance.

The same year 1804 saw the huge advent of *Jerusalem*. Of that terrible " emanation," hitherto the main cornerstone of offence to all students of Blake, what can be said within any decent limit? or where shall any traveller find a rest for feet or eyes in that noisy and misty land? It were a mere frenzy of discipleship that would undertake by force of words to make straight these crooked ways or compel things incoherent to cohere. *Supra hanc petram*—and such a rock it is to begin any church-building upon! Many of the unwary have stumbled over it and broken their wits. Seriously, one cannot imagine that people will ever read through this vast poem with pleasure enough to warrant them in having patience with it.

Several things, true in the main of all the " Prophetic Books," are especially true and memorable with regard to those written or designed during the "three years' slumber" at Felpham. They are the results of intense and active solitude working upon

x 2

the capricious nerves and tremulous brain of a man
naturally the most excitable and receptive of men.
They are to be read by the light of his earlier work
in the same line ; still more perhaps by the light of
those invaluable ten letters printed in Vol. II. of the
" Life," for which one can hardly give thanks enough.
The incredible fever of spirit under the sting and
stress of which he thought and laboured all his life
through, has left marks of its hot and restless
presence as clearly on this short correspondence as
on the voluminous rolls of prophecy. The merit or
demerit of the work done is never in any degree
the conscious or deliberate result of a purpose.
Possessed to the inmost nerve and core by a certain
faith, consumed by the desire to obey his instinct of
right by preaching that faith, utterly regardless of
all matters lying outside of his own inspiration, he
wrote and engraved as it was given him to do, and
no otherwise. As to matter and argument, the
enormous *Jerusalem* is simply a fervent apocalyptic
discourse on the old subjects—love without law and
against law, virtue that stagnates into poisonous
dead matter by moral isolation, sin that must exist
for the sake of being forgiven, forgiveness that must
always keep up with sin—must even maintain sin
that it may have something to keep up with and
to live for. Without forgiveness of sins, the one
thing necessary, we lapse each man into separate
self-righteousness and a cruel worship of natural
morality and religious law. For nature, oddly
enough as it seems at first sight, is assumed by this

mystical code to be the cruellest and narrowest of
absolute moralists. Only by worship of imaginative
impulse, the grace of the Lamb of God, which
admits infinite indulgence in sin and infinite forgive-
ness of sin—only by some such faith as this shall
the world be renewed and redeemed. This may be
taken as the rough result, broadly set down, of the
portentous book of revelation. Never, one may
suppose, did any Oriental heretic drive his deduc-
tions further or set forth his conclusions in obscurer
form. Never certainly did a man fall to his work
with keener faith and devotion. Sin itself is not so
evil—but the remembrance and punishment of sin !
"Injury the Lord heals ; but vengeance cannot be
healed." Next or equal in hatefulness to the
division of qualities into evil and good (see above,
" Marriage of Heaven and Hell ") is the separation
of sexes into male and female : hence jealous love
and personal desire, that set itself against the
mystical frankness of fraternity : hence too (contra-
dictory as it may seem till one thinks it out) the
hermaphroditic emblem is always used as a symbol
seemingly of duplicity and division, perplexity and
restraint. The two sexes should not combine and
contend ; they must finally amalgamate and be
annihilated.* All this is of course more or less

* One may fear that some such symbolic stuff as this is really at
the root of the admirable poem christened by its editor with the
name of *Broken Love* : which I gravely suspect was meant for
insertion in some fresh instalment of prophetic rhapsody by way of
complement or sequel to *Jerusalem*. The whole tone of it, and
especially that of some rejected stanzas, is exactly in the elemental

symbolic, and not to be taken in literal coarseness
or folly of meaning. The whole stage is elemental,

manner of the scenes (where scene is none) between Albion,
Jerusalem, and Vala the Spectre of Jerusalem (books 1st and
2nd) :

> " Thou hast parted from my side—
> Once thou wast a virgin bride :
> Never shalt thou a true love find—
> My Spectre follows thee behind.

> " When my love did first begin,
> Thou didst call that love a sin ;
> Secret trembling, night and day,
> Driving all my loves away."

These two stanzas (recalling so many other passages where Blake
has enforced his doctrines as to the fatal tendency of the fears and
jealousies, the abstinence and doubt, produced by theoretic virtue
and hatched by artificial chastity) stood originally as third and
fourth in the poem. They are cancelled in Blake's own MS. ; but
in that MS. the poem ends as follows, in a way (I fear) conclusive
as to the justice of my suggestion ; I mark them conjecturally, as I
suppose the dialogue to stand, by way of helping the reader to
some glimpse of the point here and there.

> " When wilt thou return and view
> My loves and them to life renew ?
> When wilt thou return and live ?
> When wilt thou pity as I forgive ? "

> " Never, never, I return ;
> Still for victory I burn.
> Living, thee alone I'll have ;
> And when dead I'll be thy gra

> " Through the heaven an
> Thou shalt never, n
> I will fly and th
> Night and m

(This I take to be
speaking through
again.)

the scheme one of patriarchal vapour, and the
mythologic actors mere Titans outlined in cloud.
Reserving this always, we shall not be far out in

> " And I, to end thy cruel mocks,
> Annihilate thee on the rocks,
> And another form create
> To be subservient to my fate.

> " Till I turn from female love
> And root up the infernal grove,
> I shall never worthy be
> To step into eternity."

(This stanza ought probably to be omitted ; but I retain it as
being carefully numbered for insertion by Blake: though he by
some evident slip of mind or pen has put it before the preceding
one.)

> " Let us agree to give up love
> And root up the infernal grove,
> Then shall we return and see
> The worlds of happy eternity.

> " And throughout all eternity
> I forgive you, you forgive me ;
> As our dear Redeemer said,
> This the wine and this the bread."

That is perfect *Jerusalem* both for style and matter. The struggle
of either side for supremacy—the flight and pursuit—the vehemence
and perversion—the menace and the persuasion—the separate
Spectre or incarnation of sex " annihilated on the rocks " of rough
law or stony circumstance and necessity—the final vision of an
eternity where the jealous divided loves and personal affections
"born of shame and pride" shall be destroyed or absorbed in
resignation of individual office and quality—all this belongs but too
clearly to the huge prophetic roll. Few however will be desirous,
and none will be wise, to resign for these gigantic shadows of form-
less and baseless fancy the splendid exposition given by the editor
(p. 76 of vol. ii). Seen by that new external illumination, though
it be none of the author's kindling, his poem stands on firmer feet
and is clothed with a nearer light.

interpreting Blake's dim creed somewhat as above. One distinction it is here possible to make, and desirable to keep in mind: Blake at one time speaks of Nature as the source of moral law, "the harlot virgin-mother," "Rahab," "the daughter of Babylon," origin of religious restrictions and the worship of abstinence; mother of "the harlot modesty," and spring of all hypocrisies and pro-hibitions; to whom the religious and moral of this world would fain offer up in sacrifice the spiritual Jerusalem, the virgin espoused, named among men Liberty, forbidding nothing and enjoying all, but therefore clean and not unclean: by whom comes indulgence, after whom follows redemption. At another time this same prophet will plead for free-dom on behalf of "natural" energies, and set up the claims of nature to energetic enjoyment and gratification of all desires, against the moral law and government of the creative and restrictive Deity — "Urizen, mistaken Demon of Heaven." With a like looseness of phrase he uses and trans-poses the words "God" and "Satan," even to an excess of laxity and consequent perplexity; not, it may be suspected, without a grain of innocent if malign pleasure at the chance of inflicting on men of conventional tempers bewilderment and offence. But as to this question of the term "Nature" the case seems to lie thus: when, as throughout the "Marriage of Heaven and Hell," he uses it in the simple sense of human or physical condition as opposed to some artificial state of soul or belief, he takes it as the contrary of conventional ideas and habits (of religion and morality as vulgarly conceived or practised) ; but when, as throughout the *Milton* and *Jerusalem*, he speaks of nature as opposed to inspiration, it must be taken as the contrary of that higher and subtler religious faith which he is bent on inculcating, and which itself is the only perfect opposite and efficient antagonist to the conventional faith and (to use another of his quasi-technical terms) the " deistical virtue" which he is bent on denying.   Blake, one should always re-member, was not infidel but heretic ; his belief was peculiar enough, but it was not unbelief; it was farther from that than most men's.   To him, though for quite personal reasons and in a quite especial sense, much of what is called inspired writing was as sacred and infallible as to any priest of any church.   Only before reading he inverted the book.

> " Both read the Bible day and night,
>   But thou read'st black where I read white."
>   (*Everlasting Gospel*, MS.)

Thus, by his own showing, in the recorded words of Christ he found authority for his vision and sympathy with his faith ; in the published creed of reason or rationalism, he found negation of his belief and antipathy to his aims.   Hence in his later denunciation he brackets together the Churches of Rome and England with the Churches of Ferney and Lausanne ; it was all uninspired—all " nature's cruel holiness—the deceits of natural religion " ; all

irremediably involved, all inextricably interwoven
with the old fallacies and the old prohibitions.

Such points as these do, above most others,
deserve, demand, and reward the trouble of clearing
up ; and these once understood, much that seemed
the aimless unreflecting jargon of crude or accidental
rhetoric assumes a distinct if unacceptable meaning.
It is much otherwise with the external scheme or
literal shell of the *Jerusalem*. Let no man attempt
to define the post or expound the office of the
"terrible sons and daughters." These, with all
their flock of emanations and spectrous or vegetating
shadows, let us leave to the discretion of Los ; who
has enough on his hands among them all. Neither
let any attempt to plant a human foot upon the soil
of the newly-divided shires and counties, partitioned
though they be into the mystic likeness of the
twelve tribes of Israel. Nor let any questioner of
arithmetical mind apply his skill in numbers to the
finding of flaws or products in the twelves, twenty-
fours, and twenty-sevens which make up the sum
of their male and female emanations. In earnest,
the externals of this poem are too incredibly gro-
tesque — the mythologic plan too incomparably
tortuous—to be fit for any detailed coherence of
remark. Nor indeed were they meant to endure it.
Such things, and the expression of such things, as
are here treated of, are not to be reasoned out ;
the matter one may say is above reasoning ; the
manner (taken apart from the matter) is below it :
the spirit of the work is too strong and its form

too faulty for any rule or line. It will upon the
whole suffice if this be kept in mind ; that to Blake,
in a literal perhaps as well as a mystical sense,
Albion was as it were the cradle and centre of all
created existence ; he even calls on the Jews to
recognize it as the parent land of their history and
their faith. Its incarnate spirit is chief among the
ancient giant-gods, Titans of his mythology, who
were lords of the old simple world and its good
things, its wise delights and strong sweet instincts,
full of the vigorous impulse of innocence ; lords of
an extinct kingdom, superseded now and trans-
formed by the advent of moral fear and religious
jealousy, of pallid faith and artificial abstinence.
In this manner Albion is changed and overthrown ;
hence at length he dies, stifled and slain by his
children under the new law. His one friend, not
misled or converted to the dispensations of bodily
virtue and spiritual restraint, but faithful from of
old and even after his change and conversion to
moral law, is Time ; whose Spectre, or mere out-
side husk and likeness, is indeed (as it must needs
be) fain to range itself on the transitory side of
things, fain to follow after the fugitive Emanation
embodied in these new forms of life and allied to
the faith and habit of the day against the old
liberty ;* but for all the desire of his despair and

* In the mythologic scheme, also, Los god of time and Albion
father of the races of men are rival powers; and the "Spectre" or
satellite deity reproaches his lord with resignation of the world and
all its ways and generations (which should have been subject only

fierce entreaties to be let go, he is yet kept to work,
however afflicted and rebellious, and compelled to
labour with Time's self at the building up within
every man of that spiritual city which is redemption
and freedom for all men (ch. i.). All the myth of
this building of "Golgonooza," (that is, we know,
inspired art by which salvation must come) is
noticeable for sweet intricacy of beauty ; only after
a little some maddening memory (surely not pure
inspiration this time, but rather memory?) of the
latter chapters of Ezekiel, with their interminable
inexplicable structures and plans, seizes on Blake's
passionate fancy and sets him at work measuring
and dividing walls and gates in a style calculated
to wear out a hecatomb of scholiasts, for whole
pages in which no subtilized mediæval intellect,
though trained under seraphic or cherubic doctors,
could possibly find one satisfactory hair to split.
For it merely trebles the roaring and rolling con-
fusion when some weak grain of symbolism is turned
up for a glimpse of time in the thick of a mass of
choral prose consisting of absolute fancy and mere
naked sound.

Not that there is here less than elsewhere of the

---

to the Time-Spirit) to the guidance of the nations sprung from the
patriarch Albion (called in Biblical records after Jewish names,
here spoken of by their English or other titles, more or less
burlesque and barbaric) who have taken upon themselves to subdue
even Time himself to this work and divide his spoils. So closely
is the bare mythical construction enwound with the symbolic or
doctrinal passages which are meant to give it such vitality and
such coherence as they may.

passion and beauty which redeem so much of these
confused and clamorous poems. The merits and
attractions of this book are not such as can be
minced small and served up in fragments. To do
justice to its melodious eloquence and tender subtlety,
we should have to analyze or transcribe whole
sections : to give any fair notion of the grandeur
and variety of its decorations would take up twice
the space we can allow to it. Let this brief pro-
logue stand as a sample of the former qualities.

> " Reader ! lover of books ! lover of heaven
> And of that God from whom all things are given ;
> Who in mysterious Sinai's awful cave
> To man the wondrous art of writing gave ;
> Again he speaks in thunder and in fire,
> Thunder of thought and flames of fierce desire ;
> Even from the depths of Hell his voice I hear
> Within the unfathomed caverns of my ear ;
> Therefore I print ; nor vain my types shall be ;
> Heaven, Earth, and Hell henceforth shall live in harmony."

" We who dwell on earth," adds the prophet,
speaking of the measure and outward fashion of his
poem, " can do nothing of ourselves ; everything is
conducted by Spirits no less than digestion or sleep."
It is to be wished then that the spirits had on this
occasion spoken less like somnambulists and uttered
less indigested verse. For metrical oratory the plea
that follows against ordinary metre may be allowed
to have some effective significance ; however futile if
applied to purer and more essential forms of poetry.
It will be enough to understand well and bear
well in mind once for all that the gist of this poem,

regarded either as a scheme of ethics or as a mytho-
logical evangel, is simply this : to preach, as in the
Saviour's opening invocation, the union of man with
God :—(" I am not a God afar off ;—Lo ! we are One ;
forgiving all evil; not seeking recompense ") : to
confute the dull mournful insanity of disbelief which
compels " the perturbed man " to avert his ear and
reject the divine counsellor as a " Phantom of the
over-heated brain." This perverted humanity is in-
carnate in Albion, the fallen Titan, imprisoned by his
children ; the " sons of Albion " are dæmonic qualities
of force and faith, the " daughters " are reflex
qualities or conditions which emanate from these.
As thus ; reason supplants faith, and law, moral or
religious, grows out of reason ; Jerusalem, symbol
of imaginative liberty, emanation of his unfallen
days, is the faith cast out by the " sons " or spirits
who substitute reason for faith, the freedom trodden
under by the " daughters " who substitute moral law
for moral impulse : "Vala," her Spectre, called
"Tirzah" among men, is the personified form in
which " Jerusalem " becomes revealed, the perverted
incarnation, the wrested medium or condition in
which she exists among men. Thus much for the
scheme of allegory with which the prophet sets out ;
but when once he has got his theogony well under
way and thrown it well into types, the antitypes all
but vanish : every condition or quality has a god or
goddess of its own ; every obscure state and allego-
rical gradation becomes a personal agent : and all
these fierce dim figures threaten and complain, mingle

and divide, struggle and embrace as human friends
or foes. The main symbols are even of a mono-
tonous consistency ; but no accurate sequence of
symbolic detail is to be looked for in the doings and
sayings of these contending giants and gods. To
those who will remember this distinction and will
make allowance for the peculiar dialect and manner
of which some account has already been taken, this
poem will not seem so wholly devoid of reason or of
charm.

For its great qualities are much the same in text
as in design : plenteous, delicate, vigorous. There
is a certain real if rough and lax power of dramatic
insight and invention shown even in the singular
divisions of adverse symbol against symbol ; in such
allegories as that which opposes the "human ima-
gination in which all things exist "—do actually exist
to all eternity—and the reflex fancy or belief which
men confound with this ; nay, which they prefer to
dwell in and ask comfort from. These two the poet
calls the " states " of Beulah and Jerusalem. As the
souls of men are attracted towards that "mild
heaven" of dreams and shadows where only the
reflected image of their own hopes and errors can
abide, the imagination, most divine and human, most
actual and absolute, of all things, recedes ever
further and further among the clouds of smoke,
vapours of "abstract philosophy," and is caught
among the " starry wheels " of religion and law,
whose restless and magnetic revolution attracts and
absorbs her.

" O what avail the loves and tears of Beulah's lovely daughters?
They hold the immortal form in gentle bands and tender tears,
But all within is opened into the deeps "—

the deeps of "a dark and unknown night " in which
" philosophy wars against imagination." Here also
the main myth of the *Europe* is once more rehandled ;
to " create a female will," jealous, curious, cunning,
full of tender tyranny and confusion, this is " to hide
the most evident God in a hidden covert, even in the
shadows of a woman and a secluded holy place, that
we may pry after him as after a stolen treasure,
hidden among the dead and mured up from the paths
of life." Thus is it with the Titan Albion and all
his race of mythologic men, when for them " Vala
supplants Jerusalem," the husk replaces the fruit,
the mutable form eclipses the immutable substance.

But into these darker parts of the book we will
not go too deep. Time, patience, and insight on the
part of writer and reader might perhaps clear up all
details and lay bare much worth sight and study ;
but only at the expense of much labour and space.
It is feasible, and would be worth doing ; but not
here. If the singular amalgam called Blake's works
should ever get published, and edited to any purpose,
this will have to be done by an energetic editor with
time enough on his hands and wits enough for the
work. We meantime will gather up a few strays
that even under these circumstances appear worth
hiving. In the address (p. 27) to the Jews, &c.,
Blake affirms that " Britain was the primitive seat of
the patriarchal religion :" therefore, in a literal as

well as in a mystical sense, Jerusalem was the ema-
nation of the giant Albion. (This it should seem
was, according to the mythology, before the visible
world was created; in the time when all things were
in the divine undivided world of the gods.) "Ye
are united, O ye inhabitants of Earth, in one Reli-
gion: the most Ancient, the Eternal, and the Ever-
lasting Gospel. The Wicked will turn it to Wicked-
ness; the Righteous, to Righteousness." If there
be truth in the Jewish tradition, he adds further on,
that man anciently contained in his mighty limbs all
things in heaven and earth, "and they were separated
from him by cruel sacrifices; and when compulsory
cruel sacrifices had brought Humanity into a feminine
tabernacle in the loins of Abraham and David, the
Lamb of God, the Saviour, became apparent on
earth as the prophets had foretold: the return of
Israel is a return to mental sacrifice and war," to
noble spiritual freedom and labour, which alone can
supplant "corporeal war" and violence of error.

The second address (p. 52) "to the Deists" is
more singular and more eloquent. Take a few ex-
tracts given not quite at random. "He," says
Blake, "who preaches natural religion or morality
is a flatterer who means to betray, and to perpetuate
tyrant pride and the laws of that Babylon which he
foresees shall shortly be destroyed with the spiritual
and not the natural sword; he is in the state named
Rahab." The prophet then enforces his law that
"man is born a spectre or Satan and is altogether
an Evil," and "must continually be changed into his

Y

direct contrary." Those who persuade him other-
wise are his enemies. For "man must and will have
some religion; if he has not the religion of Jesus
he will have the religion of Satan." Again, "Will
any one say, Where are those who worship Satan
under the name of God?—where are they? Listen.
Every religion that preaches vengeance for sin is the
religion of the enemy and avenger, and not of the
forgiver of sin : and their God is Satan named by
the Divine Name." This, he says, must be at root
the religion of all who deny revelation and adore
nature ; * for mere nature is Satanic. Adam the first
man was created at the same time with Satan, when
the earth-giant Albion was cast into a trance of sleep :
the first man was a part of the universal fluent nature
made opaque ; the first fiend, a part contracted ; and
only by these qualities of opacity and contraction
can man or devil have separate natural existence.
Those, the prophet adds in his perverse manner, who
profess belief in natural virtue are hypocrites ; which
those cannot be who "pretend to be holier than
others, but confess their sins before all the world."
Therefore there was never a religious hypocrite!
"Rousseau thought men good by nature ; he found
them evil, and found no friend. Friendship cannot
exist without forgiveness of sins continually." And
so forth.

---

* Who adore nature as she appears to the Deist, who select
this and reject that, assume and presume according to moral law
and custom, instead of accepting the Pantheistic revelation which
consecrates all things and absorbs all contraries.

At p. 66 is a passage recalling the myth of the
"Mental Traveller," and which seems to bear out
the interpretation we gave to that misty and
tempestuous poem. This part of the prophecy,
describing the blind pitiful cruelty of divided
qualities set against each other, is full of brilliant
and noble passages. Even the faint symbolic
shapes of Tirzah and all her kind assume now and
then a splendour of pathos, utter words of stately
sound, complain and appeal even to some recog-
nizable purpose. So much might here be cited that
we will prefer to cite nothing but this slight touch of
myth. In the world of time "they refuse liberty to
the male : not like Beulah,

Where every female delights to give her maiden to her husband."

The female searches sea and land for gratification to
the male genius, who in return clothes her in gems
and gold and feeds her with the food of Eden : hence
all her beauty beams. But this is only in the "land
of dreams," where dwell things "stolen from the
human imagination by secret amorous theft:" and
when the spectres of the dead awake in that land,
"all the jealousies become murderous:—forming a
commerce to sell loves with moral law; an equal
balance, not going down with decision: therefore
—mutual hate returns and mutual deceit and mutual
fear." In fact, the divorce batteries are here open
again.

The third address "to the Christians" is too long
to transcribe here ; and should in fairness have been

given in the biography. Its devout passion and beauty of words might have won notice, and earned tolerance for the more erratic matter in which it lies embedded. "What is the joy of heaven but improvement in the things of the spirit? What are the pains of hell but ignorance, bodily lust, idleness, and devastation of the things of the spirit?" Mental gifts, given of Christ, "always appear to the ignorance-loving hypocrite as sins; but that which is a sin in the sight of cruel man is not so in the sight of our kind God." Every Christian after his ability should openly engage in some mental pursuit; for "to labour in knowledge is to build up Jerusalem; and to despise knowledge is to despise Jerusalem and her builders." A little before he has said: "I know of no other Christianity and no other Gospel than the liberty both of body and mind to exercise the divine arts of imagination." God being a spirit, and to be worshipped in spirit and in truth, are not all his gifts spiritual gifts? "The Christians then must give up the religion of Caiaphas, the dark preacher of death, of sin, of sorrow, and of punishment, typified as a revolving wheel, a devouring sword; and recognize that the labours of Art and Science alone are the labours of the Gospel." As to religion, "Jesus died because he strove against the current of this wheel—opposing nature; it is natural religion. But Jesus is the bright preacher of life, creating nature from this fiery law, by self-denial and forgiveness of sin." So speaks to the prophet "a Watcher and a Holy One;" bidding him

"Go therefore, cast out devils in Christ's name,
Heal thou the sick of spiritual disease ;
Pity the evil ; for thou art not sent
To smite with terror and with punishments
Those that are sick.   *   *   *   *
But to the publicans and harlots go :
Teach them true happiness ; but let no curse
Go forth out of thy mouth to blight their peace.
For hell is opened to heaven ; thine eyes behold
The dungeons burst, the prisoners set free.
  England, awake ! awake ! awake !
   Jerusalem thy sister calls ;
  Why wilt thou sleep the sleep of death
   And chase her from thy ancient walls ?
  Thy hills and valleys felt her feet
   Gently upon their bosoms move ;
  Thy gates beheld sweet Zion's ways ;
   Then was a time of joy and love.
  And now the time returns again ;
   Our souls exult ; and London's towers
  Receive the Lamb of God to dwell
   In England's green and pleasant bowers."

Much might also be said, had one leave of time, of the last chapter ; of the death of the earth-giant through jealousy, and his resurrection when the Saviour appeared to him revealed in the likeness and similitude of Time : of the ultimate deliverance of all things, chanted in a psalm of high and tidal melody ; a resurrection wherein all things, even "Tree, Metal, Earth and Stone," become all

"Human forms identified ; living, going forth, and returning wearied
Into the planetary lives of years, months, days, and hours : reposing
And then awaking into his bosom in the life of immortality.
And I heard the name of their emanations : they are named Jerusalem."

We will add one reference, to pp. 61–62, where God shows to Jerusalem in a vision "Joseph the carpenter in Nazareth, and Mary his espoused wife." Through the vision of their story the forgiveness of Jerusalem also, when she has gone astray from her Lord, is made manifest to her.

"And I heard a voice among the reapers saying, 'Am I Jerusalem the lost adulteress? or am I Babylon come up to Jerusalem?' And another voice answered saying, 'Does the voice of my Lord call me again? am I pure through his mercy and pity? am I become lovely as a virgin in his sight, who am indeed a harlot drunken with the sacrifice of idols?—O mercy, O divine humanity, O forgiveness and pity and compassion, if I were pure I should never have known thee: if I were unpolluted I should never have glorified thy holiness, or rejoiced in thy great salvation.'" The whole passage—and such are not so unfrequent as at first glimpse they seem—is, if seen with equal eyes, whether its purport be right or wrong, "full of wisdom and perfect in beauty." But we will dive after no more pearls at present in this huge oyster-bed; and of the illustrations we can but speak in a rough swift way. These are all generally noble: that at p. 70 is great among the greatest of Blake's. Spires of serpentine cloud are seen before a strong wind below a crescent moon; Druid pillars enclose as with a frame this stormy division of sky; outside them again the vapour twists and thickens; and men standing on desolate broken ground look heavenward or earth-

ward between the pillars. Of others a brief and
admirable account is given in the " Life," more final
and sufficient than we can again give ; but all in fact
should be well seen into by those who would judge
fitly of Blake's singular and supreme gift for purely
imaginative work. Flowers sprung of earth and lit
from heaven, with chalices of floral fire and with
flower-like women or men growing up out of their
centre; fair large forms full of labour or of rest;
sudden starry strands and reaches of breathless
heaven washed by drifts of rapid wind and cloud ;
serrated array of iron rocks and glorious growth of
weedy lands or flowering fields ; reflected light of
bows bent and arrows drawn in heaven, dividing
cloud from starlit cloud ; stately shapes of infinite
sorrow or exuberant joy ; all beautiful things and all
things terrible, all changes of shadow and of light,
all mysteries of the darkness and the day, find place
and likeness here : deep waters made glad and
sad with heavy light that comes and goes ; vast
expansion of star-shaped blossom and swift aspira-
tion of laborious flame ; strong and sweet figures
made subject to strange torture in dim lands of
bondage ; mystic emblems of plumeless bird and
semi-human beast; women like the daughters of
giants, with immense shapeliness and vigour of
lithe large limbs, clothed about with anguish and
crowned upon with triumph ; their deep bosoms
pressed against the scales of strong dragons, their
bodies and faces strained together in the delight of
monstrous caresses ; similitudes of all between angel

and reptile that divide illimitable spaces of air or
defile the overlaboured furrows upon earth.

It is easier to do complete justice to the minor
prophecies than to give any not inadequate concep-
tion of this great book, so vast in reach, so repellent
in style, so rich, vehement, and subtle beyond all
other works of Blake ; the chosen crown and trea-
sured fruit of his strange labours. Extracts of
admirable beauty might be gathered up on all hands,
more eligible it may be than any here given ; none I
think more serviceable by way of sample and exposi-
tion, as far as such can at all be attained. That the
book contains much of a personal kind referring in
a wild dim manner to his own spiritual actions and
passions, is evident : but even by the new light of
the Felpham correspondence one can hardly see
where to lay finger on these passages and separate
them decisively from the loose floating context.
Not without regret, yet not with any sense of wilful
or scornful oversight, we must be content now to
pass on, and put up with this insufficient notice.

The only other engraved work of a prophetic
kind did not appear for eighteen years more. This
last and least in size, but not in worth, of the whole
set is so brief that it may here be read in full.

THE GHOST OF ABEL.

A REVELATION IN THE VISIONS OF JEHOVAH.

SEEN BY WILLIAM BLAKE.

To Lord Byron in the Wilderness.—What dost thou here, Elijah ?
Can a Poet doubt the Visions of Jehovah? Nature has no Outline :

But Imagination has. Nature has no Time ; but Imagination has.
Nature has no Supernatural, and dissolves ; Imagination is Eternity.

SCENE.—*A rocky Country.* EVE *fainted over the dead body
of* ABEL *which lays near a grave.* ADAM *kneels by her.*
JEHOVAH *stands above.*

JEHOVAH. Adam !
ADAM. It is in vain : I will not hear thee more, thou Spiritual
Voice.
Is this Death ?
JEHOVAH. Adam !
ADAM. It is in vain ; I will not hear thee
Henceforth. Is this thy Promise that the Woman's Seed
Should bruise the Serpent's Head ? Is this the Serpent ? Ah !
Seven times, O Eve, thou hast fainted over the Dead. Ah ! Ah !

(EVE *revives.*)

EVE. Is this the Promise of Jehovah ? O it is all a vain
delusion,
This Death and this Life and this Jehovah.
JEHOVAH. Woman, lift thine eyes.

(A VOICE *is heard coming on.*)

VOICE. O Earth, cover not thou my blood ! cover not thou
my blood !

(*Enter the* GHOST of ABEL.)

EVE. Thou visionary Phantasm, thou art not the real Abel.
ABEL. Among the Elohim a Human Victim I wander : I am
their House,
Prince of the Air, and our dimensions compass Zenith and Nadir.
Vain is thy Covenant, O Jehovah : I am the Accuser and Avenger
Of Blood ; O Earth, cover not thou the blood of Abel.
JEHOVAH. What vengeance dost thou require ?
ABEL. Life for Life ! Life for Life !
JEHOVAH. He who shall take Cain's life must also die, O Abel ;
And who is he ? Adam, wilt thou, or Eve, thou, do this ?
ADAM. It is all a vain delusion of the all-creative Imagination.
Eve, come away, and let us not believe these vain delusions.
Abel is dead, and Cain slew him ; We shall also die a death
And then—what then ? be as poor Abel, a Thought ; or as

This? O what shall I call thee, Form Divine, Father of Mercies,
That appearest to my Spiritual Vision? Eve, seest thou also?

EVE. I see him plainly with my mind's eye: I see also Abel
living;
Tho' terribly afflicted, as we also are: yet Jehovah sees him
Alive and not dead; were it not better to believe Vision
With all our might and strength, tho' we are fallen and lost?

ADAM. Eve, thou hast spoken truly; let us kneel before his
feet.

(*They kneel before* JEHOVAH.)

ABEL. Are these the sacrifices of Eternity, O Jehovah? a
broken spirit
And a contrite heart? O, I cannot forgive; the Accuser hath
Entered into me as into his house, and I loathe thy Tabernacles.
As thou hast said so is it come to pass: My desire is unto Cain
And he doth rule over me: therefore my soul in fumes of blood
Cries for vengeance: Sacrifice on Sacrifice, Blood on Blood.

JEHOVAH. Lo, I have given you a Lamb for an Atonement
instead
Of the Transgressor, or no Flesh or Spirit could ever live.

ABEL. Compelled I cry, O Earth, cover not the blood of Abel.

(ABEL *sinks down into the grave, from which arises* SATAN
armed in glittering scales with a crown and a spear.)

SATAN. I will have human blood and not the blood of bulls
or goats
And no Atonement, O Jehovah; the Elohim live on Sacrifice
Of men; hence I am God of men; thou human, O Jehovah.
By the rock and oak of the Druid, creeping mistletoe and thorn,
Cain's city built with human blood, not blood of bulls and goats,
Thou shalt thyself be sacrificed to me thy God on Calvary.

JEHOVAH. Such is my will—(*Thunders*)—that thou thyself go
to Eternal Death
In self-annihilation, even till Satan self-subdued put off Satan
Into the bottomless abyss whose torment arises for ever and ever.

(*On each side a Chorus of Angels entering sing the following.*)

The Elohim of the Heathen swore Vengeance for Sin! Then thou
stood'st
Forth, O Elohim Jehovah, in the midst of the darkness of the oath
all clothed

In thy covenant of the forgiveness of Sins. Death, O Holy! is
    this Brotherhood?
The Elohim saw their oath eternal fire ; they rolled apart trembling
    over the
Mercy-Seat, each in his station fixed in the firmament, by Peace,
    Brotherhood, and Love.

The Curtain falls.

(1822.   W. Blake's original stereotype was 1788.)

On the skirt of a figure, rapid and "vehemently
sweeping," engraved underneath (recalling that
vision of Dion made memorable by one of Words-
worth's nobler poems) are inscribed these words—
"The Voice of Abel's Blood." The fierce and
strenuous flight of this figure is as the motion of
one "whose feet are swift to shed blood," and the
dim face is full of hunger and sorrowful lust after
revenge. The decorations are slight but not in-
effective ; wrought merely in black and white. This
small prose lyric has a value beyond the value of its
occasional beauty and force of form ; it is a brief
comprehensible expression of Blake's faith seen from
its two leading sides ; belief in vision and belief in
mercy. Into the singular mood of mind which made
him inscribe it to the least imaginative of all serious
poets we need by no means strive to enter ; but in
the trustful admiration and the loyal goodwill which
this quaint inscription seems to imply, there must be
something not merely laughable : as, however rough
and homespun the veil of eccentric speech may seem
to us at first, we soon find it interwoven with threads
of such fair and fervent colour as make the stuff of

splendid verse ; so, beyond all apparent aberrations
of relaxed thought which offend us at each turn,
a purpose not ignoble and a sense not valueless
become manifest to those who will see them.

Here then the scroll of prophecy is finally wound
up ; and those who have cared to unroll and de-
cipher it by such light as we can attain or afford
may now look back across the tempest and tumult,
and pass sentence, according to their pleasure or
capacity, on the message delivered from this cloudy
and noisy tabernacle. The complete and exalted
figure of Blake cannot be seen in full by those who
avert their eyes, smarting and blinking, from the
frequent smoke and sudden flame. Others will see
more clearly, as they look more sharply, the radical
sanity and coherence of the mind which put forth its
shoots of thought and faith in ways so strange, at
such strange times. Faith incredible and love in-
visible to most men were alone the springs of this
turbid and sonorous stream. In Blake, above all
other men, the moral and the imaginative senses were
so fused together as to compose the final artistic
form. No man's fancy, in that age, flew so far and
so high on so sure a wing. No man's mind, in that
generation, dived so deep or gazed so long after the
chance of human redemption. To serve art and to
love liberty seemed to him the two things (if indeed
they were not one thing) worth a man's life and
work ; and no servant was ever trustier, no lover
more constant than he. Knowing that without
liberty there can be no loyalty, he did not fear,

whether in his work or his life, to challenge and to
deride the misconstruction of the foolish and the
fraudulent. It does not appear that he was ever at
the pains to refute any senseless and rootless lie
that may have floated up during his life on the
muddy waters of rumour, or drifted from hand to
hand and mouth to mouth along the putrescent
weed-beds of tradition. Many such lies, I am told,
were then set afloat, and have not all as yet gone
down. One at least of these may here be swept
once for all out of our way. Mr. Linnell, the truest
friend of Blake's age and genius, has assured me—
and has expressed a wish that I should make public
his assurance—that the legend of Blake and his
wife, sitting as Adam and Eve in their garden, is
simply a legend—to those who knew them, repulsive
and absurd ; based probably, if on any foundation at
all, on some rough and rapid expression of Blake's
in the heat and flush of friendly talk, to the effect
(it may be) that such a thing, if one chose to do it,
would be in itself innocent and righteous—wrong or
strange only in the eyes of a world whose views and
whose deeds were strange and wrong. So far Blake
would probably have gone ; and so far his com-
mentators need not fear to go. But one thing does
certainly seem to me loathsome and condemnable ;
the imputation of such a charge as has been brought
against Blake on this matter, without ground and
without excuse. The oral flux of fools, being as it
is a tertian or quotidian malady or ague of the
tongue among their kind, may deserve pity or may

not, but does assuredly demand rigid medical treat-
ment. The words or thoughts of a free thinker and
a free speaker, falling upon rather than into the ear of
a servile and supine fool, will probably in all times
bring forth such fruit as this. By way of solace or
compensation for the folly which he half perceives and
half admits, the fool must be allowed his little jest
and his little lie. Only when it passes into tradition
and threatens to endure, is it worth while to set foot
on it. It seems that Blake never cared to do this
good office for himself; and in effect it can only
seem worth doing on rare occasions to any workman
who respects his work. This contempt, in itself
noble and rational, became injurious when applied
to the direct service of things in hand. Confidence
in future friends, and contempt of present foes, may
have induced him to leave his highest achievements
impalpable and obscure. Their scope is as wide and
as high as heaven, but not as clear ; clouds involve
and rains inundate the fitful and stormy space of air
through which he spreads and plies an indefatigable
wing. There can be few books in the world like
these ; I can remember one poet only whose work
seems to me the same or similar in kind ; a poet as
vast in aim, as daring in detail, as unlike others,
as coherent to himself, as strange without and as
sane within. The points of contact and sides of
likeness between William Blake and Walt Whitman
are so many and so grave, as to afford some
ground of reason to those who preach the tran-
sition of souls or transfusion of spirits. The great

American is not a more passionate preacher of sexual or political freedom than the English artist. To each the imperishable form of a possible and universal Republic is equally requisite and adorable as the temporal and spiritual queen of ages as of men. To each all sides and shapes of life are alike acceptable or endurable. From the fresh free ground of either workman nothing is excluded that is not exclusive. The words of either strike deep and run wide and soar high. They are both full of faith and passion, competent to love and to loathe, capable of contempt and of worship. Both are spiritual, and both democratic; both by their works recall, even to so untaught and tentative a student as I am, the fragments vouchsafed to us of the Pantheistic poetry of the East. Their casual audacities of expression or speculation are in effect wellnigh identical. Their outlooks and theories are evidently the same on all points of intellectual and social life. The divine devotion and selfless love which make men martyrs and prophets are alike visible and palpable in each. It is no secret now, but a matter of public knowledge, that both these men, being poor in the sight and the sense of the world, have given what they had of time or of money, of labour or of love, to comfort and support all the suffering and sick, all the afflicted and misused, whom they had the chance or the right to succour and to serve. The noble and gentle labours of the one are known to those who live in his time; the similar deeds of the other deserve

and demand a late recognition. No man so poor
and so obscure as Blake appeared in the eyes of
his generation ever did more good works in a more
noble and simple spirit. It seems that in each of
these men at their birth pity and passion, and relief
and redress of wrong, became incarnate and innate.
That may well be said of the one which was said
of the other: that "he looks like a man." And
in externals and details the work of these two
constantly and inevitably coheres and coincides.
A sound as of a sweeping wind; a prospect as over
dawning continents at the fiery instant of a sudden
sunrise; a splendour now of stars and now of
storms; an expanse and exultation of wing across
strange spaces of air and above shoreless stretches
of sea: a resolute and reflective love of liberty in
all times and in all things where it should be; a
depth of sympathy and a height of scorn which
complete and explain each other, as tender and as
bitter as Dante's; a power, intense and infallible,
of pictorial concentration and absorption, most rare
when combined with the sense and the enjoyment
of the widest and the highest things; an exquisite
and lyrical excellence of form when the subject is
well in keeping with the poet's tone of spirit; a
strength and security of touch in small sweet
sketches of colour and outline, which bring before
the eyes of their student a clear glimpse of the
thing designed—some little inlet of sky lighted by
moon or star, some dim reach of windy water or
gentle growth of meadow-land or wood; these are

qualities common to the work of either. Had we place or time or wish to touch on their shortcomings and errors, it might be shown that these two are nearly akin; that their poetry has at once the melody and the laxity of a fitful stormwind; that, being oceanic, it is troubled with violent ground-swells and sudden perils of ebb and reflux, of shoal and reef, perplexing to the swimmer or the sailor; in a word, that it partakes the powers and the faults of elemental and eternal things; that it is at times noisy and barren and loose, rootless and fruitless and informal; and is in the main fruitful and delightful and noble, a necessary part of the divine mechanism of things. Any work or art of which this cannot be said is superfluous and perishable, whatever of grace or charm it may possess or assume. Whitman has seldom struck a note of thought and speech so just and so profound as Blake has now and then touched upon; but his work is generally more frank and fresh, smelling of sweeter air, and readier to expound or expose its message, than this of the "Prophetic Books." Nor is there among these any poem or passage of equal length so faultless and so noble as his "Voice out of the Sea," or as his dirge over President Lincoln—the most sweet and sonorous nocturn ever chanted in the church of the world. But in breadth of outline and charm of colour, these poems recall the work of Blake; and to neither poet can a higher tribute of honest praise be paid than this.

We have now done what in us lay to help the

z

works of a great man on their way towards that
due appreciation and that high honour of which in
the end they will not fail.   Much, it need not be
repeated, has been done for them of late, and
admirably done; much also we have found to do,
and have been compelled to leave undone still more.
If it should now appear to any reader that too much
has been made of slight things, or too little said of
grave errors, this must be taken well into account :
that praise enough has not as yet been given, and
blame enough can always be had for the asking;
that when full honour has been done and full thanks
rendered to those who have done great things, then
and then only will it be no longer an untimely and un-
seemly labour to map out and mark down their short-
comings for the profit or the pleasure of their inferiors
and our own; that however pleasant for common
palates and feeble fingers it may be to nibble and
pick holes, it is not only more profitable but should
be more delightful for all who desire or who
strive after any excellence of mind or of achieve-
ment to do homage wherever it may be due; to let
nothing great pass unsaluted or unenjoyed; but as
often as we look backwards among past days and
dead generations, with glad and ready reverence to
answer the noble summons—"Let us now praise
famous men, and our fathers who were before us."
Those who refuse them that are none of their sons;
and among all these "famous men, and our fathers,"
no names seem to demand our praise so loudly as
theirs who while alive had to dispense with the

thanksgiving of men. To them doubtless, it may
be said, this is now more than ever indifferent ; but
to us it had better not be so. And especially in the
works and in the life of Blake there is so strong
and special a charm for those to whom the higher
ways of work are not sealed ways that none will
fear to be too grudging of blame or too liberal of
praise. A more noble memory is hardly left us ;
and it is not for his sake that we should contend to
do him honour.

LIST OF AUTHORITIES

1. LIFE OF WILLIAM BLAKE. By Alexander Gilchrist. 1863.
2. POETICAL SKETCHES. By W. B. 1783.
3. SONGS OF INNOCENCE. 1789.
4. THE BOOK OF THEL. 1789.
5. THE MARRIAGE OF HEAVEN AND HELL. 1790.
6. VISIONS OF THE DAUGHTERS OF ALBION. 1793.
7. AMERICA: A PROPHECY. 1793.
8. SONGS OF EXPERIENCE. 1794.
9. EUROPE: A PROPHECY. 1794.
10. THE FIRST BOOK OF URIZEN. 1794.
11. THE BOOK OF AHANIA. 1795.
12. THE SONG OF LOS. 1795.
13. MILTON: A POEM IN TWO BOOKS. 1804.
14. JERUSALEM, AN EMANATION OF THE GIANT ALBION. 1804.
15. IDEAS OF GOOD AND EVIL. (MS.)
16. TIRIEL. (MS.)

PRINTED BY
SPOTTISWOODE AND CO. LTD., NEW-STREET SQUARE
LONDON